Beyond Brushtalk

With love to my parents
William and Margaret Keaveney
and to Shigeko, Bridget and Erica

Beyond Brushtalk
Sino-Japanese Literary Exchange in the Interwar Period

Christopher T. Keaveney

香港大學出版社
HONG KONG UNIVERSITY PRESS

Hong Kong University Press
The University of Hong Kong
Pok Fu Lam Road
Hong Kong
https://hkupress.hku.hk

© 2009 Christopher T. Keaveney

ISBN 978-962-209-928-9 (*Hardback*)

All rights reserved. No portion of this publication may be reproduced or transmitted in any form or by any means, electronic or mechanical, including photocopying, recording, or any information storage or retrieval system, without prior permission in writing from the publisher.

British Library Cataloguing-in-Publication Data
A catalogue record for this book is available from the British Library.

Digitally printed

Contents

A Note about Romanization		vii
Acknowledgements		ix
Introduction		1
Chapter 1	The Hub: Uchiyama Kanzō's Shanghai Bookstore and Its Role in Sino-Japanese Literary Relations	23
Chapter 2	Musings of a Literary Pilgrim: Tanizaki Jun'ichirō's Discoveries in China and Their Records	45
Chapter 3	The Allure of the White Birch School to May Fourth Writers	65
Chapter 4	Greener Pastures: The New Village Ideal and May Fourth Intellectuals	85
Chapter 5	The Art of Wanderlust: Hayashi Fumiko's Encounters with China	97
Chapter 6	Satō Haruo's "Ajia no ko" and Yu Dafu's Response: Literature, Friendship and Nationalism	117
Chapter 7	Return to the Brush: The Polarization of the Chinese and Japanese Literary Communities in the 1930s	129

Epilogue: Dream of a Dream	157
Notes	163
Appendix: Glossary of Selected Terms from Chinese and Japanese	187
Bibliography	193
Index	201

A Note about Romanization

In rendering Chinese in this text I have used the *pinyin* system. All Chinese names, titles, and terms in the document itself have been rendered in *pinyin*, but in the bibliographic references and in quotations from English language sources I have retained the original romanization system, with the *pinyin* equivalent in parentheses, where appropriate. In rendering Japanese I have used the standard Hepburn system and have indicated long vowel sounds by means of a macron.

Acknowledgements

It is fitting that my own stubborn efforts to see this project through to completion should in some meager way parallel Uchiyama Kanzō's persevering efforts at sustaining relations between the Japanese and Chinese literary communities. However, I must acknowledge that this book would never have been completed without the help and support of many wonderful people. This is my opportunity to recognize and thank those individuals who helped to make this book possible.

First of all, I would like to thank the editors of the following journals for permission to use material from these previously published articles: "Satō Haruo's 'Ajia no ko' and Yu Dafu's Response: Literature, Friendship and Nationalism," which appeared in *Sino-Japanese Studies,* Volume 13, No. 2, Spring 2001; "Uchiyama Kanzō's Shanghai Bookstore and Its Impact on May Fourth Writers," which appeared in *E-ASPAC*, Vol. 1, February, 2002; and "Musings of a Literary Pilgrim: Generic Variations in Tanizaki Jun'ichirō's Travel Writings from China," which appeared in *B.C. Asian Review,* No. 14, 2003–2004.

In the autumn of 2004 I pursued research and writing at Wenzhou University, Linfield College's partner institution in Zhejiang, China. Many of my colleagues there helped me with Chinese texts, particularly Professor Ye Miao. In the summer of 2006 I pursued research at Kyoto Bunkyo University, Linfield College's partner institution in Kyoto, Japan. Once again, I received the assistance of a number of faculty members at the university, including Professors Lu Jun and Elizabeth King, who helped me to locate texts and provided me with library space to pursue research. Furthermore, I appreciated the opportunity to give a presentation about my research provided by Mr. Suzuki Nobuyuki who also supplied invaluable logistical support during my stay in Kyoto. In the spring of 2007 Dr. Li Xinde from Wenzhou University spent an academic year at Linfield College. During his stay, Dr. Li helped me locate a number of articles that proved very useful for my research, and I am extremely grateful for all of the help that he provided. I would also like to extend my thanks to Dr Li for introducing me to Mr. Meng

Tiexia of the *Shanghai Daily* who was instrumental in obtaining permission from the Lu Xun Museum in Shanghai to use the cover photograph. My sincere appreciation goes to Mr. Wang Xirong, Curator of the Lu Xun Museum for permission to use that photograph.

I am also very indebted to Dean Barbara Seidman and my colleagues in the Department of Modern Languages at Linfield College who encouraged me to complete this project. In particular, I owe a debt of gratitude to John Sagers in the Department of History for all of his excellent advice about academic publishing. Many thanks also to Bahram Refaei and Kathleen Spring from the Educational Media Services Office and to Saiyare Refaei for help in preparing the photographs included in this book. Many thanks also to Linfield student Yang Shi for all of his assistance identifying and communicating with sources in China. Without institutional and departmental help and support, this book would not have been possible. I also would like to thank Dr. Rebecca Copeland from Washington University in St. Louis for sharing insights into the role of women writers in Japan during the war, and to my father, Dr. William P. Keaveney, for carefully reading and editing the draft manuscript in preparation for submission.

I must also express appreciation to the anonymous reviewer of the manuscript whose insightful comments and constructive suggestions guided me during the revision stage. Moreover, my sincere appreciation goes to Dr. Colin Day and Hong Kong University Press for publishing this book. Dr. Day was a firm supporter of this project and helped me to resolve a number of editorial issues along the way. Many thanks also to Ms. Clara Ho for guiding me through the final critical publication stages. I would like to express my most heartfelt thanks to Dr. Ian Lok, a former editor at Hong Kong University Press, for his support throughout this process. Ian believed in this work from the very beginning, and his efforts to see that my work was published exemplify the qualities that every scholar hopes to find in an editor.

Finally, I reserve my deepest, most heartfelt gratitude for my parents William and Margaret Keaveney who always supported and cultivated my intellectual interests, and to my wife Shigeko and my daughters Bridget and Erica who have always been and will always remain my sweet muses.

Introduction

The interwar period (1919–1937) was, in a number of significant ways, the nadir of Sino-Japanese relations. The idealistic façade of Jazz Age abandon and "Taishō Democracy" of the twenties masked the systematic expansion of militarism in Japan that ultimately would threaten stability on the continent and stymie efforts at cultural interaction among Chinese and Japanese intellectuals. In China, the various manifestations of Japanese aggression and imperialism met with waves of stiff and increasingly well orchestrated resistance that led first to invasion by the Japanese and then to war in 1937.

Given the severity of the political relations between the two nations it is ironic and surprising that there should have been such frequent and salubrious interactions between Chinese and Japanese writers during this period. The positive exchange that emerged between writers from the two literary communities proved to be an ultimately futile challenge to the Japanese militarist juggernaut. Nevertheless, it was an admirable and noteworthy essay at cultural bridge building between China and Japan where political and diplomatic measures had failed. For the first time in the long history of relations between these two East Asian neighbors, the cultural touchstone for both nations was no longer China and traditional Confucian values, but the West, and this in turn created increased opportunities for writers to interact in more equitable, less culturally bound ways than ever before, as both communities of writers sought to fashion a new modern literature based on Western models.

This is the story of attempts on the part of writers from the two literary communities to overcome formidable historical, cultural, ideological and political obstacles in order to engage in dialogues emphasizing literary cooperation and mutuality. It is a story, or rather a series of stories, that was destined to end in failure, crushed beneath the moraine of inevitable forces. Nevertheless, it is a tale worth telling insofar as it provides an example of positive interaction between two countries whose modern history of relations has been marred all too often by miscommunication, dogmatic adherence to ideological posturing and outright conflict.

The Golden Age of Sino-Japanese Literary Exchange

The "interwar period," as defined in this study, lasted from the May Fourth Movement in China, which came about in the wake of the Versailles Treaty in 1919, to the formal declaration of war on China by Japan in 1937. A number of the writers who would eventually go on to become pivotal figures in modern Chinese letters studied in Japan and embarked on their literary careers while in Japan during the May Fourth period. The period under consideration in this study ends, tragically, with the breakdown in communications between the literary communities that was the result of Japanese imperialism of the 1930s. The writers examined in this book include a number of the most celebrated authors of the era from both China and Japan. Ultimately, although this study examines relations involving famous writers such as Lu Xun and Tanizaki Jun'ichirō, the figure who emerges as the unsung hero of Sino-Japanese literary relations was a little-known bookstore owner named Uchiyama Kanzō, whose bookstore in Shanghai became the hub of relations between writers in the two communities during the interwar period.

The stories told here revolve around communication — face-to-face communication — and attempts at cultural understanding. For the first time in the long history of cultural relations between the two nations, intellectuals and artists attempted to transcend traditional biases and conventional assumptions about the other in order to communicate via a new Western aesthetic vocabulary. To the degree that historical rigidity and political exigencies allowed, they attempted to meet as equals and to communicate as modern artists who shared common aesthetic aspirations. In order to accomplish this goal they first had to go beyond the limitations inherent in the traditionally esteemed mode of cultural communication, written classical Chinese, and to literally lay their brushes aside and communicate directly to effectively confront a new array of cultural issues. In so doing, they were able to go beyond "brushtalk" in order to achieve a true meeting of the minds.

Brushtalk: Traditional Cultural Communications in East Asia

Traditionally, the ink brush had served as the chief tool of literary expression in East Asia and was valued as one of the "four treasures" of the scholar. Furthermore, written literary Chinese was the medium for intercultural exchange among intellectuals throughout East Asia. "Brushtalk" (Chinese, *bitan;* Japanese, *hitsudan*) was the vehicle through which ideas, both profound and mundane, were exchanged during the Chinese dynastic period among Chinese of different regions and between Chinese and visitors from their tributary and neighbor states including Koguryo, Paekche and Silla on the Korean Peninsula, Vietnam, and Japan.

Brushtalk refers specifically to the practice of communication in East Asia among literate individuals, incapable of speaking one another's language, by means of written classical Chinese. In actual practice, of course, it need not be classical Chinese. A simple exchange of written Chinese characters would often suffice to convey a point or to make an inquiry. All educated people in East Asia in premodern times possessed the ability to read and write in classical Chinese. As Joshua Fogel suggests, one should not underestimate the power of written Chinese characters and of the ink brush itself as a flexible tool for asking questions, exchanging ideas and proffering formal greetings.[1] This is a phenomenon that has its origins in the earliest exchanges among literate individuals in the Sinitic world. Even today, one can see this scenario played out regularly in East Asia in which, for example, Japanese visiting China are able to ask the whereabouts of a particular kind of store or site of cultural interest, or to identify themselves by means of a name card, all without having to speak a word.[2]

Such modes of communication have their roots in very early cross-linguistic encounters in East Asia. Chinese records suggest that the first Japanese visited China as early as the second century BCE.[3] Although the Japanese of the period were as yet preliterate and could not avail themselves of this mode of communication, one can conjecture that the Chinese themselves of the Han Dynasty (206 BCE–220 CE), hailing from different regions with radically different spoken dialects, employed classical Chinese as a mode of communication when none in the party could speak the dialect of the party with whom they were conversing.[4]

The phenomenon of brushtalk was already fairly well established by the fourth century when Paekche, the dominant power on the Korean Peninsula in that period, began to send embassies to the Chinese court. Chinese historical sources, for instance, speak about formal interactions between successive Chinese courts and the Korean kingdom of Paekche, when Paekche was an independent power on the peninsula between the late fourth and mid-seventh centuries in the common era.[5] Paekche's period of ascendancy coincided with the Six Dynasties period (222–589 CE) in China, thus Paekche embassies to China presented tribute and exchanged classical Chinese poems with a number of different dynastic regimes.[6]

Paekche presents an example of the model of a tributary state in terms of its relations with the Chinese dynasties with which it interacted. For a tributary state, such as Paekche, presentation of tribute and poetry to the dynastic court was the cost of recognition by the ruling emperor. In exchange for tributary gifts, Paekche leaders received grandiose titles that both confirmed their right to rule and increased their prestige back home and in the eyes of the Chinese court.[7]

The model of Paekche's interactions with China was well known to the early Japanese. Paekche envoys regularly visited both China and Japan, and Paekche provided the Japanese court with the concepts and teachers needed to introduce an advanced civilization based on the Chinese dynastic model.[8] The Japanese, for their part, traveled to Paekche at the same time that they were beginning to send envoys to China. The journey from Japan to Paekche and onward to China was a long and dangerous one for Japanese of the era. An account of one such trip made in 659 and recorded in the *Nihon shoki* (Chronicles of Japan, 720) describes how the two ships making the journey were blown off course and separated, with one ending up in present-day Jiangsu Province and the other in Zhejiang. After reuniting at Yuyao, it took the party two months before reaching the capital near Luoyang.[9] Japanese records also recount trips made from Japan to Paekche in 608, 615, and 654.[10]

In such visits to their civilized neighbors, the Japanese, still in the nascent stages of court culture, were learning the fundamental structures and conventions of Sinitic court culture along with Chinese linguistic skills from Paekche and from the Sui and Tang courts. Through interactions with neighboring states the Japanese acquired the requisite skills to communicate in an acceptable manner during formal court visits, including the ability to communicate via classical Chinese.

The Tang court, anxious to foster appropriate communications skills among its neighbors, established academies in which scholars from tributary and neighboring states could acquire the skills necessary to interact in appropriate ways. One such institution was the Zhongwenguan, a Confucian academy established by Emperor Taizang (627–50) in the Tang capital of Chang'an in order to educate students from China's neighboring states. Korean and Japanese monks studied at the academy, and although little information survives about specific aspects of the academy's curriculum or pedagogical methods, for example the language(s) of instruction, the fact remains that many foreign students received their education there. Jonathan Best suggests that the academy educated as many as 8000 students during its existence in the Tang Dynasty.[11]

Although Japan was never officially a tributary state of China, it was nevertheless clearly within the cultural orbit of China and was in close contact with the Chinese court during the Nara period (710–794) and the former part of the Heian Period (794–1185). Actually, the first official Japanese visit to China took place at the end of China's Sui Dynasty in the year 600. The Japanese court dispatched the mission in 600 to the Sui court, and this served to establish a tradition of court sanctioned visits that would continue for the next two centuries.[12] These envoys to the Sui and Tang courts and to the courts of Paekche and Silla, served as the principal channel for study and trade in China and bolstered Japan's status as a civilized member of the East Asian community.[13] These official embassies to the Tang capital of Chang'an known in Japanese as *kentōshi*, allowed Japan to remain abreast of political developments and intellectual currents in China. The Japanese court eventually would dispatch a total of six such embassies to the Sui court and fifteen to the Tang Court, with the last, a huge mission including over six hundred men and various forms of tribute, coming in 801.[14] Emperor Kammu died in 806 and with his death ended the dependence on Tang dynasty cultural models.

Written classical Chinese served as the true language of exchange between the Japanese visitors and their Chinese hosts. Thus, the ability to read and write *kanbun* and the ability to write a passable Chinese poem, *kanshi*, were considered indispensable skills for the Heian courtier. The ability to read and write classical Chinese poetry required a certain mastery of Chinese prosody and of the conventions of Six Dynasties and Tang Dynasty poetry. Nevertheless, most of the *kanshi* written by Heian courtiers were public and formal and undistinguished.[15] The composition of poetry in Chinese remained, then, something of a parlor trick for Japanese aristocrats and its currency among Heian courtiers did not imply any real proficiency in the Chinese language, and presumably few in the Heian court could actually communicate in spoken Chinese.

There were notable exceptions to this fact, and there were among intellectuals of the Heian period some who possessed genuine proficiency in the Chinese language. Of these, the two best known are the monk Kūkai and the courtier Sugawara no Michizane. Kūkai, also known as Kōbō Daishi (774–835), is one of the truly remarkable figures in Japanese cultural history and holds a legendary status in Japan. Kūkai is counted among the *sanpitsu*, the three great calligraphers in Japanese history along with Tachibana no Hayanari and Emperor Saga. Kūkai is also credited with having developed the *kana* syllabaries which, along with the *kanji* (Chinese characters), comprise the modern Japanese writing system. The total veracity of Kūkai's achievements notwithstanding, his introduction of Shingon Buddhism to Japan and his overall influence on Buddhism in Japan are undeniable. Well documented also was Kūkai's ability in Chinese.

Kūkai and Saichō (767–822), who established the Tendai (Chinese, Tiantai) sect of Buddhism in Japan, participated in the mission from the Heian court to the Tang Court that lasted in total from 801 to 806. This final mission to the Tang court ultimately encountered some problems, as had earlier missions, due to Japan's refusal to adopt an attitude of subordination befitting tributary states.[16] The men who participated in this and other missions to the Tang court were chosen either on the basis of birth or significant scholarly achievement.[17] Kūkai, whose scholarship and spiritual aspirations were beyond reproach, was also a valuable member of the mission due to his facility with written Chinese. Saichō, who was traveling to China in order to study in greater depth Tendai, brought along a disciple proficient in Chinese in order to facilitate communications with his hosts. However, there is no mention of Kūkai having such an intermediary, suggesting his ability to communicate sufficiently well in spoken Chinese.[18]

The importance of brushtalk in these intercultural exchanges, and Kūkai's ability to communicate skillfully via this medium, is suggested by a brief anecdote from the 801 mission to China. One of the ships containing nearly half of the emissaries was blown off course and ended up in the small southern port city of Fuzhou. The local officials, unaware of the arrival of the mission, and skeptical of its true objectives, were reluctant to allow the emissaries to continue en-route to Chang'an, until Kūkai composed an elegant appeal describing the goals of the mission in mellifluous Chinese prose, which convinced the authorities to allow the mission to continue on to its destination.[19]

Kūkai spent time in various places in China and studied for a year and one month in the capital of Chang'an. After leaving Chang'an, Kūkai traveled to Yuezhou before returning to Japan via the entry port of Dazaifu in October of 806. It is a testimony to his cultural importance in Japan and to the recognition of his stature as a cultural bridge between the two countries that even today there is a memorial to Kūkai in the city of Xi'an.[20]

An even more significant figure in terms of the discussion of brushtalk and the use of Chinese by Japanese intellectuals of the Heian period is Sugawara no Michizane (845–903). Michizane is often posited as an exemplar of true understanding of the Chinese literary tradition and one of the few eminent Japanese of any period to master the complexities of Chinese prosody. In fact, Michizane's grandfather, Kiyokimi, had been an eminent Sinologist in the Heian court prior to Michizane's time. Kiyokimi visited the Tang court as a member of the 801 mission along with Kūkai, and his use of the contemporary colloquial Chinese term *bufen*, in a surviving *kanbun* attributed to him, is often raised as proof of his facility with spoken Chinese.[21] Among teachers active during Michizane's day also, there is mention of a teacher by the name of Wang Tu, who was apparently an immigrant from China living among a community of Chinese near the capital of Heiankyō (present day Kyoto). He was apparently among those who taught Chinese at a local imperial institution, suggesting that Michizane had the opportunity to study spoken Chinese along with his exposure to the most recent developments in Chinese prosody.[22]

Michizane was recognized as a master of both *kanshi* and *kanbun* among Heian courtiers, but in fact all Heian courtiers were expected to have a certain level of conversance with the Chinese canon. Heian period courtiers were comfortable with the poetic forms of the Six Dynasty Period and were increasingly familiar and comfortable with the Tang dynasty poetic forms and conventions, including the five and seven character *jueju* form which rose to prominence in the Tang Dynasty. Nevertheless, no poet of the age was as comfortable and adept at producing *kanshi* as Michizane. Even when convention did not demand the composition of Chinese poetry, Michizane often chose that mode of literary expression. For example, on a twelve-day journey to Japan's southern provinces undertaken in 898 Michizane produced *kanshi* while his companions composed poems in the representative Japanese *waka* form.[23]

The court recognized Michizane's genius for *kanbun* and *kanshi* and exploited his skills in those areas in cultural interactions with dignitaries from neighboring countries. For example, Michizane was among a group who welcomed a visiting delegation from the kingdom of Parhae who visited in 883. Parhae flourished northeast of the Tang border and was comprised of leaders who had fled from Koguryo in 696.[24] The welcoming of the visitors from Parhae began with an exchange of Chinese poems between Michizane and the other Japanese hosts and the dignitaries from Parhae. Only when Chinese poetry had been exchanged could formal negotiations begin.[25] Depending on the availability of interpreters, it can easily be imagined that both parties might be compelled to depend on the writing brush as the sole means of conducting negotiations.

One of the great tragedies of cultural exchange between Japan and China is the fact that Sugawara no Michizane, Sinophile and cultural bridge between Japan and China, never had the opportunity to visit the country the culture of which he so exquisitely interpreted to his generation. Michizane had been appointed chief ambassador for a large-scale mission that was to take place in 894. However, the instability in China due to the An Lushan Rebellion led Michizane to suggest that the mission be cancelled, and that aborted mission turned out to be the last chance for Michizane to visit China. The infamous exile which marked his final years spelled not only the end of Michizane's influence at court, it also effectively led to the abandonment of such official Japanese court missions to China and a virtual break of official contact between China and Japan that would last for nearly five centuries.[26]

Thereafter, interaction between Japan and China became sporadic and did not adhere necessarily to the formal trappings of cultural exchange that had developed during the Tang Dynasty. The Ashikaga shogunate sent representatives to the Ming Court in the fourteenth century, and the abiding interest in *kanshi* can be seen in the phenomenon of Five Mountain (*gozan*) Chinese language poetry that flourished among Zen Buddhist monks in Japan during the Medieval period.

Certainly, even with the cession of formal relations between Japan and China, Japanese writers and scholars remained keenly interested in cultural developments on the continent as can be witnessed, for example, in the influence of the Neo-Confucian thought of Wang Yangming on Tokugawa thought.[27] The trappings of traditional cultural interactions and the central importance attached to the writing brush remained as well. During the Tokugawa period (1603–1868) when the shogunate officials received visiting envoys from the Yi (Choson) Court in Korea, they were received in the traditional manner and Chinese poetry was exchanged. Such practices at a time when Japan effectively had cut itself off from the rest of the world, including the Chinese court, suggests the persistence of classical Chinese and of brushtalk as the ultimate medium and mediator of cultural exchange in East Asia.[28]

During the same period that modern Japanese writers were journeying to China and writing about their experiences there with increasing frequency, *kangakusha* or "scholars of Chinese learning," particularly in the realms of history and culture, were also venturing to China and producing accounts of their visits. These visits by *kangakusha* and the body of writing that resulted from their visits provides an intriguing corollary to the parallel body of writing by members of the *bundan* (literary community).[29]

The visits of *kangakusha* to China actually preceded those of Japanese writers and can be traced to the visit of the Senzaimaru mission in 1862. Such *kangakusha* as Takasugi Shinsaku (1839–1867) and Hibino Teruhiro (1838–1912) were included in the mission by the shogunate because of their broad knowledge of traditional Chinese culture and history and because of their facility in communicating with the Chinese they encountered via the brush in the form of *hitsudan*. Their role in the mission and their subsequent responses to the realities of the China they encountered in Shanghai often differed in radical fashion from those of the merchants and government officials who accompanied them on the journey.[30]

Although the Senzaimaru mission included *kangakusha,* who produced accounts of their visit upon their return to Japan, the real genre of *kangakusha* accounts of visits to China developed in the decades that followed in the works of several of the most renowned *kangakusha* of the Meiji period. Visits by Takezoe Shin'ichirō (1842–1917) in 1876, Oka Senjin (1832–1913) in 1884 and Naitō Konan (1866–1934) in 1899 provided Japanese readers with nuanced and informed perspectives on contemporary China in the context of a thoroughgoing knowledge of traditional Chinese culture and society.

Some of these accounts, such as Oka Senjin's *Kankō Kiyū* (Trip Report, 1884) expressed despair at the contrast between the robust splendor of traditional China and the squalor he encountered during his visit to China. Other accounts, however, offer a contrasting viewpoint. In Naitō Konan's *Enzan sosui* (Mountains of North China and the Rivers of South China) Naitō wrote openly about the problems gripping contemporary China, but never despaired of China's ability to return to its former position of glory.[31]

One of the most fascinating and weighty pieces of writing produced by *kangakusha* in the wake of an extended stay in China was written by Uno Tetsuto (1875–1974) in 1907 entitled *Shina bunmei ki* (A Record of Civilization in China). The work describes Uno's eighteen months of study in Beijing in 1906–07. An intriguing and comprehensive description of China which extends to nearly four hundred pages, *Shina bunmei ki* recounts in painstaking detail the various phenomena that Uno observed including people, places, festivals and sites of cultural interest. One important quality of the work, which it held in common with other accounts of China by *kangakusha*, was Uno's dogged attempts to consciously root out those elements of tradition that still existed in some fashion.³² The most symbolically important manifestation was Uno's visit to Mount Tai. Mount Tai, China's most sacred mountain, was the destination of a pilgrimage by Confucius, 2500 years earlier, and by following in the footsteps of the master, Uno had "returned, figuratively, to the fount of civilization itself."³³

Kangakusha continued to visit China in the first half of the twentieth century, and their accounts provide a corollary to the body of writing by Japanese writers. In some ways, the two bodies of writing validate and challenge one another in such themes as the attempt to use traditional culture as a touchstone for contemporary China. For *kangakusha*, the brush and brushtalk provided the immediate means of exchange and cross cultural and literary exchange with the host. Unlike many of the Japanese writers treated in this text, the *kangakusha* possessed a facility with classical Chinese unrivaled in Japan. These scholars thus felt no great need to go beyond brushtalk; brushtalk remained an apposite and effective means of communication with Chinese hosts.

Bridge Building: Factors Contributing to the Ease of Interaction between Chinese and Japanese Writers in the Interwar Period

A variety of factors contributed to the ease with which Japanese and Chinese writers were able to meet and interact in the interwar period. Among the most significant issues that contributed to effective interaction between the two literary communities was the opportunity for a number of bright, promising young Chinese students to study abroad in Japan. This happily coincided with increased opportunities for Japanese writers to visit China, and many important Japanese writers of the period did, in fact, avail themselves of this opportunity. Moreover, for a variety of reasons, some of which will be touched upon here, Chinese writers were interested in Japanese intellectual and cultural currents and were even more interested in keeping abreast of Western intellectual trends and reading Western literary works in Japanese translations. As a consequence of this, maintaining the Japanese language proficiency achieved while studying in Japan was of critical importance to many Chinese writers.

The phenomenon of Chinese students returning from years of study in Japan to embark on careers as writers is part of the larger phenomenon of Chinese studying abroad in the first quarter of the twentieth century. Of the significant writers of the May Fourth period, it has been suggested that nearly half of them had some overseas study experience either before they started their careers as writers, or soon after they had begun writing.[34] Although the majority went to study when they were between the ages of twenty and thirty, presumably already having committed themselves to their craft, nearly a quarter of May Fourth writers who studied abroad went when they were under the age of twenty.[35] Significantly, many of the latter cohort went to Japan, and among them are some of the most influential literary and intellectual figures of that generation including, Lu Xun (1881–1936), Tian Han (1898–1979) and Guo Moruo (1892–1978).

In fact, of the Chinese who studied abroad in the period under discussion, the overwhelming majority did so in Japan. Of the writers of the May Fourth Era, 66 studied in Japan as opposed to 32 in France, 30 in the United States and only 19 in England.[36] Of course the reasons why the decision was made to study in a certain country, often by the provincial government officials who sponsored the student, were complex. The decision to study in Japan was primarily an economic one, bolstered by cultural and linguistic affinities, which were presumed to facilitate the process of acculturation on the part of the students.

For the few fortunate enough to be chosen to participate in study abroad, there were innumerable benefits, including direct contact with artists and intellectuals in the host country, which influenced their individual decisions to write. These encounters in turn parlayed into the development and organization of China's new literature. The benefit of living abroad for these young writers included a direct engagement with foreign literature and literary theory, an openness to new ideas and influences, a willingness to question and criticize authority, and a worldliness and sophistication borne of the experience of negotiating in a foreign society and culture.[37]

Nevertheless, there were certain aspects of the experience abroad for those who studied in Japan that were unique to Japan and which are germane to this study. While in Japan, the students' encounter with contemporary Japanese literature affected their conceptualization of literary organizations in terms of the structure of both specific literary coteries and also of the social status and obligations of writers as a class. Moreover, because of their proximity to Japan, many students were able to later revisit Japan in order to keep abreast of recent literary and intellectual developments. It is, however, in terms of language that the experience in Japan most profoundly influenced those who returned to China and became writers. The Japanese language primarily influenced Chinese literary style as May Fourth writers sought to create a new vernacular literary language.[38] The ability to speak and read Japanese also proved to be of paramount importance to these young writers. Not only did it allow them to pursue studies in Japan and to read contemporary Japanese literature, it also gave them access to the substantial and increasing body of Western literature in Japanese translation which in turn profoundly affected the speed with which Chinese writers were able to hasten the development of China's own modern literature.[39]

Given the number of May Fourth era writers who had lived and studied in Japan in the late Meiji and Taishō periods it is not surprising that the Japanese writers who they openly admired and whose works they sought to translate should correspond to those who enjoyed a strong reputation in Japan. However, it is a source of some interest that some of the most acclaimed writers in Japan, including naturalist writers such as Tayama Katai (1872–1930) and Shimazaki Tōson (1872–1943) did not receive critical attention in China commensurate to their status in Japan while a less celebrated writer such as Mushanokoji Saneatsu, should have been so highly regarded.

It was Zhou Zuoren and Lu Xun in their translations from contemporary Japanese literature and their critical essays from the teens and early twenties who helped establish tastes in Japanese literature among May Fourth readers. In fact, it was Zhou Zuoren's speech delivered at Beijing University in 1918, "Japanese Literary Developments in the Past Thirty Years" (Riben jin sanshinian xiaoshuo zhi fada), published as an essay in *New Youth* (Xin qingnian) in the following year, that provided the initial introduction to literary currents in contemporary Japan and established a hierarchy of Japanese writers. In this essay and in the essays and translations produced by the Zhou brothers through the early twenties, the Japanese writers who emerge as the most influential figures, including some of those treated in this study, are Natsume Sōseki, Tanizaki Jun'ichirō, Akutagawa Ryūnosuke and Kikuchi Kan from the Shinshichō (New Currents of Thought) School, and Mushanokōji Saneatsu and Arishima Takeo from the White Birch School. Since Mushanokōji, Arishima and Tanizaki are all treated in this study, I will restrict my remarks to the reception of other Japanese writers in the May Fourth literary milieu.

The individualism and humanism of Natsume Sōseki (1867–1916) resonated with May Fourth readers in much the same way as they did with Japanese readers. The influence of Sōseki in the May Fourth literary world came largely filtered through the essays of Zhou Zuoren. The influence of the humanism of Sōseki is particularly apparent in Zhou's humanist manifesto, "Ren de wenxue" (Humane Literature), in which Zhou advocates a realistic literary approach that delineates human experience from an individual's perspective.[40]

Like his brother, Lu Xun too was initially drawn to Sōseki's thought, but, as Zhou Zuoren asserts, "The True Story of Ah Q" and other works of fiction by Lu Xun also clearly reflect the style of Sōseki. Lu Xun appears to have been most attracted to Sōseki's essays and *shōhin,* and he translated several of these pieces for the Japanese literature volume in the *Shijie wenxue daxi* (Compendium of World Literature) in 1922 including "Yume jūya" (Ten Nights of Dreams) and "Kureegu sensei" (Craig sensei).[41] Both of these pieces are characterized by Sōseki's unmistakable and engaging narrative voice which, despite other difference between the two writers, is a quality that he clearly shares with Lu Xun.[42] Lu Xun's admiration for Sōseki helped to establish in China the same aura of high regard for Sōseki in which the writer was held in Japan.

In a similar way, Akutagawa Ryūnosuke garnered critical and popular attention in May Fourth China comparable to that which he received in Japan. Lu Xun translated Akutagawa's story "Hana" (The Nose) in *Chenbao fukan* (The Morning News Supplement) between May 11 and June 14, 1921. In the appendix that accompanied his translation Lu Xun stated that what appealed to him about this and other stories by Akutagawa was his artful recasting in contemporary terms of historical material in which a thoroughly modern, realistic style brought the historical moment to life.[43]

Starting with "The Nose," Lu Xun and Zhou Zuoren translated several stories by Akutagawa in the twenties. Due to their endorsement of Akutagawa and the sensation caused by his suicide, Akutagawa enjoyed an exalted status among Chinese readers in the interwar period.[44] Moreover, to a greater degree than other Japanese writers from the prewar era, Akutagawa's appeal continued in China long after the war, and he appeared as the subject of a number of critical essays in the 1980s and 1990s.

While his appeal was ultimately not as enduring as Akutagawa's, during the interwar period fellow Shinshichō writer Kikuchi Kan (1888–1948) also enjoyed a strong reputation among May Fourth readers. While in Japan, prior to the formation of the Creation Society, Yu Dafu read and admired Kikuchi Kan and apparently intended to produce a literary magazine modeled on *Shinshichō* (New Currents), the literary organ of the coterie group of the same name.[45] Interestingly, Yu Dafu and the other Creationists, who read Japanese literary magazines as students in Japan, had developed their own tastes in contemporary Japanese literature independent of the influence of Lu Xun and Zhou Zuoren prior to their return to China in 1921 and 1922.[46] As he had with Akutagawa, Lu Xun translated two of Kikuchi Kan's stories in the early twenties: "Miura Uemon no saigo" (The End of Miura Uemon) and "Adauchi kinshirei" (A Proscription on Revenge). Lu Xun stated that what he admired about Kikuchi Kan was that he was less consciously aesthetic than Akutagawa and that Kikuchi possessed a genius for portraying the complexities of the human condition.[47] Kikuchi's reputation in China was further enhanced by the introduction to his plays by Tian Han and Ouyang Yuqian and other young Chinese dramatists who were drawn to the social realism of Kikuchi's plays.

Ironically, Japanese linguistic ability ultimately offered a further benefit for these writers. The high level of Japanese linguistic proficiency that these writers were able to attain while students in Japan allowed them to go beyond the traditional brushtalk to communicate directly with Japanese writers who flocked to China in increasing numbers in the Taishō and early Shōwa periods. Accounts by Japanese writers as diverse as Tanizaki Jun'ichirō (1886–1965) and Ibuse Masuji (1898–1993) comment on the remarkably high levels of Japanese linguistic ability of these Chinese writers, even years after their return to China.

The phenomenon of Chinese writers of the May Fourth period who had studied in Japan and possessed not only a familiarity with Japanese literature and intellectual currents, but also strong Japanese proficiency was accompanied by increased opportunities for Japanese writers to visit China. Travel to China on the part of the Japanese had actually recommenced in 1862, five years before the fall of the Tokugawa shogunate. Following the Senzaimaru mission to China which, in the manner of the traditional *kentōshi*, included Japanese officials and eminent Sinologists, an increasing number of Japanese writers and thinkers traveled to China in the late Meiji period.[48] The number of Japanese writers who visited China increased even more dramatically in the Taishō period (1912–1926) and through 1936, the first decade of the Shōwa period (1926–1989).

Japanese writers who traveled to China in this period visited for a variety of reasons. Japan's influence in China had widened, and Japanese had easy entry into such ports as Shanghai and Ningbo. Shanghai in the first half of the twentieth century was one of the world's truly cosmopolitan cities, the fifth largest city in the world and a metropolis "shrouded in glamour and mystery."[49] Part of the attraction of Shanghai was its diversity, and it attracted ambitious, adventurous people from around the world. The International Settlement, which was home to large foreign populations, represented for visiting Japanese the illusion of visiting the West.

However, Japanese were also anxious to visit the China of tradition, which they envisioned as a place with which they had strong cultural affinities. Japanese writers, in their description of various sites they visited during this era were likely to speak of it in terms of a common cultural homeland, and the places they were naturally drawn to were places with which they were already familiar through their conversance with traditional Chinese culture and literature. Japanese writers spoke of *kanji bunka*, the culture of Chinese characters, which ostensibly linked all men of letters in East Asia. Japanese writers professed to possess an intuitive knowledge of China which came via the written Chinese characters themselves and which emboldened them to adopt the role of apologists for China to their readers back in Japan.[50]

There were other, internal factors that made travel to China possible and desirable for Japanese writers. These writers were sometimes dispatched to China and had their passage paid by organizations and institutions that wished to enlist the aid of well-known writers to develop some image of China. For instance, newspapers would sometimes send writers to China as special literary correspondents. One celebrated example of this was Akutagawa Ryūnosuke, who visited China from late March to early July of 1921. He was sent by the *Osaka Mainichi Shinbun* in order to visit famous sites in China and to write a series of articles on the cultural life of contemporary China.[51]

The South Manchurian Railway (SMR) Company was another organization which made it possible for writers to visit China from the late Meiji period into the Shōwa period, as something of a public relations strategy. The most celebrated of these literary visitors who came via the offices of SMR was Natsume Sōseki (1867–1916). Sōseki visited China in 1909 at the invitation of Nakamura Zeko (1867–1927), the president of SMR.[52] Although the company paid for Sōseki's visit and presumably hoped that he would say flattering things about their efforts in China, they had no control over what he actually wrote.[53] In fact, one of the striking features of the body of writing by Japanese writers who visited China in the early twentieth century was the startling range of responses that the experience of travel in China elicited among them, which ran the gamut from unbridled adulation to outright disgust, and often featured a little of the two.

One final impetus for travel to China on the part of Japanese writers in the first half of the twentieth century was the increasing vigilance of authorities and the skewed reportage of China in the media. Writers traveled abroad in order to see the realities of contemporary China with their own eyes and to offer their readers an alternative perspective, one that differed from that provided by official channels, one that often consciously hearkened back to the traditional relationship between the two countries and was designed to elicit a sympathy for China sadly lacking in that militarist era. Intellectuals in the Taishō period perceived themselves as leaders in the "rising trend of individual consciousness and spoke increasingly of the social function of *zaya gakuha*, independent artists and intellectuals."[54] The Taishō Democracy movement, in fact, urged universal suffrage, and the end of censorship and social equality for all.[55] The phenomenon of Japanese writers visiting China is profitably seen, in one sense, as an attempt to foster greater autonomy on the part of the writers from authority.

Furthermore, the phenomenon of Japanese writers visiting China was accompanied by several academic efforts to learn more about contemporary China and to go, by means of Chinese language education, beyond the limitations and stiff formality of traditional brush talk encounters in order to engage contemporary China. One such example of this was the Tōa Dōbun Shoin (East Asian Common Culture Academy) in Shanghai which educated Japanese youth in Chinese language, including the spoken Chinese, and culture.[56] The purpose of the academy, established by the parent institution Tōa Dōbunkai in Tokyo (1898–

1945), was to train young Japanese for business and government service. More than five thousand students received training at the institute between 1900 and 1945.[57] Some of the graduates of Tōa Dōbun Shoin became academics, others went into business and banking. Moreover, the school maintained a strong connection with the military, and many graduates ended up serving in Manchuria.[58] What is critical to this study is that at the time when the study of vernacular Chinese was seen as "crazy" and Chinese language education in Japan still emphasized written classical Chinese, there were isolated academic attempts in Japan also to go beyond the limitations of brushtalk.[59]

The various factors described in this section converged in the interwar period (1919–1937) to create an environment of relations between China and Japan in which writers were able to meet and to exchange ideas directly, sometimes employing the time-tested practices associated with the tradition of brushtalk interaction, but often eschewing them in order to develop a new, modern idiom of cultural exchange and to create a climate in which writers from both Japan and China could interact above of the political imbroglio in the development of their respective vernacular literatures.

In the Name of Progress: The Sordid Realities of Sino-Japanese Political Relations in the Interwar Period

The attempts at cultural bridging by Japanese and Chinese writers described in this study were enacted against a backdrop of increasing tension and impending conflict between the two countries. These efforts at direct communication between writers from the two literary communities can only be interpreted as vain and ultimately futile attempts to avoid and transcend the various obstacles that lay between writers from the two countries. For a short period, corresponding to the first half of the period covered in this study, roughly from 1919 to 1929, writers were able to sidestep these larger issues in their dealings with one another, clinging to the safe haven of a shared aesthetic vision, whether an art-for-art's sake aesthetic or a socialist realism based on European models. Ultimately, however, this flouting of political realities became less and less tenable with the increasing tensions of the 1930s.

Sino-Japanese relations during the interwar period have been characterized as a "many layered cake, impossible to eat all at once."[60] To be certain, relations between the two countries during this period were enormously complex, with the cultural relations described in this study representing but one facet of a network of interrelations that also included political and diplomatic relations, economic and social relations, most of which were marred by increasingly severe pressures that were constantly threatening the fragile balance that allowed for dialogue between members of the two literary communities. Writers in both communities attempted to justify their efforts by resorting to a time-honored argument, appealing to affinities between the two countries. Likewise, propagandists in Japan sought to legitimize their imperialist activities in East Asia by drawing upon cultural affinities, racial similarities and geographical proximity to underscore an assumed sense of closeness. Both literati and propagandists couched these appeals by resorting finally to written characters as the source of closeness as manifested in the term *dōbun dōshu* (common script, common race).[61]

The history of political and diplomatic relations between the two countries in the interwar period is a litany of missteps, betrayals and diplomatic failures as the two countries moved inexorably toward open conflict. One commentator describes the "psychological warfare" waged by both Japan and China between 1905 and 1945 in regard to relations with the other in order to sway opinion both at home and in the other nation.[62] This propaganda often took the form of an appeal to pan-Asian doctrine. That writers too should have appropriated this rhetoric, which had a certain appeal as an antidote to the hegemony of Western values, should not be surprising.

Sino-Japanese relations in the interwar period have their roots in the late nineteenth century in the aftermath of China's humiliating defeat at the hands of the Japanese in the Sino-Japanese War (1894–95). This defeat, in conjunction with unflattering reports about China sent back by an increasing number of Japanese visitors to China resulted in a dramatic change in the Japanese conceptualization of China. Whereas China had traditionally been held in awe by the Japanese, who referred to their giant neighbor as a "sleeping lion," in the modern period "Shina," itself a culturally weighted designation, was portrayed as the home to a backward race of people unable to modernize whom the Japanese came to refer to derisively as *chankoro* (pig-tailed fellows).[63]

In August of 1914 Japan launched an invasion force against the German forces in China and captured Qingdao on November 7 of the same year. The infamous "Twenty-one Demands" presented to Yuan Shikai on January 18, 1915 brought Sino-Japanese relations to a new low.[64] Among Japan's demands of China were unprecedented privileges in Manchuria and the transfer of control of the resource-rich and culturally important Shandong Peninsula.[65] When Yuan Shikai (1859–1916) caved in to the Japanese demands, the response among the Chinese populace was both immediate and widespread. A great number of Chinese students returned from studies in Japan and become involved in anti-Japanese activities, which included a boycott of Japanese goods and nationwide demonstrations.[66]

When the Terauchi Masatake (1852–1919) cabinet came to power in Japan in 1916 there was an attempt to improve relations with China and to alleviate some of the tensions caused by the Twenty-one Demands. Toward that end, Prime Minister Terauchi provided political loans to the Chinese government.[67] However, the loans themselves were resented in certain quarters in China, and with the appointment of the more conservative and less accommodating Hara Kei (1856–1921) cabinet in 1918 the loans were eventually discontinued.

Tensions again rose to the boiling point in the wake of the Paris Peace Conference of 1919 when at the plenum the lease of Germany in the Shandong Peninsula was awarded to Japan rather than being returned to China despite the urging of the Chinese delegates in attendence.[68] This action again resulted in Chinese boycotts of Japanese goods and massive demonstrations in China's major cities and also served as the catalyst for the New Culture Movement, which in turn led to the rise of the May Fourth Movement which produced the writers who are the focus of this study. It was not until the Shandong Treaty of February 4, 1922 that the former German leased territory, which included the Jinan-Qingdao Railway and other assets were formally restored to China.[69] While this action served to temporarily relax tensions between China and Japan, the mistrust of Japan by the Chinese and the schism that had emerged between the two countries remained unchanged.

The cabinet of Shidehara Kijūrō (1872–1951) from 1924–1927 saw genuine attempts to cultivate more benign policies toward China and to relax some of the seething tensions between the two countries. There were several endeavors during Shidehara's administration to create a policy of "Friendship and Co-operation" with the various warlord cliques in an increasingly unstable China.[70] Although it can be argued that in fact economic considerations drove Japan's more beneficent policies in China, there is no doubt that Shidehara's diplomatic principles of co-existence and co-prosperity (kyōson kyōei-shugi) created some small measure of goodwill between the two countries. It is not surprising then that this four-year period corresponds to the high point of relations between the two literary communities. It was during these years that most of the writers addressed in this study became acquainted, and several of the Japanese writers considered in this study visited China.

The relative euphoria of the period, however, was short-lived. With the coming to power of General Tanaka Giichi (1866–1949), head of the Seiyūkai opposition party, in 1927 relations once again began to sour. Anti-Japanese demonstrations occurred once again, and when Prime Minister Tanaka sent 2000 Japanese troops in to quell the unrest in Shandong in May of 1927, tensions were further exacerbated. The Eastern Conference (Tōhō kaigi) convened by Tanaka between June and July of 1927 failed to bridge the gap between Chinese nationalist aspirations and Japanese continental expansionism.[71] Under these circumstances it was difficult for writers to meet and avoid the realities of tensions between the two countries.

Further deterioration of relations between the two countries can be inferred from the increasing frequency of "events" and "incidents" which were indications of Japan's return to wholesale intervention on the continent. These include, for instance, the Mukden Incident of September 18, 1931 in which a train traveling from Beijing to Mukden was attacked by the Japanese Guandong Army.[72] The Manchurian Crisis, which this incident precipitated, marked an important turning point in Sino-Japanese relations. The Guandong Army secured the main arteries in central and southern Manchuria, effectively taking control of all of Manchuria. Zhang Xueliang (1901–2001), the Chinese military leader in Manchuria, withdrew from Manchuria and appealed to the League of Nations. The league was unable to resolve the crisis, and Japan, emboldened by the apparent acquiescence of the international community, recognized the puppet state of Manchuguo (Japanese, Manshūkoku), effectively rendering constructive relations between the two nations impossible.[73]

Japanese intervention in the greater Shanghai area in 1932, which resulted in the lopsided Sino-Japanese Treaty of May 1932 and Japan's decision to withdraw from the League of Nations in 1933, effectively meant that international mediation in Sino-Japanese affairs was no longer possible.[74] These direct military actions and diplomatic maneuverings were accompanied by rhetoric on the Japanese side designed to consolidate Japanese legitimacy on the continent. Prime Minister Konoe Fumimaro's (1891–1945) designation of a New Order in East Asia and the concept of Japan's leadership in the Greater East Asian Co-prosperity Sphere (Daitōa kyōeiken) were intended to be seen as the justification for Japanese military maneuverings in China.[75] By the time war was officially declared in 1937, all relations between the two countries, including the personal relations between the writers described in this study, effectively had come to an end.

Writers in both China and Japan in the 1930s were faced with a staggering array of impediments to continued interactions with their colleagues in the other literary community. In Japan, increasingly vigilant censorship and pressure from the authorities made intercourse with Chinese writers virtually impossible. Although travel to China continued, it was more and more difficult for Japanese writers to have unmediated contact with their Chinese colleagues.

Ultimately, Japanese writers were faced with several choices, all unsavory. They could oppose the government's militaristic stance and rightist agenda and use their writing as a tool for political criticism. Few writers chose the path of conscience, and those who did were faced with harassment by the police, imprisonment, or even death, as in the well-known case of the proletarian writer Kobayashi Takiji (1903–1933), murdered while under incarceration. Among the other options available to Japanese writers during the 1930s were collaboration with the authorities, or silence. Writers who were associated either with "pure literature" or with the proletarian movement and had been critical of the militarist government were forced to recant and perform *tenkō*, a "conversion" from their apolitical or socialist stance to one of service to the imperialist goals of the state. A number of writers reluctantly trod that path. Other writers, including some contained in this study, who had been apolitical and had clung to an art-for-art's-sake position prior to the 1930s, did an about-face and became, in some cases, enthusiastically supportive of state policy and actively contributed to the dissemination of imperialist propaganda. Still other writers chose to withdraw and remain silent in the face of the atrocities that Japan was committing abroad. Even this seemingly passive option was a difficult one fraught with peril in the face of mounting pressure from the authorities upon artists to support their efforts and to contribute to the propaganda machine. The Japanese writers included in this study reflect the full range of choices.

In China the range of options was much more limited. A few writers aligned themselves with the Guomindang, though the majority aligned themselves with the Chinese Communist Party. Moreover, the majority of Chinese writers included in this study were associated with the League of Leftist Writers, which was formed in 1930. The mission of the league was to support the goals of the Chinese Communist Party through cultural activities and via the literary works themselves. The result was the pursuit of a variety of literature, which would reflect the goals of the party. Many of the members of both the Creation Society and Sun Society were party members, and the movement was well-organized and disciplined, with many of the members of the league active in the Cultural Party Branch in Shanghai.[76] In the late twenties and early thirties literature was seen by the Chinese Communist Party as one of the few areas where the party could assert influence, and writers were charged with the duty of fashioning literary works that reflected the principles of Western realism.[77] The term *shehuizhuyi xianshizhuyi* (Socialist Realism) was adopted from the Soviet Union in 1932 to describe the aspirations of writers to create a proletarian literature which would reflect the unpleasant realities of contemporary Chinese society. Though, as one commentator suggests, "As heirs of the May Fourth literary revolution all left-wing writers claimed to be realists, but they could not agree as to what realism meant."[78] In fact, in actual practice, the Proletarian Movement in Chinese literature was more rhetorical than real. When one looks at the most important Chinese literary works of the 1930s such as Mao Dun's *Ziye* (Midnight, 1933), Ba Jin's *Jia* (Home, 1933), and Ye Shengtao's *Ni Huangzhi* (1929), they all are about the bourgeoisie and cannot properly be called proletarian literature.[79]

Many of the figures included in this study made substantial efforts to avoid and overcome the manifold obstacles that hampered positive interaction between the two literary communities in the 1930s, but ultimately all were forced to submit. Increasingly, during the interwar period in both China and Japan, any interactions with writers in the other literary community were seen as collaboration with the enemy, and writers were forced to abandon their hopes for positive communications with their counterparts in the other literary community and either turn to the task of supporting their state or turn inward away from the horrors that threatened their very existence.

Ian Nish, in writing about relations between China and Japan during this period, adroitly assesses the realities that lay beneath the ideological posturing:

> Few, if any, periods of sustained friendship can be detected. ... However much Japanese thought — and spoke — in terms of co-existence and co-prosperity, it is not evident that China thought in similar terms or reciprocated. There was always some degree of illusion or self-deception in the more benign policies which some Japanese tried to apply to China.[80]

The relations between Chinese and Japanese writers described in this book represent the exception in terms of Sino-Japanese relations during the interwar period. The writers under discussion earnestly sought, at least initially, to put aside ideological differences and endeavored to rise above the fray of political posturing in order to communicate directly and to cooperate in the creation of a common modern East Asian aesthetic vocabulary. Although all writers were forced to abandon this undertaking, many did so only reluctantly, when it became clear that to cling to hopes of the resumption of positive cultural relations was an endeavor fraught with danger. Yu Dafu's death at the hands of Japanese authorities in 1945 was the result in part of his facility with the Japanese language and the close ties he retained with influential Japanese despite his abhorrence of Japanese policies. Yu Dafu was the ultimate victim of this period of failed relations although, as I hope to demonstrate, writers in both communities suffered while trying to sustain relations with colleagues across the political divide.

Beyond Brushtalk: Writer to Writer in the Interwar Period

This work examines Chinese and Japanese literary relations during the interwar period from a variety of perspectives. Among those are direct encounters between writers from the two communities, including relations cultivated during those turbulent years. Also included are considerations of intriguing parallels between writers from the two literary worlds and analyses of important dimensions of writers' oeuvre informed by their experience with the other literary community. Nevertheless, neither is this an exhaustive study of the complex web of cultural relations between the two countries nor will it suggest that the ties between the two literary worlds were organized or officially sanctioned by either country. Finally, it must be admitted that these informal relations between two small cohorts of writers had no effect on slowing the juggernaut of Japanese imperialism in China. Nevertheless, the relationships themselves were sincere and affected the lives and works of all of the writers involved.

Chapter 1 introduces the key figure in literary exchange during the interwar period, Uchiyama Kanzō (1885–1959), and describes how his bookstore served as the unofficial hub for interactions between Chinese and Japanese writers. Moreover, it describes Uchiyama's relationship with Lu Xun, China's most important modern writer and a writer much admired by contemporaries in Japan. The chapter further describes how the relationship between these two men, which hearkened back to the tradition of literati friendships in pre-modern East Asia was tested in the fires of political intrigue and scrutiny by the authorities and was strengthened in the process. Without exception, every writer treated in this study was in some way indebted to the efforts of Uchiyama Kanzō at cultural bridging.

Unlike Chapter 1, which focuses on a specific literary relationship involving two writers, Chapter 2 examines the impact of travel to China on one Japanese writer. Tanizaki Jun'ichirō traveled to China on several occasions, and his interactions with Chinese writers and his encounters with specific places of cultural import informed his literary output at a time that he was gradually turning from the fascination with the West that informed his early works to a return to Eastern aesthetics. The pieces resulting from the first visit fall neatly into the *kikōbun* (travel diary) and *nikki* (literary diary) varieties and are representative examples of a body of such work penned by Japanese writers in the modern period based on their travels, both domestic and overseas. On the other hand, the most significant work produced following Tanizaki's second visit, in its frank description of the Chinese literary community and of specific Chinese writers with whom Tanizaki became acquainted, constitutes a valuable record of cultural exchange between the Chinese and Japanese literary communities during the twenties. The final section of this chapter examines Tanizaki's perspective on the significance of his encounters with those Chinese writers from the vantage point of the War period.

Chapter 3 describes the impact of Japan's White Birch School (Shirakabaha) on the contemporary Chinese literary world. The White Birch School was one of the best organized and ideologically focused of the Taishō period coteries. The idealism and humanism they espoused had an immediate impact on Chinese writers. The brothers, Zhou Zuoren (1885–1967) and Lu Xun, translated and championed the works of various of the School's members, although the writers to whom each of the brothers was attracted too reflect some fundamental aesthetic and ideological differences between the two men.

These differences are even more apparent when contrasting each brother's reaction to Mushanokōji Saneatsu's (1885–1976) New Village movement in aesthetic communal living, a movement derided by Lu Xun, but championed by

Zhou Zuoren, which had an impact on Chinese intellectuals as diverse as Zhou Zuoren, Chen Duxiu (1879–1942) and Mao Zedong (1893–1976). Chapter 4 examines the impact of the New Village experiment on May Fourth intellectuals and gauges the level of interest in the Village among writers and revolutionaries and conjectures on the reasons that enthusiasm for the possibilities of such an experiment quickly cooled in May Fourth China.

Chapter 5 considers the impact of travel experiences in China on the writer, Hayashi Fumiko (1903–1951). Moreover, the chapter considers the reception of Hayashi's work by members of the League of Leftist writers, who were in the early thirties searching for literary representations of the new emancipated women. Parallels between Hayashi's most important early work *Diary of a Vagabond* and Ding Ling's classic early work, *Miss Sophie's Diary* also offer an interesting dimension for discussion of literary relations. Both works, which represent the "new woman" struggling for recognition in a society clinging to traditional values, were welcomed by leftist writers in China. The dramatic turns in the careers of both writers in the 1930s demonstrates the rift that had emerged between the two literary communities and serves as a fitting metaphor for the collapse of relations between Chinese and Japanese writers.

Chapter 6 examines the complex relationship of the Chinese writer Yu Dafu (1896–1945) and the Japanese writer Satō Haruo (1892–1964). The relationship between these two writers, which was initially one of mutual respect and admiration before deteriorating into betrayal and animosity, seems to most fully manifest the unfulfilled hopes of this period. The two writers were familiar with one another's works even before they met, and Yu's story "Sinking" exhibits a debt to Satō's signature work *Rural Melancholy*. The relationship between these two texts, which will also be addressed in this chapter, demonstrates the closeness of aesthetic goals of the two literary communities during the interwar period.

Finally, Chapter 7 will catalogue the choices that each of the writers made in the face of the tensions in the late thirties that led to outright war. The paths that writers trod in the late 1930s, ranging from political activism and collaboration to silence and withdrawal into the relative safety of aesthetics and political disengagement, correspond to the exigencies of that turbulent age. Writers, who had initiated in the 1920s a period of intercommunity dialogue in which they were able to transcend the stiff propriety and cultural orthodoxy of the writing brush in order to communicate directly as artists with similar aesthetic goals, were forced to abandon their efforts. The dream had failed. Nevertheless, for a brief space of time, during a terrible period of enmity between the two nations, Chinese and Japanese writers succeeded in carving out a charmed space in which they could negotiate questions of modernity, the creation of a new literature, and the role of the writer in the new society.

1

The Hub: Uchiyama Kanzō's Shanghai Bookstore and Its Role in Sino-Japanese Literary Relations

Any attempt to understand relations between the Japanese and Chinese literary communities in the interwar period must begin with Uchiyama Kanzō. Uchiyama, who even in his native Japan has received very little scholarly attention, was the most important single figure in Sino-Japanese literary relations during the 1920s and 1930s. The bookstore, which he established in Shanghai in 1916, became during the period in question, the focal point of relations between the Chinese and Japanese literary communities and a safe haven for those seeking some cultural common ground in the increasingly treacherous political terrain between the two countries.

The path that led Uchiyama Kanzō from rural western Japan to Shanghai and to the epicenter of Sino-Japanese cultural relations was a circuitous one. Uchiyama Kanzō was born in the township of Shitsuki in Okayama Prefecture in 1885 to a family of modest means. In elementary school Kanzō was a poor student prone to disciplinary problems. As his family attempted to extricate him from one predicament after another, his mother would invoke the example of her father, a *kangakusha* scholar from the Bakumatsu period named Hagita Ungai who had studied at a Chinese Studies Academy in Osaka and is remembered, if somewhat vaguely, for having produced a memorial for a stele that remains in Osaka to this day.[1] Despite his mother's pleas that he follow in the footsteps of his grandfather, Kanzō ultimately dropped out of school in 1897 at the age of twelve and resolved to go to Osaka to work as a laborer.

In Osaka, Uchiyama performed a variety of menial occupations, which included both factory work and delivery jobs. In 1901 Uchiyama moved to Kyoto where he found employment at a cloth wholesaler in the garment district of Karasuma Avenue.[2] During this period, Uchiyama was fully engaged in the commercial life of Kyoto, and his later reflections on the period suggest that along with other members of the working class with whom he associated, Uchiyama endorsed Japan's military ambitions on the continent. During the

Russo-Japanese War of 1904–05 Uchiyama expressed his support of the war and took part in demonstrations celebrating Japan's military victories over the Russians.[3] Although Uchiyama became an ardent pacifist only later after his move to China and his exposure to the misery brought on by civil strife in that country, several factors merged while he was living in Kyoto to lead him in that direction.

The Education of a "Japanese Coolie"

While Uchiyama's conversion to Christianity and his reading of Christian writers were the more critical factors in his deliberate movement toward pacifism, there was a more immediate impetus toward that path. The young Uchiyama, who had defied his family's wishes and left his younger brothers and sisters behind in Okayama when he moved to the Kansai region, found himself caring for the neglected children of one of his colleagues, Sekino Sanji. Sekino, who Uchiyama later described as both a poor businessman and a failed father, was often away from his home and provided little support for his wife and children.[4] Uchiyama spent more and more time caring for the neglected daughter of the family, even providing shelter for her in the boarding house where he was staying during a particularly trying time for the family.[5] When the third son of the Sekino family, who was a student in Yokohama, fell ill, it was Uchiyama who was sent to look after the boy, staying with him for over two months while he convalesced.[6]

While Uchiyama was shouldering these responsibilities and was adapting naturally to his role as protector and mentor, he was becoming increasingly disillusioned with his work. He had recently switched to newspaper sales and delivery, which did nothing to ease his growing disillusionment with commerce. Just as he was struggling to find some new direction in his life, Uchiyama was introduced to Christianity by a clothier named Otani Shōzō.[7]

In January of 1912, the year which marked the transition from the Meiji period to the Taishō period, at the urging of Otani, Uchiyama visited the Kyoto Church (Kyoto Kyōkai), a day that Uchiyama would later describe somewhat hyperbolically as the "first day of my life's revolution" (watakushi no shōgai no kakumei no daiichinichi).[8] It was there that Uchiyama first met Itō Katsugi and Makino Toraji, the associate pastor and pastor respectively of the Kyoto Church, who would change the course of his life and who were to set him on the path that was to lead him to China.[9]

Having turned to Christianity out of a mounting sense of futility about his life as a merchant, Uchiyama determined to abandon the commercial life and to begin to train to become a missionary, so as to better adhere to the ideals of his newly embraced Christian faith.[10] Under the mentorship of Pastor Makino, Uchiyama came closer to the church while retreating from his former mercantile life. Nevertheless, it was Makino who first suggested to Uchiyama the idea of going to China in order to serve God, and it was also Makino who suggested that Uchiyama not completely abandon business but rather serve God in China while persevering as a merchant.[11]

Makino convinced Uchiyama that the way of the Christian and the way of the merchant were not mutually exclusive, and that were he to work for the right kind of employer, he could pursue business in China without having to resort to the lies that he had come to despise or to engage in the fierce competition he had become accustomed to as a merchant in Osaka and Kyoto. Makino introduced Uchiyama to Taguchi Kenkichi, the owner of a drug company in Osaka named Santendō who was at that time looking for people to serve as sales representatives for the company in China. Uchiyama leapt at the prospect of starting anew in China.

Just as Uchiyama had begun to embrace Christianity and was starting to consider the form that a life of service might take, he was also beginning, under the influence of Makino and Itō, to read the works of several influential Christian pacifists. As with virtually every writer treated in this study, Uchiyama first became enamored with the writing of Leo Tolstoy (1828–1910), but it was his encounter with the writing of Japan's first great Christian thinker of the modern era, Uchimura Kanzō (1861–1930) that was to have the greater impact on Uchiyama's intellectual and spiritual development.

While tossing his prized ivory cigarette case and silver cigarette holder into the sewer may have been the dramatic gesture indicating Uchiyama's repudiation of the cupidity of the merchant and his acceptance of the Christian life, selling his futon and remaining possessions had a more immediately practical significance. With the small amount of money that he earned from the sale of his personal effects, Uchiyama purchased a Bible, a hymnal and the complete forty volumes of Uchimura Kanzō's *magnum opus*, *Seisho no kenkyū* (Biblical Research).[12] Thereafter, during the final days in Japan prior to his departure for China, Uchiyama maintained a strict daily regimen in which he awoke every morning at 4, read a passage from the Bible, sang a hymn and then read a selection from Uchimura's *Seisho no kenkyū*.[13]

Uchiyama's engagement with Christianity and his immersion in the writings of Uchimura Kanzō served to hasten the process of disillusionment with Japan's militarism and accelerated the attraction toward pacifism that had already been initiated in the preceding years. While working as a deliveryman, Uchiyama had been a sensitive observer of the inequities in Japanese society and had been particularly affected by the ill treatment of the Sekino children to which he had been a silent witness. By the time that Uchiyama moved to Shanghai in March of 1913 he had begun to regard pacifism as the only truly Christian way, and his observations in China of inequalities and painful examples of injustice, many the product of foreign imperialism, only served to steel his resolve to serve as a Christian.[14]

Uchiyama went to Shanghai along with two other men to serve as the company's overseas agents. The single most important duty of the overseas agents was to advertise Santendō's products and to promote new products such as the company's recently developed Daigaku eye medicine.[15] Their duties took the three agents to cities that had a Japanese concession and a substantial Japanese population. On these advertising campaign trips from Shanghai where the three were stationed, they invariably would be accompanied by several Chinese coolie (kuli) laborers, who would help post signs and distribute leaflets.

During these trips Uchiyama was often disillusioned and even shocked by the attitudes he observed among the Japanese he encountered along the way, including those of his associates, who often separated themselves from the Chinese with whom they worked, even refusing to eat with them. This separation of the Japanese from the local population was particularly apparent during a one-month sojourn in Hankou by Uchiyama in 1913.[16] Uchiyama was profoundly disappointed by the propensity of Japanese to demand adherence to Japanese protocol and customs, even outside of the concessions, and by the superciliousness that was *de rigueur* among Japanese expatriates. Uchiyama found himself sympathizing more and more with the Chinese laborers who had accompanied him.

> During the one-month advertising campaign in Hankou, I came to be referred to as a "Japanese coolie," indeed I began to so designate myself, as I spent my days shoulder-to-shoulder with the Chinese laborers. This experience would later serve as the foundation for some of my "random chat" essays, and I came to realize that my perspective was far removed from that of civil servants, soldiers, and the privileged.[17]

The consciousness informing this self-designation was an indispensable stage in Uchiyama's education in China. It was not merely Uchiyama's sympathy for the Chinese, which though rare was not unique among Japanese in that era, but rather his desire to live in and among the Chinese that set Uchiyama apart from other Japanese in the interwar period and led ultimately to his acceptance by Chinese of all classes.

Back in Kyoto, Pastor Makino and President Taguchi eagerly read Uchiyama's candid reports in letters that he sent from China and marveled at his quick assimilation to his new surroundings. The two men resolved that a young man in Uchiyama's position should marry. Makino quickly identified Inoue Miki as an appropriate marriage partner for Uchiyama. Inoue was the daughter of a failed merchant from the sake-producing region of Kyoto called Fushimi and had been the victim of neglect and abuse at home, having been sold along with her sister to a geisha house in the Gion district of Kyoto as a teenager. Inoue escaped from that life and turned to Christianity, arriving at the Kyoto Church four years earlier.[18] She worked in both the church and the Makino household and distinguished herself as a self-sufficient young women who could deal with adversity. When Uchiyama returned from China for a brief visit in February of 1915, the two were introduced and were soon engaged to be married. They married the following year in a simple Christian ceremony in Kyoto.[19]

The Uchiyamas moved to Shanghai and rented a room in an area occupied by a large number of Japanese from a man named Itani. Kanzō sold eyewash and other products for Santendō, and his sales duties took him to various cities in China, often for weeks at a time. The couple decided to open a small Christian bookstore that would be run by Miki in Kanzō's absence. The idea of opening a bookstore was made for several reasons: Miki was the daughter of a merchant and had been raised in an environment of hard work, and she worked assiduously while living with Pastor Makino. Now married, she longed to contribute to the newly established household. More immediately, both Miki and Kanzō realized that a second source of income would provide greater security while living abroad. Finally, Kanzō, for his part, had seen his own mother suffer for many years in a dependent relationship, in which she had no recourse but to serve a domineering husband. Kanzō did not want to see Miki, who had already been victimized as a child and was now so far from home, deprived of all measure of independence.[20]

The Uchiyamas rented a single room in a building adjacent to their apartment on Wusong Road. It was a modest room, which at first contained no bookshelves and fewer than one hundred texts. The entire stock was comprised of Christian texts in Japanese. At the time, there were three Japanese bookstores already established in Shanghai, although the Uchiyama shop was the only one specializing in Christian literature.[21] Despite the paucity of texts and Kanzō's frequent absences from Shanghai, the store quickly distinguished itself for integrity and a penchant for innovative policies. Among the pioneering policies that set the Uchiyama shop apart from other bookstores was their willingness to sell merchandise on credit to anyone, regardless of race. Other Japanese stores in Shanghai at that time were wont to maintain separate policies regarding credit sales depending on the race of the customer.[22]

All of the Christian texts sold at this first incarnation of Uchiyama bookstore were sent to them from Kyoto by Pastor Makino. Most of the initial clientele were Japanese who worked at the two major Japanese banks in Shanghai, Mitsubishi and Shōkin. While these customers appreciated the proximity of a bookstore specializing in Japanese literature, some customers expressed dissatisfaction with the selection of texts, and requested works of philosophy and literature to supplement the store's stock of Christian volumes.[23]

Just as the store was beginning to prosper, Uchiyama's sales job was becoming more trying due to the tensions among the various colonial powers and the reverberations from the war raging in Europe, which led to escalating restrictions on mobility. As Uchiyama was becoming disillusioned with the life of the traveling salesman, it was becoming more and more difficult for him to execute his duties. Uchiyama became increasingly involved in the activities of the store and began to respond to the requests of his customers to diversify their stock from solely Christian texts to include a variety featuring works of philosophy, literature, and economics, along with Japanese translations of works from Western languages.[24] The shop's clientele began to diversify too, with an influx of young Chinese intellectuals recently returned from study abroad in Japan. Eventually, with the increasing popularity of the shop, they outgrew the confines of the original space and moved to a more spacious location on Sichuan Road in 1924. It was this modest shop on Sichuan road that was soon to become the center of lively cultural exchange between the Chinese and Japanese literary communities (see Photo 1, p. 153).

The period in which the shop prospered coincided with the maturation of Uchiyama's political and social views. Uchiyama's encounters with the Christian pacifism of Tolstoy and Uchimura and his attraction to socialist thought led him to sympathize openly and unabashedly with the plight of the workers whom he encountered during his travels while a salesman and in the neighborhood in which he and Miki lived and worked. At the time of the Twenty-One Demands and throughout the May Fourth Era, the Uchiyamas' support of Chinese student activists and workers often put them at odds with other members of the Japanese community, even his colleagues at Santendō.[25] By the time of the first May Day celebration in China in 1920, Uchiyama, now age 35, was clearly "on the side of the Chinese people."[26]

This sympathy for the Chinese worker on the part of Uchiyama Kanzō and the perception that he was a friend to the Chinese bore fruit in a variety of ways. Even when, during moments of crisis between China and Japan, mail delivery to Japanese living in Shanghai was halted, the Uchiyamas never stopped receiving his letters and parcels, and there never was a time during these tumultuous years when Uchiyama had to close his shop for any extended period of time or when the customers stopped coming.

By the time the bookstore began to flourish in the 1920s, Uchiyama Kanzō had encountered Chinese of all classes during his years as a sales representative and had already attained a level of knowledge about contemporary China that few Japanese possessed.[27] Uchiyama, as a keen observer of China, had concluded that in blindly following the dictates of Western Sinology, Japanese Sinologists had abandoned the opportunity to judge Chinese values in the context of contemporary China. As Uchiyama embraced China, as he sought to serve as a cultural liaison between the two nations, he clung tenaciously to the belief that in order to understand China, one could not merely approach it through traditional channels; one had to be willing to confront the complexities of a living, breathing China.

Uchiyama Shudian: Book Sales and Publishing

In Shanghai in the 1920s, the Japanese population outnumbered other ethnic communities and represented a wide demographic spectrum. Uchiyama Shudian (bookstore; Japanese, *shoten*) was the premier center for Sino-Japanese literary encounters and Uchiyama himself became the broker for meetings between writers from the two communities.[28] Moreover, Uchiyama's shop on Sichuan Road boasted the largest collection of Japanese books and periodicals in China and provided its customers with access to most recent intellectual and literary currents from Japan and, via Japanese translation, from the West.[29] Uchiyama sold more books on Marxism, literature and medicine than any other subjects. Furthermore, during this period many bookstores in China also served as book publishers, and Uchiyama Shudian was soon widely known for publishing left-wing works.[30]

Appreciating Uchiyama's contributions to Sino-Japanese cultural relations implies an understanding of the clientele he sought to reach. Strictly speaking, there were two groups to which his store appealed during the interwar period: Japanese residents of Shanghai and young Chinese intellectuals returned from extended periods of study in Japan who possessed a facility with Japanese language. Uchiyama Shudian was soon a fixture in Shanghai and attempts on the part of Uchiyama and his wife Miki to reach out to the Shanghai community, which included serving tea out in front of the shop everyday to the local rickshaw pullers, made them popular among Chinese of all classes. One of Uchiyama's former associates explained that the Chinese appreciated the work that Uchiyama and his wife did to encourage mutual understanding between the Japanese residents of Shanghai and the Chinese, and their shop was one of the few Japanese establishments not targeted during the various anti-Japanese campaigns during the period that their shop was in operation in Shanghai.[31]

The variety of texts that Uchiyama's store could boast of in the interwar period certainly would have appealed to the shop's Chinese clientele, comprised for the most part of former exchange students to Japan. Periods of study in Japan varied among these former students, as did their Japanese proficiency levels. Their interests were also wide ranging. Many of the Chinese customers to Uchiyama Shudian were interested in reading Japanese translations of Western politics, economics, law, and medicine; others were interested in reading Western literature or philosophy in Japanese translation. A significantly smaller number of Chinese customers were interested in Japanese literature and thought *per se*.

The question of what the Chinese customers to Uchiyama's bookstore were reading and the amount of time required to obtain the requisite skills to read those materials was a question that interested Tanizaki Jun'ichirō in his interactions with Chinese writers during his visit to Shanghai in 1926. According to what the Chinese writers whom he met during that visit told him, the majority of Chinese readers of Japanese really only sought to get the gist of Japanese texts concerning law, science, or other specific practical fields of study. In order to acquire that level of proficiency, they contended, only required an educated Chinese learner six months to a year of concentrated study of Japanese. On the other hand, they continued, in order to read literary texts, or to unravel the intricacies of literary criticism in Japanese required at least three years of study in the Japanese educational system.[32] Although one might argue with this optimistic assertion, the fact remains that the Chinese writers treated in this study spent substantially more time in Japan than the time they suggest was required to attain the skills needed to read literary works. Writers such as Tian Han and Zhou Zuoren could effortlessly negotiate the intricacies of literary Japanese, including classical Japanese, and their levels of linguistic proficiency apparently verged, in some cases, on native speaker proficiency.

Lu Xun and Zhou Zuoren, whose translations of and essays about Japanese literature helped to initially disseminate knowledge about contemporary Japanese literature, both had received much of their higher education in Japan. Lu Xun pursued medicine in Tokyo and Sendai between 1902 and 1909, and Zhou Zuoren studied literature in Japan from 1906 to 1911. The generation of Chinese exchange students to Japan that followed, who were to return to China as writers in the early 1920s, had spent even more extended periods of study in Japan. Representative of this generation were the members of the Creation Society, who spent an average of nine years in Japan and received both their secondary and university education there.[33] Japanese commentators as varied as Tanizaki Jun'ichiro and Ōda Takeo commented on the stunning proficiency levels of the Creationists, who had even contributed Japanese language stories of their own to student literary magazines in Japan.

While, admittedly, Chinese customers to Uchiyama Shudian with the proficiency levels of the Zhou brothers or the Creationists were exceptional, there were a great number of Chinese customers who could at least get the gist of the content of the materials in Uchiyama's shop, and Chinese customers continued to comprise a substantial portion of his customer base through the twenties and thirties.

Preeminent among Uchiyama Kanzōs activities at his Shanghai bookstore was the sale and distribution of Japanese books and periodicals along with works translated into Japanese from Western languages. Uchiyama also published a journal under the auspices of the Chinese Drama Research Society, which served as the mouthpiece for that organization of which he was a founding member and which met at his shop.

The year 1927 marked the high point of Uchiyama's activities in Shanghai and his bookstore was, by that time, well established. Part of the success of Uchiyama's shop in this period had to do with an increase in the number of periodicals he was able to sell to Japanese residents. These included such large circulation magazines as *Chūō kōron* (Central Review), *Kaizō* (Reform), and *Bungei shunjū* (Literary Quarterly), along with poetry and haiku magazines.[34] Uchiyama carried a variety of Japanese translations of works from Western languages in his shop, which appealed to young Chinese intellectuals and often served as the basis for their translations into Chinese. In the diary of that period called *Kakōroku*, Uchiyama made reference to collections of poetry from Western literature, which had been translated into Chinese based upon works from his shop. Uchiyama's contention was supported by his close familiarity with such writers/translators as Lu Xun (1881–1936), Tian Han (1898–1979), Zhang Ziping (1893–1959), and Guo Moruo (1892–1978), among others. For instance, Uchiyama suggested, with no small amount of pride, that he was acquainted with many of the Chinese writers who translated the over eight hundred poems which had, by that time, been translated into Chinese. These translators became regular customers at his shop from during its twenty years of existence in Shanghai.[35] Furthermore, Uchiyama purported that of the two hundred and twenty Chinese writers, by his estimation, who translated foreign literature during the May Fourth era, at least forty-three had studied in Japan.[36] What Uchiyama was suggesting of course was that the works contained in his shop, both original Japanese works and Western works in Japanese translation, contributed in a critical way to the emergence of a body of foreign literature translated into Chinese during the 1920s.

The Second Floor: Education and Scholarship

With the increasing popularity of the low priced *enpon* (one yen) books in the late 1920s, the stock of Uchiyama's store changed as, subsequently, did the focus of his activities at the shop. The bookstore contained two floors, and for the most part sales were confined to the first floor. The second floor was a flexible space that could be used for other purposes. This was the second way in which Uchiyama's shop contributed to Sino-Japanese cultural relations. The second floor of Uchiyama Shudian was used at various times as a meeting space for cultural organizations, as an exhibit space, and as a salon for entertaining visiting writers from Japan.

Japanese writers who came to visit China in the modern era generally started their journey in the port of Shanghai. In some cases, writers used the second floor of Uchiyama's store as a starting point, where Uchiyama would introduce the Japanese visitors to his acquaintances in the Chinese literary community. Uchiyama envisioned himself as a student of traditional Chinese culture, as an educator charged with the duty of delivering Japanese language materials to contribute to China's new vernacular literature emerging in the 1920s, and as a liaison between the two literary communities.

The convergence of these roles led Uchiyama to form the Chinese Drama Research Society (Shina geki kenkyūkai). Originally, this group of aficionados of Chinese theater met at the Japanese Christian Church in Shanghai but later moved to the second floor of Uchiyama's shop. Formed in 1924, the purpose of the society, as articulated in the articles of their charter, was to research the rich tradition of Chinese drama, to make presentations about Chinese theater, and to sponsor performances. The group boasted various levels of membership revolving around a central cohort consisting of seven members, four Chinese and three Japanese, who paid regular membership fees and contributed to the coterie magazine.[37] Although membership in the society fluctuated, it included besides Uchiyama, the well-known Chinese dramatists Tian Han and Ouyang Yuqian (1889–1962) as well as Xie Liuyi (1900–1945), the Chinese translator of *The Tale of Genji*.

Another interesting activity undertaken by Uchiyama in his capacity as educator and scholar was the opening of a Japanese language school in Shanghai in 1935–36. According to Uchiyama's account, Japanese language schools catering to Chinese students already existed in substantial numbers in Shanghai at that time, but were generally academically unsound. The idea behind such schools was that much from the West had already been translated into Japanese, so that a high level of proficiency in reading Japanese would provide a key to understanding the West. This would, in turn, prepare young men to better contribute to China's modernization. The idea for the school came from Zheng Boqi, writer, member of the Creation Society and a close friend of Uchiyama's. Uchiyama, whose impetus to open the Shanghai bookstore had included a desire to furnish Japanese texts for an audience of young Chinese readers, heartily supported the plan. With the monetary and logistical support of the Japanese Study Association (Nihon benkyōkai) in Shanghai, they were able to procure five rooms on the second floor of the Buyer's Association (Kōbai kumiai). With Zheng as the headmaster and five other instructors on the staff, they opened the school and quickly had classes filled.[38] This was accompanied by an attempt to create a strong library of Japanese language texts, and they were soon able to boast a collection of over seven thousand Japanese texts. Just as they were beginning to succeed, fighting in Manchuria and the anti-Japanese backlash that followed led to a mass exodus of students from the school, and so, reluctantly, they had to close the school in 1936.[39] Naturally enough, during Uchiyama's thirty years in Shanghai, many of his attempts to foster good will and cultural interchange between Japan and China were cut short due to sudden shifts in the political climate between the two countries.

Uchiyama as Cultural Liaison

One area in which Uchiyama expended considerable energy during the 1920s, and perhaps his most lasting contribution to Sino-Japanese relations, was in his capacity as a liaison between the two literary communities and as a guide and facilitator for visiting Japanese writers.

Japanese writers in the modern era had visited China from the late nineteenth century onward, including visits by such luminaries in the Meiji period *bundan* as Natsume Sōseki (1867–1916) and Futabatei Shimei (1872–1912). However, it was during the 1920s that the pace of such visits dramatically increased, with the great majority of literary travelers beginning their journeys in Shanghai. Perhaps it was natural, under such circumstances, that someone in Uchiyama's position should play a crucial role in bringing these visiting Japanese writers together with the Chinese writers with whom he was acquainted. The Japanese writers who passed through Shanghai during the 1920s and 1930s and were the recipients of Uchiyama's efforts at cultural exchange included Akutagawa Ryūnosuke (1892–1927), Tanizaki Junichirō (1886–1965), Satō Haruo (1892–1964) and Hayashi Fumiko (1904–1951).

Of course, such attempts at bringing visiting Japanese writers into contact with Chinese writers would have been impossible had Uchiyama's connections with the May Fourth literary community not been so extensive. In fact, to some degree or another, Uchiyama was acquainted with virtually all of the leading Chinese writers of the day who were active in Shanghai. Many of these writers had studied in Japan and were drawn to his store originally out of a desire to remain abreast of recent Japanese translations and intellectual currents. These included not only the aforementioned Tian Han and Ouyang Yuqian but also the Creation Society members Guo Moruo and Yu Dafu (1896–1945) as well as Chen Duxiu (1879–1942), Zhou Zuoren (1885–1967) and his brother Lu Xun (1881–1936). They found in Uchiyama Kanzō a kindred spirit and passionate advocate for contemporary Chinese literature. It was his relationship with Lu Xun, with whom Uchiyama exchanged poetry and spoke about literature during the last decade of Lu Xun's life, that Uchiyama referred to as the greatest joy in his life.[40]

The degree to which writers themselves recognized Uchiyama as a liaison and came to depend upon him as an intermediary can be inferred from correspondences from several writers to Uchiyama. In each of these letters, Uchiyama's capacity as a cultural liaison is alluded to either implicitly or explicitly. For example, in a letter to Satō Haruo on March 1928, Yu Dafu refers to a manuscript about Chinese poetry by a colleague of his, which was then in the possession of Mushanokōji Saneatsu. Yu asks Satō to have Mushanokōji return the manuscript by sending it to Uchiyama's shop where he can go and retrieve it.[41] In other words, Uchiyama's shop seemed to Yu the most secure place in Shanghai to send this important document.

In a short note from Yu Dafu to the Japanese writer, Ōda Takeo (1900–1979), on 1937, Yu who was living in Fuzhou at the time, is apparently advising the Japanese writer on a planned visit to China. He recommends that if Ōda travels in April, Yu might be able to go and meet him in Shanghai. Shanghai, he suggests, would be the best place to stay because he could easily travel from there to Hangzhou. However, in a telling piece of final advice, Yu suggests that Ōda consult carefully with Uchiyama before making any travel plans.[42]

In correspondences from Lu Xun to Uchiyama also we see a similar recognition of Uchiyama's role in intercultural relations. In a brief note in 1931, Lu Xun, then visiting a sick family member, asks Uchiyama to pass along some enclosed photographs to a mutual acquaintance in Shanghai.[43] A second letter in 1932 to Uchiyama, who had returned to Japan for an extended visit, was apparently written as a response to an invitation from Satō Haruo and other Japanese writers. Lu Xun asks Uchiyama to inform Satō and the other writers that he must regretfully decline their invitation to visit Japan. He explains that he is afraid to inconvenience people while in Japan, and he is reluctant to put aside his writing regimen. He also urges Uchiyama to hurry back to Shanghai because although he has been visiting Uchiyama's shop everyday, he admits that he misses the random discussions (*mandan*) that the two share when together.[44]

The content and tone of these correspondences tend to confirm the fact that Japanese and Chinese writers respected and trusted Uchiyama in this capacity as an intermediary. They naturally came to perceive him as the link to the other literary community and as the one person who could be entrusted to convey information and materials across the political and cultural divide that separated the two communities.

Chinese writers in the May Fourth era were most eager to meet visiting Japanese writers. On the Japanese side also, for those who chose to visit China, there was a desire to meet and discuss literature with the leading figures of the new vernacular literary movement about which, admittedly, they knew little. In that sense, Uchiyama's role was a logistical one — he served as a conduit between the two literary communities, ensuring that writers on both sides of the cultural divide had the opportunity to meet and interact with their counterparts. Uchiyama apparently had a genius for creating opportunities for writers to meet and converse, and for introducing visiting Japanese writers to precisely those Chinese counterparts with whom they would likely be compatible and conceivably forge lasting relationships.

One of the most interesting visits by a Japanese writer to Shanghai during this era was Tanizaki Jun'ichirō's 1926 visit, which is described in detail in Chapter 2. The visit of another Japanese writer, Satō Haruo, in the following year further underscores Uchiyama's role as liaison during such visits.

Satō's visit was recorded by several people involved in the trip, including Satō himself and Uchiyama. Much about the visit can also be gleaned from a letter to the literary scholar Itō Toramaru by Satō Haruo's niece, Chieko, who accompanied the writer and his wife to China. Chieko relates that soon after they arrived in Shanghai, they called on Uchiyama's shop and were introduced to several Chinese writers. They stayed at a hotel called the Wansuiguan where Akutagawa and other Japanese writers had stayed during their visits. Tian Han, Yu Dafu and others took them around to various places during their stay including meals at well-known restaurants and visits to Shanghai's foreign concessions. They also attended a play sponsored by the Chinese Drama Research Society and attended a banquet in their honor at the Japanese Club sponsored by the local Japanese community.[45] After returning to Shanghai from a sojourn with Yu Dafu to Hangzhou and the West Lake they again called upon Uchiyama Shudian. It was during this visit to Uchiyama's store that Satō and his party learned of the suicide of Akutagawa Ryūnosuke.[46] Akutagawa, one of the most famous Japanese writers of his day, was both a friend and rival of Satō, and one can imagine that the shock that Satō received from the news was indeed great. It is interesting to note that Satō received this news from Uchiyama, who had become acquainted with both men during their respective visits to Shanghai.

Looking at Satō's 1927 journey, it appears to follow the same basic pattern as Tanizaki's visit of the previous year. Interestingly enough, by the time of Satō's visit, Uchiyama's position as liaison between the two communities had been established and was immediately recognized by Japanese writers traveling to China. Satō, who had been introduced to Uchiyama by Tanizaki, immediately checked in with Uchiyama upon his arrival. During his visit, he was dependent on Uchiyama for arranging his schedule and for acting as an intermediary in meetings with Chinese writers who in fact did much of the actual day-to-day organizing of activities. This "hands-off" approach seemed to serve Uchiyama's ultimate objective particularly well. He created opportunities for Japanese and Chinese writers to meet, without interfering in actual interactions between them. He usually seemed to remain at his shop, which served as a home base for these visitors.

Uchiyama wrote about Satō's visit along with the visits of other writers and about interactions between Chinese and Japanese writers. Uchiyama's records of his own activities, his reminiscences about writers, and his observations on various facets of contemporary China were the last significant contributions by Uchiyama to Sino-Japanese relations.

Uchiyama's first writings about China were not published until after the other contributions described above had already been made. His first essay, published in *Kaizō* in 1934, entitled "Shanhai seikatsu nijū nen" (Twenty Years Living in Shanghai), was a portrait of cultural interchange in Shanghai during the two tumultuous decades that his store had been the hub of interaction between Chinese and Japanese writers. The success of this and subsequent articles and books can be interpreted as a manifestation of a continuing interest in contemporary China on the part of Japanese writers in the 1930s despite increasingly volatile political relations between the two nations. A number of similar articles, most of which were published in *Kaizō*, offered further observations about Chinese culture and reminiscences about Uchiyama's relationships with individual cultural figures under such names as "Shanhai manwa" (Random Talk in Shanghai) and "Shanhai mango" (Random Chatter in Shanghai). After returning to Japan permanently in late 1945, Uchiyama continued to write about his twenty years at the bookstore, including the diary *Kakōroku* published in 1960, which served as the most comprehensive record of Uchiyama's years in China.

From Disciple to Friend: Uchiyama Kanzō's Relationship with Lu Xun

At the epicenter of relations between the Japanese and Chinese literary communities in the interwar period was the friendship between Uchiyama Kanzō and Lu Xun. The relationship was one in which two like-minded individuals were able to surmount linguistic and national boundaries and in which literature itself and shared values, aesthetic and personal, brought the two writers together. Examples of such relations can be seen in other places at other times. Nevertheless, the relationship between Uchiyama and Lu Xun exhibits qualities that seem, in some inscrutable ways, peculiar to the East Asian literary tradition. From the beginning of their association, both men had a clear sense of their status vis-à-vis the other. Uchiyama recognized Lu Xun's genius and saw himself as the protégé fated to foster that genius. Furthermore, Uchiyama, as protégé and advocate for the master, was willing to sublimate his own interests in order to facilitate the genius of the master. Lu Xun, for his part, appeared to regard Uchiyama as a friend and confidante with whom he could speak openly and candidly about virtually any issue, whether it was traditional Chinese literature, contemporary Western thought or even the delicate political relations between their respective nations.

The interdependence of the two men was a critical factor in fostering relations between the two literary communities. It is telling that the relationship between these two men of letters, one of whom was China's first great modern writer and outspoken advocate for cultural reform, the other whose bookstore was so central for the introduction of Western thought in Shanghai, should hearken back to the model of the traditional literati friendship. The friendship between these two men, sustained and fostered during the most acrimonious years of the interwar period, provided the foundation for the whole network of relations during this period.

The period prior to the one in which Lu Xun and Uchiyama Kanzō became acquainted was a relatively quiet period for Lu Xun as a writer. He had moved from Guangdong to Shanghai. There were personal changes in his life, and he had all but ceased the writing of fiction which had made him the most famous cultural figure in May Fourth China.[47] Lu Xun's move to Shanghai and his acquaintance with Uchiyama signaled an important and productive new phase in his career.

In 1927, the year of Akutagawa's death and of Satō Haruo's visit to Shanghai, Lu Xun moved from Guangdong to Shanghai. Apparently it was soon after he arrived in Shanghai that Lu Xun became aware of the existence of Uchiyama's shop and determined to pay a visit. Uchiyama would later describe that first meeting, during which Lu Xun purchased a large number of books totaling fifty yuan. Uchiyama did not recognize the rather nondescript man who made such a large purchase as the famous Lu Xun, a writer whom he had long admired. It was only when the customer provided his delivery address and name, Zhou Shuren, that Uchiyama recognized who it was with whom he was dealing.[48] Thereafter, until his death, with the exception of periods in which other duties or concerns prevented him, Lu Xun was an almost daily visitor to Uchiyama's shop, sometimes calling in several times a day.[49]

The relationship between Lu Xun and Uchiyama was complex and has been described variously by observers and scholars. Whereas Lu Xun considered Uchiyama a friend, and colleague, and sometimes protector, Uchiyama perceived himself as something of a disciple to the sensei Lu Xun, and this affected their interactions. Another dimension of their complex relationship was that Uchiyama acted as an agent for Lu Xun both for visiting Japanese and other visitors including George Bernard Shaw during his visit to Shanghai in February 1933.[50]

What is remarkable about the relationship between the two men is how quickly they came to depend on one another. In 1931, after the Guomindang execution of five young leftist writers which included Ding Ling's husband Hu Yepin (1904–1931) and Lu Xun's young protégée Rou Shi, it was Uchiyama who first received news of the incident and broke the tragic news to Lu Xun.[51] Moreover, fearing for Lu Xun's safety, Uchiyama burned some possibly incriminating documents of Lu Xun's and arranged for him and his family to stay in a hotel in the foreign settlement for a period that eventually extended to thirty-nine days until Uchiyama deemed it safe for them to return to their home.

During that interim in the hotel, Uchiyama was the one person Lu Xun entrusted with knowledge of his whereabouts.[52]

This pattern of Lu Xun having to go into hiding in order to avoid arrest and Uchiyama helping to provide a safe haven for him and his family was to be repeated several times in the remaining six years of Lu Xun's life. The execution of the five young leftists in 1931 was just one indication that the dangers to a writer of Lu Xun's political leanings were very real. Wang Baolian, an employee at Uchiyama's shop on Sichuan Road, described how Guomindang spies disguised as students would show up at the shop and pretend to browse the shelves. Often middle-aged and well dressed, those "students," when challenged to read the Japanese texts aloud, would flee the store.[53]

In order to provide immediate protection for Lu Xun in times of impending danger Uchiyama and his wife always made provisions for Lu Xun's refuge. Because Lu Xun was such a regular visitor to the shop on Sichuan Road, this sometimes meant harboring Lu Xun in a less conspicuous place. One such safe spot was Uchiyama's branch shop in the British Concession. During hostilities with the Japanese in 1932 Lu Xun stayed briefly in the back room of Uchiyama's branch shop, sleeping on the floor there until it was safe for him to leave the International Settlement.[54]

It has been posited that part of the appeal of Lu Xun upon the Christian Uchiyama was that he saw in Lu Xun an artist and a man with deeply held convictions. His predictions for Chinese society and his prescriptions for China's social ills must have appeared to Uchiyama like the testimonial of a true prophet. His words had the ring of authority.[55] Moreover, the fervor and zeal with which Lu Xun approached questions having to do with the reform of Chinese society deeply moved Uchiyama.[56]

Lu Xun would sit in the rattan chair in Uchiyama's shop set aside for his exclusive use. Setting aside the book he was reading, he would call over the store's *laoban*, Uchiyama, and the two men would converse, sometimes for hours at a time. Occasionally, they would be joined by others, but more often than not the conversation involved only the two of them.[57] Students who would see them talking together in this manner, noting their unassuming demeanor and indifference to appearance, characterized the two as "poor gentlemen."[58] In this way, the two men of letters, engrossed in conversation and indifferent to all except the lively exchange of ideas, embodied the age-old qualities of the East Asian literati, who took pleasure in the company of words and of one another. The ease that the two men felt in one another's company is apparent in the many photographs that remain of the two from the period of their decade-long friendship (see Photo 2, p. 153).

The animated discussions of the two men soon drew others, which led to the emergence of the lively literary and artistic salon, centered on the second floor of Uchiyama's shop described earlier in this chapter. One of the most significant artistic activities promoted by Uchiyama and Lu Xun was woodblock printing. Lu Xun's interest in woodblock prints dated to his years in Japan, but the collecting and production of woodblock prints coincided with Lu Xun's move to Shanghai in 1927. It was one of many such felicitous coincidences that characterized the relationship between Uchiyama and Lu Xun that Uchiyama's youngest brother Kakichi was himself an artist who worked in that medium.[59] Uchiyama and Lu Xun collaborated in the appreciation and promotion of this art form throughout the decade of their acquaintance.

In August of 1931, Uchiyama Kanzō sponsored a weeklong workshop about woodblock printmaking in Shanghai. Kakichi gave a series of lectures and demonstrations about printmaking with Lu Xun translating.[60] Kakichi was at that time teaching crafts at the Seijō Institute in Tokyo and used his summer break to visit his older brother in Shanghai and to lead the workshop.[61] Lu Xun studied with Kakichi during that period and thereafter established an artistic salon of woodblock print artists with younger Chinese artists that was to be the outlet for much of his creative energies during his final years. Lu Xun and the circle of artists met on the second floor of Uchiyama's shop and Uchiyama occasionally sponsored exhibits. The last gathering of the group, in fact, took place on October 8, 1936, eleven days before Lu Xun's death. There is a well-known photograph from this final meeting showing Lu Xun speaking with young Chinese artists along with the Austrian artist Ruth Weiss.[62]

Nevertheless, the most significant contribution made by Uchiyama Kanzō and Lu Xun to Sino-Japanese literary relations during the decade of their interaction were the lively conversations themselves. The *mandankai* (Random Chat Meetings), which Uchiyama established, brought together a variety of people for discussions in regular gatherings that continued even after Lu Xun's death. These gatherings suggest the atmosphere of mutual trust and engagement that characterized Uchiyama's bookstore salon in the interwar period.

Initially, Uchiyama and Lu Xun engaged in these convivial discussions at a table at the front of the shop. Others would be invited to join them or would merely stop in their perusal of books to listen to the easy banter of the two men which alternately sounded like the conversation of old friends, or the weighty dialogue of a teacher and his favored disciple.[63] It was Lu Xun who eventually suggested that all the participants jot down their versions of these chat sessions in order to retain some record, however sketchy, of these conversations.[64]

Eventually, Uchiyama produced his own personal essays reflecting his perspectives on the subjects discussed at those Random Chat Meetings. Uchiyama published his *zuihitsu* (miscellanea) collection *Ikite iru Shina no sugata* (Portrait of a Living China) in 1935, which included records of those conversations. Among Japanese readers, just the presence of Lu Xun among the participants in these *mandan* sessions and the forward that he provided for the collection were enough to ensure sales of Uchiyama's book.⁶⁵

In defining the term *mango* and explaining his intentions in producing these personal essays, Uchiyama had the following to say in the preface to his 1941 collection *Shanhai mango* (Random Chatter in Shanghai):

> Recently at the request of *Kaizō* I wrote something called *Random Chatter in Shanghai*. This "random chatter" was truly nothing more than "chatter". It was not history, nor was it geography; it was not travel writing, and it goes without saying that it did not qualify as philosophy. In fact, no matter how many times I went back and looked over what I had written, I found it to amount to nothing more than my random prattle.⁶⁶

The topics covered by Uchiyama in his *manwa* and *mango* collections were as varied as the very conversations that spawned them, but all were delivered in Uchiyama's distinctive voice. The first few lines in a piece called "Shina kinyūkai" (The Chinese Financial World), which appeared in *Shanhai mango*, are typical of the familiar tone that Uchiyama cultivated in these essays, reflecting the practiced insouciance of the dilettante:

> Whenever I play cards I inevitably end up losing. I can never figure out why I lose. Even when I go at it with great enthusiasm, for some reason I find myself losing again … Kind folks will caution me about this propensity again and again, but being so full of myself I never quite get it.⁶⁷

In the *mandan* that took place in the salon of Uchiyama's shop and in the essays by Uchiyama that followed, the figure of Lu Xun is always looming in the background. Lu Xun seemed to delight in the opportunity to contribute to the records of these discussions for the sake of Uchiyama who had long relished the idea of making a literary name for himself. Lu Xun felt a debt of gratitude to Uchiyama for protecting him, and enabling him to pursue his own artistic inclinations during those final years when pain racked his body and the fragile community ties that the two men who worked so tirelessly to establish were threatened by forces that conspired to undermine their efforts.

Conclusion

Finally, any discussion about Uchiyama's role as a liaison between the Japanese and Chinese literary communities during the years in question must attempt to account for his politics. Cultural and literary activities, claims of "pure literature" notwithstanding, were in a sense inseparable from politics. In the *Kakōroku*,

Uchiyama eschews discussion of political issues, for the most part, but an examination of those occasions when his political views were revealed suggests some contradictions in his political positions. When Uchiyama arrived in Shanghai in 1913 he was a Christian socialist and in some ways he always remained true to his initial political views and was sympathetic with the cause of the young Chinese communists with whom he was acquainted. He found it ironic and deeply satisfying, for example, that Chen Duxiu, founder of the Chinese Communist Party and former exchange student to Japan, initially read a number of communist tracts in translations purchased at his shop.[68]

On the other hand, given these sympathies, Uchiyama was not as critical of Japan's imperialist aggression in China as might be expected. When confronted with anti-Japanese reactions to Japanese imperialism in China in the 1920s and 1930s, Uchiyama all too often tended to regard the events as a nuisance that upset the balance of life in Shanghai rather than to condemn the Japanese aggression which gave rise to those circumstances. This apparent insensitivity on the part of Uchiyama toward the situation in China can be seen also in the timing of the attempt to open the Japanese school referred to earlier. Even before he and Zheng attempted to open the school, anti-Japanese sentiment was running high in Shanghai. The most charitable interpretation one might make was that he and Zheng were trying to alleviate some of the ill will toward Japan by suggesting that Japan was not simply an imperial aggressor and that it still had much to offer in terms of providing a model for China's modernization.

A question that emerges when one considers the significance of Uchiyama's shop in the cultural life of Shanghai in the thirties and forties, and Uchiyama's special relationship with politically active Chinese writers was whether or not Uchiyama Kanzō was ever coerced by the Japanese military authorities to have his bookstore serve as a surveillance hub to oversee the activities of the leftist writers who frequented his shop. The absence of any allusion to such coercion in either Uchiyama's candid and voluminous writing from the period or in the reminiscences of the period by Chinese writers suggests that his shop never served in that way.

Certainly, there is ample evidence to suggest that the Japanese military authorities were adept at managing the propaganda portion of the "thought war" (shisōsen) that accompanied their military activities, and they readily enlisted writers and artists to serve in that capacity.[69] In Shanghai, which was a center of intellectual and political foment, the Japanese did in fact see the surveillance of bookstores as a potentially effective means of controlling the dissemination of thought. In 1941 the Japanese military authorities in Shanghai requested Uchiyama to take management of two foreign bookstores on Nanjing Road, Kelly and Walsh and the American Publishing Company. Uchiyama initially balked at this offer and only after much dragging of feet did he finally accept management of the latter store.[70]

Uchiyama's unusual status in Shanghai in the interwar period and the reputation that he had cultivated and proudly flaunted as a friend to Chinese of all classes, almost certainly deterred the Japanese authorities from charging him with further duties or from enlisting him as a spy during the war.[71] The Japanese community in Shanghai in the years leading up to the war was not monolithic, and could be divided into two groups: the *kaishaha* or "company clique" which included recent arrivals of wealthy capitalists who had virtually no interaction with the Chinese, and the *dochakuha* or "native clique" who were more established in Shanghai, often permanent residents, and possessed ties with the Chinese community.[72] Uchiyama was clearly a well respected member of the latter group and enjoyed a special status that effectively exempt him from some of the pressures to comply and collaborate with the authorities that were directed at others in Shanghai.

Ultimately, it is apparent that Uchiyama was not nearly as interested in politics as he was in larger cultural and social issues, and would have avoided thorny, divisive issues altogether were he able. Certainly his friends and acquaintances among Chinese intellectuals ran the full gamut on the political spectrum. In the final analysis, Uchiyama apparently felt that his vocation as cultural ambassador transcended such mundane concerns as political ideology. This can be inferred from the fact that the one association which he founded and in which he was actively engaged was not a political society but rather a literary coterie comprised of both Chinese and Japanese members and dedicated to the understanding and appreciation of Chinese drama.

In conclusion, Uchiyama Shudian, specializing in Japanese texts, including translations, was the finest store of its kind in Shanghai. However, by the time the store was well established in the 1930s, there were ten such Japanese bookstores competing for customers.[73] By that point, Uchiyama's store already had become, via word of mouth, something of an institution — a "must-see" for visiting Japanese writers and one of the first stops for Chinese students repatriated from study abroad in Japan. An examination of Uchiyama's voluminous writings about his life in China provides evidence that he envisioned himself as something of a missionary for the cause of Sino-Japanese cultural relations, and he attacked the duties of fostering cultural interchange and good will with evangelical zeal.

In his various capacities as writer, educator, scholar and liaison between the two cultural communities, Uchiyama strove to bring Japanese and Chinese writers together. There is nothing among the writings about Uchiyama, either contemporary or subsequent, to suggest that his motives were anything less than altruistic. For the Sinophile Uchiyama, the simple opportunity to bring Chinese and Japanese writers together for positive dialogue and interaction seems to have been motivation enough. Unfortunately, there is little to suggest that Uchiyama's mission to bring the two literary communities had any lasting impact. Tensions between the two countries in the 1930s and 1940s made it at first difficult and then impossible to continue the kind of interaction that had been achieved in Shanghai in the 1920s and early 1930s largely through the intercession of Uchiyama. The cultural exchange achieved in Uchiyama's shop during the interwar period stands as both a watershed and, unfortunately, as something of an anomaly in terms of cultural relations between China and Japan. Nevertheless, for the period in question, Uchiyama Kanzō's bookstore served as the hub of a lively exchange between Chinese and Japanese writers that found expression in ways as varied as the writers whom he brought together.

2

Musings of a Literary Pilgrim: Tanizaki Jun'ichirō's Discoveries in China and Their Records

Tanizaki Jun'ichirō (1886–1965) visited China on two occasions, once in 1918 at the age of thirty-two and again in 1926 at the age of forty. In both cases, experiences in China were recast in literary works representing a variety of genres. The pieces resulting from the first visit fall neatly into the *kikōbun* (travel diary) and *nikki* (literary diary) varieties and are representative examples of a body of such work penned by Japanese writers in the modern period based on their travels, both domestic and overseas. On the other hand, the most significant work produced following Tanizaki's second visit, in its frank description of the Chinese literary community and of specific Chinese writers with whom Tanizaki became acquainted, constitutes a valuable record of cultural exchange between the Chinese and Japanese literary communities during the interwar period. Tanizaki's travels to China and the relationships with writers that he forged during his second visit not only influenced the works immediately following his return, they also continued to affect him as an artist and as a man long after his final visit. The works resulting from Tanizaki's trips represent moments of discovery; however, what he discovered — about China and about himself — during each of his two trips proved to be fundamentally different.

The Tradition of Travel Writing in Japan: Conventional Genre Distinctions

The *kikōbun* and the *nikki* produced by Tanizaki in the wake of his first trip fit into a long and illustrious body of such writing in Japan, whose classical precedents include Ki no Tsurayuki's *Tosa nikki* (Tosa Diary) and Matsuo Bashō's *Oku no hosomichi* (Narrow Road to the Deep North). Tanizaki applies the terms *nikki* and *kikōbun* to the pieces from the first trip, and certainly fine distinctions between these two forms are sometimes less than obvious. In general, the *nikki* refers to the variety of literary diary represented by the *Tosa Nikki*, in what amounts to a belletrized record of days.¹ On the other hand, the *kikōbun*, a travel diary which had its beginnings as a sub-genre of the *nikki* form, emerged during the thirteenth century as such a popular form in its own right that "the larger class designated as the diary [*nikki*] gradually yielded to its subclass."²

One of the noteworthy qualities of the *kikōbun* is its careful depiction of the local color of a specific place with pointed references to its literary and cultural associations — specifically those with which the audience would be expected to be familiar; there is less attention to encapsulating events into specific daily time frames than there is to the delineation of a particular locale and the qualities and associations of the place.³ Such writing about locales in China by Japanese literary men had clear precedents when Tanizaki wrote his essays in the mid-Taishō period. The earliest travel accounts of note written by Japanese travelers to China in the modern era were produced in the decades following the 1862 journey of a Japanese embassy to China aboard the Senzaimaru in the wake of the lifting of the shogunate's ban on travel abroad.⁴ The most important travel accounts of China written by Japanese during these years were by Sinologists or *kangakusha* such as Oka Senjin (1832–1913) and Naitō Konan (1866–1934) discussed in the introduction.

It seems likely that many of these writers went over for much the same reason as the *kangakusha* — to rediscover, as it were, a kind of cultural homeland. It is worth noting that Japanese literary travelers to China in the interwar period like Tanizaki were generally not great trailblazers; they painstakingly followed customary routes in the footsteps of literary predecessors in order to encounter *meisho*, famous sites of cultural importance.⁵

Moreover, Japanese intellectuals and literary men were inspired to visit China due to a sense of kinship with the culture via their familiarity with the Chinese literary canon. Integral to our understanding of the attitudes of Japanese travelers to China during the early modern period is the recognition of their ambivalence between respect for China as the seat of Asian culture on the one hand and a general disgust at the lowly state of contemporary China on the other hand. Most of the accounts of China dating from the Meiji and Taishō periods reflect this dichotomy. In writing about this phenomenon, Atsuko Sakaki characterizes this shift from the traditional veneration of China to a critical engagement with contemporary Chinese society as a shift in focus among Japanese visitors to China from "the metaphysical to the material."⁶

Concerning this ambivalence on the part of Japanese writers, Joshua Fogel suggests: "as travel writers began to tell their readers from 1862 on, China of the classics — from whence they sought cultural referents — and the real contemporary China were not the same. ... Indeed, it was a jolting, disconcerting experience for many."⁷ In his first visit to China, then, Tanizaki carried with him a variety of preconceptions of what he would find in China. This, in turn, contributed to the character of the writings that emerged following that visit.

The 1918 Trip: Encounters with Tradition

The two important essays resulting from Tanizaki's 1918 journey, "Soshū kikō" (A Record of a Visit to Suzhou) and "Rozan nikki" (A Diary of Lushan), are fairly conventional records in terms of their contents and format. One of the salient characteristics of Tanizaki's essays is the aforementioned ambivalence toward the China with which he comes in contact — the almost religious reverence with which he encounters places of cultural and historical import, and his general disgust with the economic and social realities of contemporary China.

Like the other Japanese writers included in this study, Tanizaki felt himself intellectually, aesthetically, and emotionally torn in several directions. Initially, there was Tanizaki's admiration and respect for Western culture, nurtured by his wide reading in Western literature and his regular contact with Westerners while living in Yokohama.[8] There was also an abiding adoration for native cultural achievements, which was to reach its highest expression in his renderings into modern Japanese of *Genji monogatari* (The Tale of Genji) during the 1930s, but had already been present in his youth. Along with this existed an enduring fascination with China and its culture. This latter fascination was articulated in an essay called "Shina shumi to iu koto" (This Taste for Things Chinese) from 1922. In regard to the mania for the West that was all the rage during the Taishō period, Tanizaki has this to say:

> We Japanese have almost totally adopted Western culture and in fact appear to have completely assimilated it, but it is a source of wonder to me that when all is said and done, in the depths of our veins, the attraction towards China is unexpectedly strong. Recently, I have become keenly aware of this feeling.[9]

The 1918 journey provided an opportunity for Tanizaki to come face-to-face with the China of tradition, the literary China with which he had long been acquainted. Interestingly, Tanizaki's lifelong fascination with China found expression not only in the essays under discussion here but also in a number of early works of fiction set in China including "Seiko no tsuki" (The Moon on the West Lake, 1917) and "Ningyo no nageki" (Lament of a Mermaid, 1917).[10] This travel experience was also a chance to test his mettle as a writer against both his contemporaries and predecessors from Japan who had come as pilgrims to many of the same spots in China that he visited and recorded their experiences for posterity.[11] "Rozan nikki" and "Soshū kikō" share much in common with works by other Japanese visitors in their rich evocations of place, but they also reflect Tanizaki himself, both in their style and in the quality of their perceptions.

"Soshū kikō," which first appeared in the March 1919 edition of *Chūō kōron* (Central Review), is the account of a daylong boat trip that Tanizaki took from Suzhou to Mount Tianping, a place known for its temples and rich history. A preface to this piece, "Soshū kikō maegaki," also appeared in the same issue of *Chūō kōron*. According to the work's preface, Suzhou (Soshū in Japanese) was, along with Nanjing and Shanghai, one of the places in China to which Tanizaki felt most attracted with its splendid gardens and its rich historical associations.

The preface to "Soshū kikō" further relates how the author spent four days in the city of Suzhou and its environs. During the trip, the author goes via pleasure boat down one of Suzhou's many canals to Mount Tianping, which, with its many temples was well-known as a particularly beautiful spot from which to view the trees tinged with the reds and golds of autumn. As the boat makes its way down the canal away from the city center, Tanizaki briefly describes Suzhou itself, a city of nearly 300,000 people with its own Japanese concession. His descriptions throughout are attentive to details of scenery and local custom as in the following description of a cemetery he spots near one of these villages.

> From time to time, I would go up to the bow of the ship to have a look out at the scenery of the fields on the opposite bank. The soil bank was unexpectedly high so I could not be sure, but there seemed to be paddy fields out beyond. Here and there were what seemed to be cemeteries. In the shadows of the soil bank, I could spy only the rounded grave mounds and the tops of the gravestones. Possibly due to the fact that the area was fairly wealthy, even the graves of the dirt farmers there were splendid. The graves on the plains of Manchuria were mere piles of dirt and there were practically none with gravestones. By contrast, in this region even the lowliest graves unfailingly were marked by gravestones.[12]

Regardless of whether Tanizaki's gaze is trained on a site of cultural import or some more commonplace vista, as in the description above, no significant detail of the landscape goes unnoticed before the writer's discerning eye. This celebration of landscape is a striking feature of Tanizaki's essays from China resulting from the 1918 sojourn. He tends to associate himself with those great poets from Chinese tradition who write about their encounters with the landscape itself.[13] One of the important effects of the details that accumulate in this narrative is a glimpse into the exotic, almost otherworldly quality of this neighboring country with which Japan held so much in common in terms of culture. Tanizaki describes a small forest along the way as the kind of enchanted forest one would expect to find in a fairy tale. His description of two female entertainers he sees on a moored boat they pass along the way focuses on those elements of their clothing and physical appearance that are unusual and exotic.[14] As they pass beneath successive arched bridges and move further and further away from the city, even the canal itself seems to transform into a body of water that "doesn't appear at all like a canal."[15]

Counterbalancing this delineation of the exotic is a candid appraisal of the realities of contemporary China and of Sino-Japanese relations. Ever since China's defeat at the hands of the Japanese in the Sino-Japanese War of 1895, the traditional reverence accorded to China often was accompanied by scorn at the weakness and vulnerability of contemporary China. In one of the encounters recorded in "Soshū kikō," the narrator criticizes his guide after being forced to listen to condemnations of the "national character" of China with which she hopes to win the approval of her client. Meeting a group of boorish Japanese tourists upon arriving at their mountain destination gives the author further cause to stare into the sordid realities of Sino-Japanese relations.

The remainder of the piece is spent describing the beauty of Suzhou as they return to the city from their excursion. The critical quality of the above passage is rare in the essays from the 1918 trip, and there is no direct description of political tensions between the two nations. Tanizaki's gaze is fixed firmly on the traditional China that he has come to discover. Seeing the Tiger Hill Pagoda from the outskirts of the city, Tanizaki recalls a stanza from a well-known poem about the pagoda. As the boat passes beneath the final arched bridge and enters the city, Tanizaki spies a pair of paper lanterns hanging before the Han Shan Temple and a copse of pine trees — a rarity in China, he remarks. The sun is setting behind a pagoda and the beauty of the scene inspires him to produce a Chinese poem comprised of sets of couplets of seven-character lines.

In the "Soshū kikō," Tanizaki remains true to the *kikō* form, rarely interrupting the flow of description in order to interpret the unfolding events. The most telling example of this distancing occurs in the scene alluded to earlier in which the narrator witnesses the activities of the group of Japanese tourists and the unfortunate attitude of his guide. Never during that scene does Tanizaki attempt to become involved or make contact with the group. On the contrary, he is at pains to tell us that he deliberately goes off afterwards to eat his *bentō* lunch by himself, avoiding any contact with the group as if having contact with such people might in some way taint the integrity of his own experience.

In "Rozan nikki," key elements of time and place, such as references to the season and allusions to sites of historical and cultural interest, provide the framework within which the narrative develops. "Rozan nikki," which first appeared in the September 1921 issue of *Chūō kōron*, describes a three-day excursion that Tanizaki undertook with two Japanese acquaintances to visit Lushan and its environs. The entry is an orthodox, relatively pedestrian description of the locale from the perspective of a traveler. In fact this seems to be precisely the point of the diary structure Tanizaki employs in "Rozan nikki"; he is endeavoring to situate it in the tradition of such travel literature.

> Taishō 7 (1918), November 10, Clear Skies.
> I awakened at 8:00 to find the skies clear and sunny for a change. It was the first sunshine I had seen since leaving Beijing a week earlier. Throughout the morning I wrote in my diary and looked through some magazines of Lu Shan. Today being Sunday, there were a great many Chinese worshippers at the Catholic Church across the street. The church bells resounded splendidly in the morning air.
> At about 4:00 in the afternoon I went along with Ōta to visit the Chinese neighborhood in Jiujiang City. On the way from the Japanese concession to the Chinese neighborhood there were two arches. Taking a smaller road off to the left we came out in front of Dragon Pond.[16]

During this excursion, unimpeded by guides, Tanizaki and his companions are able to relish the surrounding scenery, which Tanizaki describes in detail. Returning from the excursion in late afternoon, Tanizaki details the bustle in Jiujiang's town center: the well-dressed gentlemen trying to avoid the muddy streets, vendors selling all manner of items from hastily-erected stalls separated only by blankets, and his own desperate search for the porcelain for which the area is known.

The entry for Day Two describes the climb up the mountain itself. On a cloudy morning, Tanizaki and his companions hire palanquins to carry them up the mountain. The road is narrow and treacherous, but from the safety of his palanquin Tanizaki is able to view the surrounding natural scenery along with the temples and pagodas along the way. Throughout, Tanizaki's description provides the precise names for the lakes, rivers, valleys and temples that they encounter. The narrator also provides lists of flora and fauna he comes across — varieties of birds, trees and plants are all carefully cataloged.

The final passage, describing their descent, is representative of the entire work's lyrical quality:

> In the ravine before us, the white fog was still thickening and, as if animated, rushed into the caves where the mountain priests were said to be dwelling. Departing from there, it seemed to return before the steles and, passing behind the peak, spread out both above and below. The wind started to pick up and the fog began to pass from right to left and crossed the peak. At this point, the valley below cleared a little and the fog cloud, as it hit the protruding angle of the peak and began to rise into the heavens, had the appearance of a dragon ascending into the Empyrean.[17]

The language of this passage is not only rich and descriptive, but its generous use of Chinese character compounds and dragon imagery echoes the cadences of *kanbun*. In its wealth of descriptive terminology, the overall beauty of its language and its careful delineation of place, "Rozan nikki" has much in common with "Soshū kikō."[18] Both are ultimately celebrations of specific locales in China. However, there are several telling differences as well, which have to do with the conventions of the form Tanizaki adopted. In "Rozan nikki" the element of time plays a more integral role in the development of the narrative. Tanizaki is careful to record not only the passing of the days, but also the sequence of events within each day. Unimportant blocks of time are left out and important events are described in detail, the cumulative effect being that the selectivity and management of time in the *nikki* becomes, in a sense, a self-portrait of the author, accentuating those qualities that, in Tanizaki's view, define the place.[19] "Soshū kikō," on the other hand, downplays the passing of time, focusing rather on lengthy descriptions of specific scenes and people.

The essays from this first journey, "Soshū kikō" and "Rozan nikki," fit quite neatly into two conventional Japanese literary genres. The forms of both pieces were inspired by Tanizaki's experience during this 1918 journey, although in later reminiscences by Tanizaki it appears he had different hopes in mind for this trip. In the following passage from an essay resulting from the 1926 trip, Tanizaki considers the irony of having the opportunity to meet so many Chinese writers during the second trip, despite having failed to do so during the first trip:

> I refer to this as "ironic" because, during my previous 1918 trip to China, I had hoped to meet young Chinese writers in either Beijing or Shanghai and sought the good offices of various people towards that purpose, but at the time in the Republic of China there was not even one person fitting that description.[20]

Thus informed, it would appear that Tanizaki, thwarted in this desire to meet Chinese writers during this 1918 visit, was left with no alternative but to play the role of literary pilgrim and to convey his experience in China via the conventional discourse of the traveler rather than to attempt to write about limited and superficial contacts with a handful of Chinese. During Tanizaki's second visit, however, the community of young writers and artists that he sought in vain during the first trip was now flourishing. In the interim since Tanizaki's last visit, there was an influx of returning overseas students from Japan who had embarked on their literary careers while still in Japan. Even more ironically, since the majority of these young writers and intellectuals had received their higher education in Japan, they not only spoke Japanese, but were also familiar with Tanizaki's work and extended him a welcome that left him utterly dumbfounded.

The 1926 Visit: Encounters and Engagement with Chinese Writers

"Shanhai kōyūki" (Record of Friendly Exchange in Shanghai), the most important piece based upon Tanizaki's second journey to China in 1926, appeared in two installments in the June and August issues of the magazine *Josei* (Woman). The piece describes events spanning several weeks and focuses on the friendly relations Tanizaki develops with members of the Chinese literary community in Shanghai. Much longer than the pieces resulting from this previous trip (thirty-five pages in the *Collected Works*), it is an intriguing footnote in the history of Sino-Japanese cultural relations, and provides one of the richest portrayals of encounters between writers from the two communities in the interwar period. Tanizaki's account provides a sympathetic and balanced portrait of the young writers active in Shanghai during the twenties and the depth of their knowledge of the contemporary Japanese literary scene.[21]

On this occasion, he had the good fortune of being introduced to Uchiyama Kanzō. Tanizaki mentions in the "Record of Friendly Exchange in Shanghai" how impressed he was with Uchiyama during his first visit to the shop, and how he was able to glean from their conversation a great deal of information not only about young Chinese writers, but also about their educational experiences in Japan, about the kind of Japanese books they read and the kind of Japanese works they were translating. Tanizaki learned from Uchiyama that news of Tanizaki's visit had already appeared in the newspaper and that, among the young Chinese writers, there was talk of holding a reception for him.[22]

At the reception held in his honor, he describes each of the writers in turn, referring to the linguist and medical doctor Guo Moruo as the "Mori Ōgai of China" and remarks that he, Tanizaki, had mistaken Tian Han for a Japanese when he first spoke with him.[23] He describes how Tian confessed having seen Tanizaki on a film set with filmmaker Kurihara Thomas in Yokohama but at the time he did not have the nerve to go up and speak with the famous writer. When Tanizaki asks about tastes in contemporary Japanese literature in China, he is told that Mushanokōji Saneatsu (1885–1976) and Kikuchi Kan (1889–1948) are particularly popular.[24]

Later, out walking with Guo and Tian, the talk turns to remuneration for writers in China as compared to Japan. Tanizaki is astounded at how little Chinese writers and translators get paid for their efforts. Tian further explains that although he and writers like Zhou Zuoren (1885–1967) have already translated much from contemporary Japanese literature, little has as yet found its way into print. The conversation then takes a political turn and when Tanizaki attempts to praise China for its recent efforts at modernization he is roundly rebuked by Guo, who heaps blame on both the imperialists who have divided up China and robbed it of its dignity, and on China itself for being so slow to respond. This is the only tense moment in the otherwise extremely amicable relations between Tanizaki and his hosts. Tanizaki responds by expressing respect for the depth of these writers' emotions toward their homeland.

Later in his speech at the reception held in his honor, Tanizaki admits the shock he received at the scope of the reception given him and his gratitude for all that these young Chinese writers had done on behalf of Japanese literature. He further states on behalf of the Japanese:

> I am sure that in the Japanese literary community there is no one who could imagine that I would be receiving the kind of welcome you have extended to me, and when I return home and relate news of this gathering as the best souvenir that I brought back with me I know my acquaintances will be shocked. At this point I would like to humbly express my deepest gratitude not only as an individual but also as a representative of the Japanese literary community. However, on second thought, there being any number of distinct literary factions in Japan at present, if I am so foolhardy as to take the position of "representative" I will probably be beaten up, so I'd better express my thanks as an individual and leave it at that.[25]

Tanizaki characterizes this essay as a *kōyūki*, a record of "friendly exchange," essentially a variety of *kiroku*, or "record" of certain events. Unlike the *kikōbun* and the literary *nikki* that resulted from the first trip, Tanizaki's concern is not with a particular place and a painstaking description of its salient features as in the *kikō*, nor is he concerned with accounting for days spent in specific locales as in the *nikki*. In "Record of Friendly Exchange in Shanghai" Tanizaki's apparent goal is to provide a more personal portrait of a community of writers in the hope that such a determined effort will foster understanding and good will between the two literary communities. Only in passing does he comment on the setting for the narrative or the time frame of events; the focus remains on individuals and much of the narrative involves descriptions of people or transcriptions of the author's conversations with these figures. Unlike the earlier essays from China in which Tanizaki is content to observe from the outside, in the "Record of Friendly Exchange in Shanghai" the narrator is a participant, relishing his status as visiting celebrity. In a photograph of that event, we see Tanizaki seated with arms folded, wearing a self-satisfied expression, and surrounded by the admiring young writers who extended to him that remarkable welcome (see Photo 3, p. 154).

In order to appreciate the significance of Tanizaki's visit and of his encounters with Chinese writers, it is important to note that the writers with whom Tanizaki associated during the 1926 visit represented some of the leading figures in the May Fourth literary world and were integral in providing direction for the new vernacular literature. Guo Moruo and Tian Han, for example, who were still students in Japan at the time of Tanizaki's first visit, were founding members of the Creation Society and now occupied positions of considerable influence in the Chinese literary world.

Guo Moruo was a leading literary critic and theorist whose collection of modern verse, *Nüshen* (The Goddesses) had revolutionized Chinese poetry upon publication in 1921. At the time of Tanizaki's visit, Guo had just resigned as the Dean of the College of Art and Letters at Sun Yatsen University in Guangdong and was poised to accept the post of Director of the Political Department of the National Republican Army.[26] Tian Han, who already disassociated himself from the Creation Society by the time of Tanizaki's visit, was a leading playwright and a pioneer in filmmaking. Tian and Ouyang Yuqian, whom Tanizaki also met during his 1926 visit, were both actively involved in the Chinese Drama Research Society which was meeting at Uchiyama Kanzō's shop.[27]

Such a record could not have been produced following Tanizaki's first visit to China; his interaction with individuals was as extensive and intensely personal during the second trip as it was sporadic and superficial during the first trip. Based on comments made by the author in "Record of Friendly Exchange in Shanghai," not only did Tanizaki consider himself an established writer to whom the young Chinese writers could look to for advice and guidance, but he saw himself as an ambassador of good will representing the Japanese literary community. It was a role he seemed to relish. The tone throughout the piece is one of sympathy and gratitude.

Tanizaki displays a prodigious range of attitudes and emotions; he seems interested in the current state of Chinese literature although, as often as not, what draws his attention is the Chinese literary community's interest in and reception of Japanese literature. In other words, Tanizaki's interest in the Chinese literary community and their activities has to be seen, at least in part, as self-reflexive. As much as anything else, Tanizaki is fascinated during this visit by the scope and depth of the interest in Japanese literature on the part of these young Chinese writers.[28] Thus, "Record of Friendly Exchange in Shanghai" is as valuable for what it tells us about Tanizaki as for what it tells us about the state of the Chinese literary community. Tanizaki's encounters with Chinese writers and his self-reflexive interest in what they have to say about the contemporary Japanese literary scene helps him to better understand his own place in Japanese literature and the role he might play in providing direction for the Japanese literary community, especially concerning relations with their Chinese counterparts. In its sympathetic portrait of the contemporary Chinese literary community and as a self-portrait of Tanizaki, "Record of Friendly Exchange in Shanghai" is invaluable.

Return to Another Homeland: Tanizaki's Fictional Representations of China after 1926

Tanizaki's 1926 visit to China was transformative for him as a writer. Although the immediate result in terms of literary output pertaining to his visit was not as dramatic as that which resulted from his 1918 visit, which resulted in several prominent stories about China, nevertheless a changed vision of China emerges in several of Tanizaki's works from the late twenties. In particular, China serves as a point of reference in the first major work of fiction Tanizaki produced after the 1926 visit, *Tade kuu mushi* (Some Prefer Nettles). The visit also contributed to Tanizaki's abiding fascination with the interplay of the cultural binaries of West and East, tradition and modernity, masculine and feminine, and Japan and the other.

In retrospect, it is not surprising that Tanizaki should have been so deeply affected by his visits to China. Like so many of his protagonists, Tanizaki was enthralled by the foreign and the exotic, and these journeys turned out to be his only visits abroad. Consequently, the impact of these visits on his aesthetic sensibilities was correspondingly great.[29] In the years just prior to and immediately following the 1918 visit, Tanizaki produced a small number of distinguished short stories that were set in China including two well-known stories mentioned earlier in this chapter, "Lament of a Mermaid" and "The Moon on the West Lake." Both of these stories and other fictional works by Tanizaki from this period set in China portray a culturally rich traditional China in almost reverential terms.[30]

Due in part to Tanizaki's admittedly limited interaction with Chinese hosts during the 1918 visit, his encounters were confined to interactions with the culturally rich topos of the places he was visiting and with an imagined China that he projected on to the real landscape. Consequently, the works from this period reflected a mythic China. The 1918 trip, in fact, seemed to largely reaffirm for Tanizaki China as a place to reinvent a mythic past. This conception of China was to remain largely unchallenged until Tanizaki's 1926 visit.[31]

The 1926 trip fundamentally changed the manner in which Tanizaki conceptualized and subsequently represented China. Contemporary China became real to Tanizaki as a result of the 1926 visit and his encounters with writers during his stay. It is a point of interest, in fact, that in the years following Tanizaki's 1926 visit, in contrast to the 1918 visit, he did not produce any works of fiction set solely in China. In fact, aside from a story entitled "Tomoda to Matsunaga no hanashi" (A Tale of Tomoda and Matsunaga, 1926), a story set partly in Shanghai, China no longer serves as a setting in Tanizaki's fiction.[32] The mystique of China that characterized Tanizaki's earlier stories, the presentation of China as an exotic place where any transformation seems possible, no longer exists.

Following Tanizaki's 1926 visit, personal essays, such as "Record of Friendly Exchange in Shanghai," replaced the short stories written after the 1918 visit. The immediacy of the personal interactions that Tanizaki had with Chinese writers during the 1926 visit seemed to beg for the unmediated candor of the essay form. As he stated on several occasions in these essays, Tanizaki wanted Japanese readers to hear about the details of his experiences and to be made aware that the Chinese were intimately familiar and concerned with what was happening in the Japanese literary community. In another essay, "Shanhai kenbunroku" (A Record of Observations in Shanghai, 1935), Tanizaki unequivocally states:

> It goes without saying that I did not write this essay simply out of a desire to please myself. I wanted my readers in Japan to know the extent to which they [i.e. Chinese writers] were familiar with the details of the Japanese *bundan*.[33]

For Tanizaki, the 1926 trip, largely centered in Shanghai, revealed to him the maddening complexities and delightful ironies of that great city caught between extreme affluence and dire poverty, between Eastern and Western sensibilities, between the sacred and the profane, and between Chinese and Non-Chinese.

This was precisely the fascinating commingling of opposites that had attracted Tanizaki to Yokohama during his early formative stage as a writer. It was the contact with the other in the form of Westerners and Chinese and the possibility of encounters with the exotic that the Yokohama and Shanghai experiences had in common for Tanizaki — the pilgrimage to forbidden spaces.[34] Shanghai, in particular, seemed to encapsulate all of the alluring complexities of the East/West binary, and encouraged Tanizaki as an artist to go beyond the realm of "either-or" categorizations in order to embrace a more encompassing "both-and" stance in regard to the dichotomies of East and West and of China and the other.[35]

Tanizaki's celebrated attraction to China only seemed to intensify with the 1926 visit as is evidenced by a letter by him to his acquaintance Tsuchiya Kei, a banker in Shanghai who had helped him during his 1926 visit and thereafter sent him materials from Shanghai. In the following passage from a letter to Tsuchiya, Tanizaki considers his attraction to China:

> It certainly must be admitted that China is an aggravating place. And yet for me this China — my affection for China — is something I have grown into. In fact, this year I am considering giving up on my plans to travel to France, and am thinking of going again to China instead.[36]

This fascination with the mystique of China and this propensity to focus on those elements of China that accentuated the exotic otherness of China that characterized the works of fiction after Tanizaki's first visit had developed into a more mature vision of China after the second visit. While in the essays written following the 1926 visit to Shanghai Tanizaki does delineate some aspects of Shanghai and of China that distinguish them from Japan, nevertheless he presents the ironies in Shanghai as particular manifestations of the ironies inherent in the modern urban space. What Tanizaki seems to be suggesting is that in Shanghai the paradoxes of the modern city and its complexities are magnified. And, as Atsuko Sakaki deftly observes, the close coexistence in Chinese culture of the "divine and the disgusting" was a "perfect match" for the aesthetic sensibility that Tanizaki had been refining for ten years as a writer.[37]

Although Tanizaki produced no overt "Chinese stories" following the second visit as he had after the first visit, nevertheless China, and particularly Shanghai, plays a role in several works of fiction that Tanizaki produced just after the 1926 visit. Tomoda, the protagonist in "A Tale of Tomoda and Matsunaga" sees in Shanghai a reflection of the Paris where he sojourned in his youth and seeks in later years the giddy cosmopolitan atmosphere that he does not find in Tokyo. Likewise, in *Tade kuu mushi* (Some Prefer Nettles, 1928–29) Shanghai hovers in the background, an important presence for the protagonist Kaname as he wrestles with a variety of yearnings, which seem initially irreconcilable, but which ultimately merge beneath his encompassing, Orientalist gaze.

Some Prefer Nettles is the story of Shiba Kaname and his wife Misako, a couple living in affluence in the suburbs of Kobe with their adolescent son Hiroshi. The novel describes, with unnerving realism, the painfully slow breakdown of a marriage and details the personal costs associated with the couple's inability to extract themselves from a marriage that has long been one in name only. While the novel's setting is Kansai, and while commentators on the novel have largely focused on the work as a manifestation of Tanizaki's increasing attraction to that region, Shanghai too plays a role in the work.

In *Some Prefer Nettles*, the attraction to China has a face — it is embodied in the character of Takanatsu Hideo, a friend of Kaname and entrepreneur based in Shanghai who sees in the metropolis a delightful, intoxicating admixture of traditional Orient and avant-garde, Jazz Age Western abandon. Takanatsu does things with flair — when he first appears in the novel he is bringing back from Shanghai the present of a greyhound to Kaname and Misako. He always dresses impeccably in the latest Western fashions, but he also subscribes to the efficacy of Chinese medicine and consumes garlic daily for its health benefits. He has the determination and swagger that Kaname lacks. As he attempts to intercede in the failing marriage and endeavors to shield the boy Hiroshi from the unpleasantness of his parents' strained relations, the strength of will that Takanatsu possesses stands in stark juxtaposition to Kaname's inertia.

Of course, the indecisiveness of Kaname, his inability to proceed in a straightforward manner with the divorce that has become an inevitability is in part a function of his being a member of an elite social class in Japan during a period in which divorce was not really a viable option. Indeed, culture — cultural differences, shifts in cultural values and clashes between cultures — is at the heart of *Some Prefer Nettles*. As Ken Ito has astutely pointed out, "marriage as a function of culture" serves as the "organizing principle" in the novel.[38] Moreover, as in two other novels by Tanizaki from the 1920s, *Chijin no ai* (A Fool's Love) and *Manji*, *Some Prefer Nettles* suggests that male-female relations and the complexities of such relations are essentially a discussion of culture.[39] In *Some Prefer Nettles* the collision of cultures and the binaries of East/West and Traditional/Modern are projected in the three female characters associated with Kaname.

Ironically, Misako, Kaname's long suffering wife, who seems to most deftly negotiate cultural ambiguities and constitutes the most graceful embodiment of the new class of cosmopolitan Japanese represented by Tanizaki himself, is shunned by Kaname for being simply too orthodox and commonplace. Kaname seems in the course of the novel to be drawn increasingly to Ohisa, the young mistress of his father who reflects those very qualities of classical Japanese culture, and of the Kansai region in particular, that would be explored in greater depth in Tanizaki's translations of *The Tale of Genji*, and in his *magnum opus, The Makioka Sisters* in the decade to follow.

Ultimately, *Some Prefers Nettles* seems to suggest that Kaname's preference for the modest and traditional, almost anachronistic Ohisa reflects a return to purely native Japanese aesthetics on the part of the author. And yet, in many ways it is Louisa, the Eurasian mistress with whom Kanami has long been involved who seems to embody the iconoclastic and intriguing intersection of cultures that had so attracted Tanizaki in Yokohama and again during his 1926 sojourn to Shanghai.

Like Naomi in *A Fool's Love* Louisa's physical appeal to the protagonist is the appeal of the exotic. Louisa's multi-ethnicity and her urbanity serve to manifest the potent and heady intersection of cultures that attracted Tanizaki to Shanghai. Louisa makes various demands of Kaname, wants only the finest things and demands his attention and constant vigilance. At the juncture in their relationship in which the novel is set, it seems that Kaname has wearied of the relationship and although she still holds an allure for him, it appears that he is prepared to break with her. The relationship and the demands of Louisa are simply too enervating and there seems to be a suggestion in the novel that the only remedy for Kaname's malaise is a return to native traditions as embodied in the kind of woman represented by the Kansai-bred Ohisa.

Scholarship has tended to associate Louisa and the exoticism, the otherness that she represents with the West. It seems more appropriate, perhaps, to envision Louisa as the personification of Shanghai chic — an amalgamation of East/West, the exotic and the familiar. Just as Kaname cannot entirely relinquish his passion for Louisa's exotic world of cabarets, Russian dancers and cognac, even as he is drawn to the comforts of native Japanese culture, Tanizaki was in no way in this novel signaling a cessation of interest in either China or the West by his relocation to Kansai. The Tanizaki scholar Noguchi Takehiko pointedly suggests that for all of his talk about a return to a native home and to the comforts of a native tradition, Tanizaki was never far from the thrall of the exotic. The return to a home, genuine or merely hoped for, coexists with the aspiration for the foreign, and just as the interplay of these two needs define Kaname they define Tanizaki also.[40]

Ken Ito suggests that ultimately for Tanizaki Kansai is best thought of as a "second homeland." It seems appropriate then to construe China as a third homeland for Tanizaki. It was not for Tanizaki like the West, an imagined place, the alien product of fanciful yearnings and or the product of novels read. China, for Tanizaki was real. The 1926 visit had transformed China for Tanizaki from a still largely imagined cultural homeland into a real one. Even at the time of the 1918 trip this closeness was clearly something to which he aspired. In the essay "Sōshū Kikō" Tanizaki described visiting China as a "return to the self" (*jiga kaiki*), and by the second trip to China, Tanizaki clearly was journeying back to the familiar.

If it is true that in moving to Kansai, Tanizaki had found a "home that was also another world," then in China Tanizaki came to possess yet another home that was both different from his true home but also uncannily homey.[41] It was a home to which he would never physically return, but one to which he would revisit again and again in reverie, even if only while gazing at a scroll rendered by a friend's hand and thinking of times passed and opportunities lost.

Toward Tomorrow: Tanizaki's "Yesterday and Today"

A fascinating postscript to Tanizaki's 1926 visit was his essay "Kinō kyō" (Yesterday and Today) that was published in *Bungei shunjū* in 1942 in serialized form from June until November. Written at a time when the scrutiny of the censors was at its most intense, the essay provides reminiscences of Chinese writers with whom Tanizaki was acquainted.[42] The composition and publication of the piece at that juncture constituted an act of bravery both on the part of Tanizaki, who risked being both ostracized and censored, and *Bungei shunjū*, for the courage to publish a piece in which Chinese writers associated with the anti-Japanese movement were treated with delicacy and sympathy. Tanizaki's conclusion, in which he boldly predicts an age in which Chinese and Japanese writers will once again be able to interact freely and on equal terms, seems an especially intrepid proclamation given the era in which it was written.

Written during the depths of war, "Yesterday and Today" is a fond recollection of the golden age of exchange between the two literary communities and a reaffirmation of the satisfaction that Tanizaki had achieved during his 1926 visit. His engaging portrayal of the Chinese writers with whom he became acquainted during that visit and the admiration he expresses for them seem to neutralize the potential propagandistic value of the piece that apparently convinced the authorities to permit the piece to be published.

Tanizaki begins the piece, interestingly, with an acknowledgement of the traditional mode of communication between writers in East Asia. He refers to a poem, which he includes in its entirety, written by Ouyang Yuqian that had been presented to Tanizaki during a visit to Ouyang's home while Tanizaki was in China in 1926. Written in the traditional *lüshi* style, Tanizaki declares that he displays the scroll containing the poem every year in the summer, and that while admiring it, he invariably recollects that visit and wonders about the present whereabouts and activities of the "old friends" from China.

> Starting with the appearance of the clouds of war which now envelop the Asian continent, every year with the arrival of summer, I look at this scroll hanging on my wall and I wonder where Ouyang, Tian, and the others that I met during that time are and what they are doing. At times like that, in spite of myself, I am overcome with powerful emotions.[43]

In this essay, Tanizaki reintroduces several of the writers whom he had introduced to his readers in "A Record of Friendly Exchange in Shanghai" fifteen years earlier including Ouyang Yuqian and Tian Han, about whom he remarks was, at the time of this visit, still recovering from the death of his wife earlier that year. The evening at Ouyang's home clearly left an impression on Tanizaki, and he relates how the traditional, ceremonial exchange of poems was one of the most treasured encounters from his 1926 visit to China.[44]

Tanizaki, in this essay, as in so many of the reminiscences of visits to Shanghai in this era by Japanese writers, relates his affection and gratitude to Uchiyama Kanzō for the great lengths to which Uchiyama went to introduce Tanizaki to Chinese writers. After briefly alluding to the banquet held in his honor that was the focus of "Record of Friendly Exchange in Shanghai," Tanizaki describes the relationship with Tian Han that developed after that evening and the friendship forged between the two writers during Tanizaki's extended visit. Tanizaki describes in detail and with obvious gratitude all that Tian did on his behalf during the visit, which included coming to his hotel and leading him around Shanghai and its environs to concerts, theaters, shopping excursions — and admiring the beautiful women who they encountered in each of those places.[45] Tanizaki was particularly appreciative of the running narrative that Tian provided on each of those occasions. Tanizaki remarks that during his visit, one of his greatest pleasures was to sit down with Tian with a pot of local wine between them and talk of literature and art, secure in the knowledge that in Tian he had found a kindred spirit. Tanizaki asserts that these conversations and this companionship served deeply felt needs for both men.

> I dare say that while there is no doubt that Tian in no small way consoled me in my travel weariness, for Tian also the appearance of a wanderer like me unquestionably diverted his attention from the loneliness that he was feeling. Tian still bore a deep spiritual wound from the death of his wife, and I was happy to be the one who listened to him open up, bit-by-bit, the pent-up yearnings of his heart.[46]

During Tanizaki's visit, on those days when Tian couldn't come to call on him, the time seemed to creep along. Even after Tanizaki's return to Japan, the two writers maintained a steady correspondence.

Two years after Tanizaki's return to Japan, he was able to return the favor when Tian and a friend came to visit Japan. The two visitors arrived in Kobe and Tanizaki, who was then living in an eastern suburb of Kobe called Okamoto, welcomed the two men to stay in his home. During their visit, Tanizaki showed Tian and his companion around Kyoto and Osaka, and they attended the Bunraku theater in Osaka. Tian, who had many years earlier studied at Waseda University in Tokyo, was anxious to visit Tokyo and to call upon friends who remained there. In Tokyo, Tian visited his old boarding house and met with Japanese writers including Kikuchi Kan, who was much admired by Tian and his fellow Chinese dramatists. Kikuchi asked Tian to write a piece about Chinese drama which was later published in *Bungei shunjū*.[47] Tian also met Satō Haruo with whom he was already acquainted from the time of Satō's visit to Shanghai, and Tanizaki remarks that he seems to recall that Satō wrote a piece about Tian's visit.[48]

In "Yesterday and Today" Tanizaki also writes briefly about Guo Moruo, a writer with whom he also became acquainted during his 1926 visit, and who Tanizaki acknowledges has become a significant political figure as well as a leading literary light in China. Tanizaki describes Guo's deep, personal ties to Japan and relates the tragedy of Guo's having to abandon his Japanese wife and children while fleeing from Japan. He also briefly outlines Guo's emergence from poet-aesthete and literary leader when Tanizaki knew him to the revolutionary Communist leader that he has become. In discussing the politicization of Tian,

Guo and other Chinese writers with whom he is acquainted, Tanizaki reveals a remarkable capacity for sympathy:

> Recently [Tian] admittedly has been involved in producing anti-Japanese films — this is an undeniable fact. That notwithstanding, these two men [Guo Moruo and Tian Han] probably understand the virtues of the Japanese better than any other [Chinese] and I truly believe that they bear no animosity toward the Japanese people.[49]

Tanizaki closes his essay by affirming his belief that the "unnatural" schism that separates the two countries and individuals will not last, and he closes with a quote from the Ouyang poem with which he opened the piece, affirming the eternal friendship between men of letters.[50]

For an established writer like Tanizaki, a writer who remained largely aloof during the war years, what was the motivation to produce such an essay? Furthermore, why did the Japanese authorities agree to publish an essay in which Chinese revolutionary leaders engaged in anti-Japanese activities are not demonized but rather portrayed in a decidedly humane manner? The answers to these questions lay in the one dimension of the essay that made it palatable to the authorities. The argument for racial affinity, which is one facet of "Yesterday and Today" was, in a sense, its saving grace. Tanizaki describes, for example, how he believes that he could never interact with Western writers in the same way that he interacts with Chinese writers, because Western writers do not share a common set of values. "To be honest," Tanizaki contends, "Western literature just doesn't seem to fit us right."[51] Moreover, this argument for racial affinity between the two peoples can be summed up in the following statement:

> Despite the existence of various differences between us [Chinese and Japanese], in the final analysis we are brothers in whose veins the same blood flows. Therefore, although relations between us have been cut completely, I am sure that in the future there will be a day when we can return to the fundamental intimacy we share.[52]

Such conventional pronouncements of racial affinity made Tanizaki's essay acceptable to authorities who were still desperately trying to justify their invasion of their neighboring nations and to garner support from the intellectual community for the Greater East Asian Co-prosperity Sphere (*Daitōa kyōeiken*). Tanizaki was obviously astute enough to recognize that his essay would be utilized as a piece of propaganda by the authorities in this manner. One gets the sense that Tanizaki realized that his inclusion of this argument was the price that he had to pay in order for this essay to be published. Tanizaki, who reluctantly expurgated his translation of *The Tale of Genji* in order to see it published, understood quite clearly what the censors wanted, and was willing to compromise in order to avoid the ignominy of being silenced.⁵³

In "Yesterday and Today" Tanizaki manipulates the censors and incorporates an argument that makes it possible to publish a piece which is ultimately not about racial affinity but about friendship. The essay celebrates collegiality and the startling capacity of literature to transcend national boundaries while it affirms traditional East Asian aesthetic values and conventions. For an established writer like Tanizaki, who already adopted a stance of non-cooperation with the authorities, there was much to lose and little to gain from a piece portraying Chinese writers with sympathy. The essay, which deliberately acknowledges traditional literary exchanges, constitutes a small act of humaneness amidst the depths of war.

Conclusion

The writings Tanizaki produced in conjunction with his travels in China demonstrate his versatility, the works produced from each journey being suited to the particular circumstances he encountered. Rather than attempting to impose a particular approach or style of writing onto his experiences in order to produce a certain effect, Tanizaki allows the circumstances of each trip to dictate the character of the writing, with some falling into recognizable genres while others defy easy categorization.

Tanizaki's 1918 trip to China brought forth several memorable, but relatively conventional, evocations of place written in the *nikki* and *kikōbun* forms. An examination of genres represented in his *Collected Works* reveals that Tanizaki used these traditional appellations quite sparingly. There are four other pieces to which he applied the name *nikki*; there is no other single work in the *Collected Works* designated as a *kikō*. The relative paucity of such traditional genres in Tanizaki's *oeuvre* suggests the relative importance of these two works in Tanizaki's overall production.

By contrast with Tanizaki's first trip to China, the 1926 trip provided Tanizaki with opportunities for direct encounters with the Chinese literary community that were unavailable to him during his 1918 visit. The resultant essay, "Record of Friendly Exchange in Shanghai," is significant for several reasons: it defies and transcends traditional generic definitions, in scope it is more far-ranging and ambitious than any of the works that resulted from the 1918 trip, and among records by Japanese visitors to China in the early modern era, it demonstrates a special sensitivity to cultural changes China was then undergoing. Most importantly, it is a vibrant, engaging record of the Shanghai literary scene in the late 1920s from the perspective of an important Japanese writer. The 1926 visit made China real for Tanizaki in a way that the 1918 visit did not and his fascination with the cultural complexities of Shanghai are evident in *Some Prefer Nettles*, the first important novel he completed after his return to Japan.

Moreover, Tanizaki's essay from 1942, "Yesterday and Today," affirms the true and lasting import of the relations with Chinese writers established fifteen years earlier. Written in the midst of war, Tanizaki skillfully constructs an artful and heartfelt portrait of relations with Chinese writers couched in terms of racial affinity that was acceptable to the censors while nevertheless looking toward a period when war would no longer divide the two countries and the two literary communities.

In Tanizaki Jun'ichirō's portrayals of China — its places, its events and its people — we glimpse Tanizaki himself as both observer and participant with the wide eyes of the pilgrim and the focused gaze of the observing artist.[54] Although the works resulting from his two journeys to China must be considered minor accomplishments in relation to his more celebrated works of fiction, they do offer insights into Tanizaki's abiding fascination with China and provide an intriguing glimpse into Sino-Japanese cultural relations in the interwar period.

3
The Allure of the White Birch School to May Fourth Writers

Although individual Japanese writers of note such as Tanizaki, Natsume Sōseki (1867–1916) and Akutagawa Ryūnosuke (1892–1927) had followers and ardent advocates among Chinese writers in the interwar period, no coterie of Japanese writers was so openly admired nor so roundly criticized among May Fourth writers as the writers associated with the Shirakaba-ha (White Birch School). The White Birch School's commingling of concerns for Western aesthetic trends and social critique, the humanistic creed championed by the school and the organizational scheme for an artistic coterie that they developed, exerted a considerable appeal on contemporary Chinese writers, particularly Zhou Zuoren and Lu Xun, both of whom translated works by White Birch School members and disseminated information about the school's achievements to a receptive audience.

The extent to which the literature and ideals of the White Birch School were known to May Fourth intellectuals was largely the result of the efforts of Zhou Zuoren and Lu Xun. The Zhou brothers, who became familiar with the White Birch School while living in Japan, found in the literary works and activities of the school the realization of the ideals that they themselves sought to convey. Moreover, they perceived in the literary productions of the Shirakaba writers, particularly Mushanokōji Saneatsu, a reflection of Tolstoyan idealism and pacifism, which they sought to manifest in their own writings.

Translations of the works of Shirakaba writers by the Zhou brothers coupled with their efforts to introduce Shirakaba humanism to Chinese readers resulted in a familiarity among May Fourth intellectuals with the values of the White Birch School. While the Zhou brothers were of one mind in their enthusiastic support of the White Birch School, the Shirakaba writers they championed and the specific works to which each was attracted betrayed fundamental ideological differences between the two brothers which became apparent in the growing schism between the two in the early twenties and the decisive split between the brothers in

1923 which is the subject of Lu Xun's 1926 story, "Xiongdi" (Brothers).[1] While Zhou Zuoren's efforts in support of the White Birch School's New Village Movement will be the focus of Chapter 4, it was Lu Xun's endorsement of Mushanokōji's pacifist play *Aru Seinen no Yume* (A Certain Young Man's Dream) and, more particularly, his championing of Arishima Takeo that led to an appreciation of the varied achievements of the White Birch School among May Fourth thinkers.

The White Birch School was a loose affiliation of writers and artists founded in 1910, which had its roots in the merging of several student groups at the prestigious Gakushūin (Peers' School). Founding members included some who would become luminaries in the Taishō period (1912–1926) literary and artistic worlds including Mushanokōji Saneatsu, Shiga Naoya (1883–1971), Yanagita Kunio (1875–1962), and Arishima Takeo (1878–1923). Soon after the White Birch School's founding in 1910, the school's literary works, its periodic art exhibits, and its eponymous journal, became magnets for other young artists disenchanted with the stifling gloom of the Naturalist School, which had dominated the Japanese literary world in the latter part of the Meiji period (1868–1912).

Although the White Birch School was just one of a number of anti-naturalist coteries that emerged in the late Meiji period which also included the writers associated with the journals *Mita bungaku* (Mita Literature), *Subaru* (Pleiades), and *Shin shichō* (New Tide) that would soon form the core of Taishō period literature, the school differed from these other anti-naturalist groups in several respects. The White Birch School was, first of all, a much larger and more organizationally complex association, which included writers, artists, cultural anthropologists, and art critics. Moreover, the school demonstrated a much greater range of activities which included, of course, creative writing and the regular production of the journal, but also extended to exhibits of painting, sculpture and ceramics and social reform activities. These latter activities were as attractive to May Fourth intellectuals as the literary works themselves.[2]

The White Birch School's initial attraction for May Fourth intellectuals was connected intimately with the Western orientation of the school's aesthetic vision. The Shirakaba members were among the first generation of Japanese writers who had received an education which was firmly grounded in Western learning. Thus, writers associated with the White Birch School betray in their writings fewer of the ambiguities and tensions in regard to tradition than do their seniors in the Japanese literary world such as Mori Ōgai and Natsume Sōseki, both of whom were the products of a more traditional educational model. The Shirakaba writers were largely uninformed about traditional Japan and impatient with the strict Confucian rigidity of the previous generation of Japanese writers.[3] For the writers associated with the White Birch School, it was Western literature and art that provided the touchstone for their own creative efforts, not the traditional native models that inspired earlier Meiji writers.[4] It was natural, given these circumstances, that Shirakaba writers should be so enthusiastic about their perceived mission to introduce knowledge about Western literature and art to their contemporaries in the Taishō intellectual world.

Significantly, the Western-style education that Shirakaba members received was the same education that the Zhou brothers, educated in Japan in the latter years of the Meiji period, had received. It is not surprising that Zhou Zuoren and Lu Xun, and the audience of young Chinese intellectuals to whom they were writing, should have discovered an affinity with these Japanese writers who were sensitive to Western aesthetic ideals and social values.

At the heart of the varied activities of the White Birch School, which included art shows and experiments in social reform, was the production of their monthly journal, *Shirakaba* (White Birch). The first issue of the magazine appeared on April 1, 1910 and continued publication as a monthly through 1923, although most of the school's founding members, including Mushanokōji Saneatsu, were no longer actively involved in regular editing by that point. Although the ordering and placement of the various sections of the journal might differ, contents usually included critical essays, along with fiction, drama, sketches and miscellanea. The final section of each issue was usually reserved for *sashie* (illustrations) and photographs of art works. The length of the journal varied from month to month, although there was a tendency toward a longer format after the first few years. Whereas the first year's issues tended to be between fifty and sixty pages, from 1911 onward the length gradually increased to between one hundred and fifty and two hundred pages.[5]

The first issue of *Shirakaba* appeared just before Zhou Zuoren and Lu Xun were poised to return to China and were preparing to embark on their own literary careers. The orientation of Shirakaba thought and values espoused by its founding members exerted an immediate appeal on the Zhou brothers, who were not only proficient enough in Japanese to appreciate the school's literary efforts but had also begun to see in Japanese literature, as had Liang Qichao (1873–1929) before them, an appropriate model for literary and linguistic reform in China.

In the early twenties the White Birch School enjoyed a distinct measure of popularity among Chinese readers. Shirakaba idealism was welcomed by May Fourth intellectuals, particularly those associated with the burgeoning socialist movement.[6] Moreover, May Fourth era writers as diverse as the dramatist Tian Han and Chen Duxiu, founder of the Chinese Communist Party, expressed their indebtedness to Mushanokōji Saneatsu, for championing pacifism and humanism in his works and living according to those ideals.[7]

The appeal of Tolstoy, of course, had been profound as well, but certainly the hunger on the part of May Fourth writers had been fed and nourished by the uncompromising humanism they found reflected in the White Birch School. Mushanokōji Saneatsu, in fact, fashioned his own writings and activities after those of Leo Tolstoy and sought in his own life an engagement with the life and achievements of Tolstoy.[8] All of the founding members of the White Birch School were impacted by Tolstoy's admixture of humanism, individualism, and sensitivity to social inequities, and if some of the members were apt to try to avoid the "perpetual conflict" between ego and the Tolstoyan concept of universal love, there is no doubt that this humanist aestheticism is the school's most enduring legacy.[9]

As significant as their own literary achievements for May Fourth writers was the considerable appeal of the Shirakaba members themselves. Mushanokōji Saneatsu, Arishima Takeo, Yanagi Sōetsu, Takamura Kōtaro (1883–1956), and Shiga Naoya were all charismatic figures who generated a loyal following at home in Japan, but were also able to exert considerable appeal in China as well. If one accepts the assertion that readers are necessarily "culturally-produced producers of texts" then May Fourth readers of Shirakaba literature brought to their reading of those works a perspective that permitted them to approach the texts through a different interpretive lens than that of contemporary Japanese readers.[10] The result was that many of the qualities of the school that appealed to a Japanese audience appealed to May Fourth readers also, but May Fourth writers ultimately found themselves attracted to facets of the school that were not seen in Japan necessarily as central to the Shirakaba mission.

What initially attracted and sustained the interest of May Fourth intellectuals about the White Birch School was the conjoining of aesthetic and political concerns. Mushanokōji's New Village experiment in socialist communal living and Arishima Takeo's giving of land to tenants on his land in Hokkaido, a la Tolstoy, are the two best known and most celebrated examples of the school's social engagement, but all of the key members of the school evinced a sensitivity to social issues.[11] Even Shiga Naoya, one of the most politically disengaged of the major figures associated with the school, had protested along with other young Japanese intellectuals, against a copper mine which in 1901 was accused of poisoning miners in Ashio.[12] Some of the school's members, such as Satomi Ton, while evincing a general sympathy for the plight of the working class and against social injustices, remained removed from actual social engagement. For Satomi Ton's older brother, Arishima Takeo, the frustrations and angst over his own inability to overcome these inequities and his overwhelming sense of guilt and powerlessness to effect social change contributed to the decision to take his own life.

What is interesting are the paradoxes that emerge in an examination of those Shirakaba writers who captured May Fourth readers' imagination and those often more highly respected writers and figures associated with the group who received relatively little attention. Mushanokōji Saneatsu and Arishima Takeo enjoyed a strong reputation among May Fourth readers, while other, equally distinguished Shirakaba figures such as Satomi Ton, Yanagi Sōetsu and Shiga Naoya were less widely acclaimed than one might expect, given their relative importance in Japan.

Yanagi Sōetsu (1889–1961), founder of the *Mingei* (folk art) movement in Japan in the late 1920s and 1930s was by no means an unknown figure in the Chinese *wentan*. Nevertheless, while he was recognized as an important figure in the White Birch School and as an important contributor to the dissemination of art through his contributions to the school's journal and occasional art exhibits, he did not serve as the catalyst for a similar reassessment of the folk art tradition in China as he had in Korea.[13] Undoubtedly, his orientation toward Korean folk art rather than Chinese folk art contributed to his lack of influence in China.

The relatively tepid reception extended to Shiga Naoya (1883–1971) in May Fourth China, however, is even more puzzling. Shiga, donned by contemporaries as the *shōsetsu no kamisama* (the god of fiction), enjoyed a reputation in the prewar Japanese *bundan* rivaled only by Akutagawa Ryūnosuke and Tanizaki Jun'ichirō. His reputation rested largely on his genius for manipulating the conventions of the *shishōsetsu*, a hallowed genre of self-referential fiction that flourished in the Taishō and Shōwa periods. The *shishōsetsu* form appealed to Chinese writers, particularly the Creation Society, and Shiga's representative works were known to Chinese readers through translations by Lu Xun and Zhou Zuoren, but he never achieved the exalted status in China attained by fellow Shirakaba writers Mushanokōji Saneatsu or Arishima Takeo. The lack of a satisfying plot resolution in his stories and the absence of any recognizable socio-political dimension in his works undoubtedly failed to reverberate among Chinese readers.

For Zhou Zuoren and Lu Xun, the initial attraction toward the social engagement of the White Birch School led to an interest in the school's literary works, and Shirakaba works were among works of contemporary Japanese literature translated by the two. Lu Xun and Zhou Zuoren, two of the most influential figures in the May Fourth intellectual world, had received much of their higher education in Meiji Japan. Lu Xun arrived in Japan in 1902 and studied medicine in Sendai before his oft-cited shift to a literary career after witnessing images of the murder of a Chinese traitor by the Japanese military during the Russo-Japanese War. Zhou Zuoren joined his older brother in Japan and the two rented a house in Nishikata while Zhou Zuoren embarked on his own studies.[14] In 1909, the year that Lu Xun returned to China, Zhou Zuoren married a Japanese woman, Hata Nobuko (1887–1962). From 1909 until his return to Shaoxing Province with his wife in autumn of 1911, Zhou concentrated on the study of Japanese literature.[15]

The two brothers' attraction to modern Japanese literature and their advocacy of it as a model to be emulated by Chinese writers differed both in degree and kind. Lu Xun, though not unaffected by Japanese literature, came to perceive it mainly as a means of introducing Western literature to China. Conversely, Zhou Zuoren found implicit value in the Japanese literary tradition and saw Japanese literature as a worthy model to emulate in the construction of a modern Chinese literary idiom.[16] These differences notwithstanding, in the 1910s the two brothers, fresh from their experience in Japan, shared a faith in the potential value of introducing contemporary Japanese literature via translation to a readership hungry for stimulation. The brothers Zhou, who had in 1909 published an anthology of translations of Western fiction entitled, *Yuwai xiaoshuoji* (Anthology of Western Fiction), decided to produce translations of contemporary Japanese fiction which were compiled and published in June 1923 under the name *Xiandai Riben xiaoshuoji* (Anthology of Modern Japanese Fiction).[17] The anthology was the first volume in the series *Shijie congshu* (Compendium of World Literature) published by the Commercial Press in Shanghai. The anthology contained thirty stories by fifteen Japanese writers, all of which were translated by either Zhou Zuoren or Lu Xun.[18]

Among the works chosen for inclusion in the anthology by the Zhou brothers were works by the White Birch School. The writers who the brothers chose to translate demonstrate the elements of the school to which each brother was drawn and point to some of the fundamental ideological differences between them. Lu Xun's Shirakaba selections were two pieces by Arishima Takeo, the essay "Chiisaki mono e" (To the Little Ones) and the story "Omatsu no shi" (The Death of Omatsu). Zhou Zuoren, on the other hand, chose four stories, one each by four members of the White Birch School. His translations include Shiga Naoya's "Seibei to hyotan" (Seibei and the Gourd), Senke Motomaro's (1888–1948) "Bara no hana" (The Rose) and stories by Mushanokōji Saneatsu and Nagayo Zenzō.[19] The disproportionately high ratio of Shirakaba stories in the collection suggests the relative importance that the brothers attached to the group as "representative" of the new anti-naturalist literature.

Although Lu Xun and Zhou Zuoren settled upon different Shirakaba writers to translate, there are some intriguing thematic parallels in the works that they chose to translate. Both the essay by Arishima Takeo that Lu Xun translated and several of the Shirakaba stories chosen to Zhou Zuoren take as their point of departure the world as seen through the eyes of children, or a father's responsibility to his children. Arishima's essay, "Chiisaki mono e," in which a father addresses his children, expresses the idea that a parent must constantly be willing to sacrifice for his children. This concept of the necessity of sacrifice for future generations is prominent in Lu Xun's work as well.[20]

Zhou Zuoren shared with his older brother this notion of the need to sacrifice for the sake of posterity. In a poem that he composed in Japanese dated August 28, 1921 entitled "Kodomo e no inori" (A Prayer for Children) he says, "Children, children, / I pray for you. / Atone for me / Please atone for my sins ..." The speaker's expectation — and indeed hope — that his children must surpass him in order to arrive at a better place, seems a direct reflection of the conclusion reached by Arishima in his essay, "Chiisaki mono e."[21]

Zhou Zuoren's choice of two Shirakaba stories about children, Shiga's "Seibei to hyōtan" and Senke's "Bara no hana" represents an interesting exercise in selectivity. While Shiga's much celebrated 1913 story was, by the time of this translation, considered a minor masterpiece, Senke's 1920 story was virtually unknown, even in Japan.[22] Nevertheless, one can argue that that these stories were included in support of Zhou's ideas about childhood development and the proper education of children based on an essay that Zhou wrote about Shiga's story that appeared in the September 22, 1921 issue of *Gankai* (Vision). Regarding the educational philosophy reflected in Shiga's story, Zhou had this to say:

> I am of the opinion that there are serious defects in the current juvenile education. ... It would seem that parents and teachers have not understood the characteristics of the target of their education, namely children. This seems true indeed. "Seibei to hyōtan" quietly depicts only one rather peaceful scene in this enormous tragedy.[23]

In short, both Zhou Zuoren and Lu Xun were attracted to Japanese works that challenged traditional values and conventional assumptions about social roles. Moreover, they saw in these translations from contemporary Japanese literature the opportunity to modify the Chinese language itself and to provide paradigms for the vernacular *baihua* movement as it sought to forge a new vernacular idiom. In discussing the social function of translation and his personal goals as a translator of fiction, Lu Xun offered the following:

> If we were only to pursue ease of understanding, it would be better to rewrite the original text and create another one. It would be better to change the incidents into Chinese ones and change the characters into Chinese. As long as we translate, our main purpose must lie in exposing readers to a wide range of foreign works. It is necessary not only to transfer the feeling of the original but also to expand the reader's knowledge.[24]

The Zhou brothers' anthology not only served to introduce the May Fourth literary world to contemporary Japanese literature, including the White Birch School, its significance as the first anthology of modern Japanese literature translated into a foreign language did not go unnoticed in Japan either. In Japan it was regarded as one manifestation of the interest on the part of May Fourth writers in contemporary Japanese culture and the seriousness with which the May Fourth literary community of writers was pursuing the creation of a modern vernacular literature. In 1925, two years after the appearance of the anthology, Akutagawa Ryūnosuke, in the magazine *Shinshichō* (New Tide) wrote a piece entitled "Nihon shōsetsu no Shina yaku" (A Chinese Translation of Japanese Stories). Translations of two of Akutagawa's own stories had appeared in the anthology.[25] What is interesting, in retrospect, is that Akutagawa praised the "accuracy" of the translations, despite the fact that he could neither speak Chinese nor read modern, vernacular Chinese. He apparently based his judgment on his limited command of classical Chinese prose *kanbun* and on the fact that the translations of his stories supply several annotations of terms that would have been unfamiliar to Chinese readers.[26]

Regardless of the ultimate accuracy of the Zhou brothers' translations, they were of critical importance in making the May Fourth literary world familiar with contemporary Japanese literature. In particular, they conveyed some of the excitement that the brothers felt about the White Birch School. Zhou Zuoren was in Japan in 1910 when the first issue of *Shirakaba* appeared and was affected by the exhilaration accompanying the publication of the journal and of Mushanokōji Saneatsu's emergence as a leading young literary voice which Akutagawa likened to opening a window and letting in fresh air on a stale literary world.[27] Both Lu Xun and Zhou Zuoren had been moved by the humanism of Mushanokōji Saneatsu, and it was Mushanokōji's powerfully expressed convictions that first attracted the Zhou brothers to the school.

Daring to Dream: Lu Xun's Translation of Mushanokōji Saneatsu's "A Certain Young Man's Dream" and Its Appeal

Mushanokōji Saneatsu (1885–1976) embodied the chief qualities of Taishō Japan (1912–1926). If Mushanokōji is remembered now primarily as the charismatic, dynamic, and often dogmatic spokesman for the White Birch School, it must be acknowledged that he initially thought of himself primarily as a creative writer whose early works included "Washi mo shiranai" (I Too Don't Know, 1914), "Sono imōto" (The Younger Sister, 1915) and the novel *Kōfukusha* (The Happy One, 1915).[28] If the White Birch Society was the most admired among Taishō literary coteries by the May Fourth literary community, then Mushanokōji Saneatsu was the most esteemed among Shirakaba writers.

Even before the inclusion of Mushanokōji's stories in the Zhou brothers' anthology of translations of contemporary Japanese literature, Mushanokōji was highly regarded among Chinese intellectuals due to their interest in the New

Village experiment in communal living, but also as a result of Lu Xun's 1919 translation of Mushnokōji's "Aru seinen no yume" (A Certain Young Man's Dream) and efforts on the part of Lu Xun and Zhou Zuoren to introduce Mushanokōji as a Japanese intellectual whose abhorrence of war and whose uncompromising advocacy of Tolstoyan idealism set him apart from the received image of Japanese writers as either staunch advocates of imperialism or as aesthetes, unconcerned about issues of social or political import.[29] Zhou Zuoren wrote the first essay introducing Mushanokōji's play in the Volume 4, Number 5, 1919 issue of *Xin qingnian* (New Youth), which was incidentally the same issue in which Lu Xun's ground-breaking vernacular story "Kuangren riji" (Diary of a Madman) appeared.[30] Lu Xun, for his part, was so moved by Mushanokōji's anti-war play that he decided to translate it. He began to translate the play in serialized form, and it appeared daily in the newspaper *Guomin gongbao* (Citizen's Public News) starting on October 20, 1919. After the play was serialized in its entirety in the newspaper, Lu Xun reworked his translation and it appeared in *Xin qingnian* over the course of four issues, starting in January 1920.[31]

Lu Xun apparently decided to translate Mushanokōji's play for several reasons. The most immediate and practical reason probably had to do with the fact that Zhou had written about the play and included references to it in his essay, but had not translated more than a few illustrative passages. Lu Xun, moved by both the play's theme and his brother's trenchant analysis of it, determined it to be a work worth introducing to the Chinese reading public. Lu Xun felt obliged to "awaken" contemporary Chinese readers to Mushanokōji's vision of permanent peace as a reflection of humanist values.[32] Moreover, there was a political dimension to Lu Xun's choice as well. During this era of Japanese jingoism and of increasing tensions between the two countries, Lu Xun sought to introduce the work of a Japanese writer whose pacifist vision and opposition to blind adherence to Japanese imperialism as portrayed in the play, were not far removed from his own views and those of his brother, Zuoren.[33]

"A Certain Young Man's Dream" was serialized in *Shirakaba* between November 1916 and January 1917. The play was said to have moved many Japanese of the day including Omaki Chikae who read it while studying in Paris.[34] The play describes the pain and loss of war and its ultimate futility from the perspective of a young man. In the play, the protagonist is introduced to the horrors of war by a stranger. His encounters with the souls of those who are the victims of war lead him to a greater understanding of the futility of war. In Act Four of the play, the young man witnesses the machinations and attempts at various potentially devastating alliances among the devil and four "brothers" who are thinly veiled personifications of England, France, Russia and Germany. In the final scene, the goddess of peace (*heiwa no megami*) appears to proclaim peace as the only path to genuine happiness.[35] Mushanokōji made his intentions in regard to the play clear in the play's preface:

What point was I trying to make in this work? I think you will understand once you have read it. I sympathize with the victims of war, and I am one of the minority who loves peace — one of the very few. If I gain one more reader, if I know that among my readers are people who love peace, I will be content.[36]

"A Certain Young Man's Dream" appealed to Lu Xun as an example of art portraying unconditional love, a love that transcended national concerns and which provided a thoroughgoing indictment of war. As with Mushanokōji, for Lu Xun creativity was by its very nature the expression of universal love.[37] The extreme individualism of Mushanokōji appealed to Lu Xun, and he remained convinced of the political efficacy of literature and sought to use literature as a means of giving expression to the spiritual and physical agony of the suffering.[38]

In the translator's preface to Mushanokōji's play that appeared in *New Youth* in January 1920 along with the translation, Lu Xun said of his reasons for initially translating the play and deciding to later rework it, "I was very moved [by Mushanokōji's play] and I felt that his thought was noble, his beliefs were resolute, and his voice was sincere."[39] This public admission of admiration for Mushanokōji was significant given a climate in which there persisted a general mistrust of the Japanese in the wake of the infamous "Twenty-One Demands" and the terms of the Paris Peace Treaty.

In his introduction to Lu Xun's translation of Mushanokōji's play, Zhou Zuoren describes the significance of the play in this way:

> A young man is conducted by a stranger to observe various things. He feels the genuine terror and coldness of war and finally concludes that "The world's people have not yet attained the level of maturity that cannot be destroyed by war ..." People ultimately are of the human race and not of a specific race or country.[40]

The Zhou brothers were in accord about the transcendent power of Mushanokōji's message of universal love. Furthermore, they were alike in their faith in the value of Mushanokōji's work to appeal to an intellectual community tired of the ravages of war and imperialist interventions and looking for an aesthetic and ideological solution to the dangers that confronted them, regardless of the source.

Nevertheless, Lu Xun was not unqualified in his endorsement of Mushanokōji's singular pacifist vision and used the occasion of this translation to question May Fourth China's ability to effectively comprehend and process Mushanokōji's message. In the aforementioned translator's preface, Lu Xun questioned whether in a China torn asunder by sectarian violence, the Chinese people were even qualified to initiate a dialogue about peace.[41] Nevertheless, in the same translator's preface, Lu Xun declared that, from the outset, his views differed fundamentally from those of Mushanokōji, and professed that he was incapable of simply accepting Mushanokōji's naïve optimism.[42] However, as a work dedicated to the search for peace it should come as no surprise that the play which proved so satisfactory to Zhou Zuoren should also have moved Lu Xun with the freshness of its vision of peace.[43]

Lu Xun's final objection to the play and the source of his misgivings about foisting the play upon his contemporaries was a product of his reluctance to countenance the source of that pacifist vision. Lu Xun could not easily accept an anti-war manifesto from an author whose nation had invaded and occupied his own.[44] Looking at the issue from Lu Xun's perspective, Mushanokōji's antiwar work seemed on one level a way to explain the Chinese "national character" in the context of a universal declaration of the injustice of war.[45]

Although Mushanokōji in "A Certain Young Man's Dream" is critical of Japan's militarism and the excesses of Japanese imperialism, he nonetheless portrays the Emperor as a potent symbol of peace. For Lu Xun, who had lived in Japan during the latter years of the Meiji period (1868–1912) and had witnessed the more heavy-handed policies of the Meiji Regime as they pertained to China, the portrayal of the Japanese Emperor as beneficent was a difficult proposition to accept.[46] Lu Xun translated Mushanokōji's play a mere two years after the Bolshevik Revolution, at a moment when both he and the leadership of *New Youth* were becoming drawn inexorably toward Marxism, and at a point in which he had already become skeptical of the capacity of ideology to effect genuine change.[47]

While Mushanokōji's play and his New Village communal experiment were much admired in China and received the endorsement of no less than Chen Duxiu (1879–1942), the founder of Chinese Communist Party, and Cai Yuanpei (1868–1940), the president of Beijing University, it is telling that Lu Xun provided no further endorsement of Mushanokōji.[48] Lu Xun's decision to translate Mushanokōji's play at this juncture, with socialist thought on the rise in China, was a conscious one, designed to act in Lu Xun's words as a "warning bell" (*qing zhong*) to Chinese readers. He seems to have had little faith in the efficacy of the play or of Mushanokōji's naïve optimism beyond that.[49]

The socialist thought of Lu Xun differed qualitatively from that of Mushanokōji Saneatsu. Although the humanism and faith in the power of universal love of the two men were similar, in practice they differed in kind. Mushanokōji gave expression, in his representative works such as *Omedetaki hito* (An Innocent) and *Yūjō* (Friendship), to a simple optimism portrayed in almost allegorical form. Mushanokōji's was an "aristocratic socialism" (*kizoku no shakaishugi*), and he wrote from the vantage point of the privileged looking with pity upon the weak. Lu Xun's socialism, on the other hand, was a fastidiously utilitarian socialism, and his perspective was from in and among the disadvantaged and disenfranchised. He tended to cast a critical eye upon everyone, whether rich or poor, high or low.[50] Although Lu Xun was constitutionally different than Mushanokōji, and although he was unable to celebrate Mushanokōji's socialist vision with the same gusto as his brother Zhou Zuoren, he nevertheless was able to find within the White Birch School another writer whose work and social vision more neatly mirrored his own — a writer who he would willingly champion even after that writer's untimely and tragic death.

Beyond Brushes, Beyond Words: Lu Xun and the Social Thought and Activism of Arishima Takeo

Despite Lu Xun's initial attraction to Mushanokōji Saneatsu's socialist thought and pacifist vision during the period of his translation of "A Certain Young Man's Dream," his ardor quickly cooled. However, Lu Xun's bond with the thought and writings of fellow Shirakaba member Arishima Takeo was of a different nature, and whereas Lu Xun's aesthetic engagement with Mushanokōji was short-lived, his admiration for Arishima's writing was to last well beyond Arishima's suicide in 1923.

Arishima Takeo (1878–1923), although among those Shirakaba members whose works were included in the first issue of *Shirakaba* in 1910, was ten or twelve years the senior of the other founding members, and was never one of the school's true insiders.[51] He had been convinced to contribute something to this first issue by his younger brothers Arishima Ikuma (1882–1974) and Satomi Ton (1888–1983), who were among the founding members of the School. The Arishima family was a prominent aristocratic family of samurai lineage, and Takeo, as with the other Shirakaba members, had been educated at the prestigious and decidedly aristocratic Gakushūin and later at the Sapporo Agricultural School in Hokkaido, an institution with a strong Christian orientation that had produced such notable Christian leaders as Uchimura Kanzō (1861–1930) and Nitobe Inazo (1862–1933).[52] It was under the influence of these Christian educators that Arishima determined to study in the United States first at Haverford College, a Quaker institution in Pennsylvania, and later at Harvard University, where he pursued graduate studies.[53]

Arishima's absorption of Christian values had a profound effect on his aesthetic and social vision, even affecting his work after his disengagement from orthodox religious belief around 1910. After returning from his studies in the United States, Arishima taught at Sapporo Agricultural College from 1907 until 1915. Although he was involved in various church-related activities while teaching at the College, he had begun to turn away from organized religion.[54]

Arishima's movement away from conventional Christian practice and his involvement in Sapporo's Christian community coincided with a departure by Arishima from adherence to expectations of conventional Christian behavior. He became involved in several ill-fated romantic relationships, which resulted in his agonizing over the loss of religious faith and ended in his suicide along with that of his married lover Hatano Akiko, a magazine editor, in Karuizawa in 1923. Nevertheless, despite his movement away from orthodox religious belief, Arishima Takeo remained committed to the goal of radical social reform until the end, and his most representative works of fiction such as *A Certain Woman* and essays such as "To the Little Ones" give expression to powerful socialist and humanist convictions that profoundly influenced not only the thought of his contemporaries in Japan but also affected Lu Xun. Lu Xun, like many of Arishima's Japanese readers, applauded Arishima's decision to turn over his vast land holdings in Hokkaido inherited from his father to his tenants.[55]

Lu Xun was first exposed to the writing of Arishima Takeo during his sojourn in Japan when the first issue of *Shirakaba* appeared. Essays by Arishima appeared in the earliest issues of the journal, and the earliest version of Arishima's masterpiece *A Certain Woman* first appeared in 1911 in *Shirakaba* under the title, "Aru onna no gurinpusu" (A Glimpse of a Certain Woman).[56] Lu Xun's real engagement with the thought of Arishima was revealed in his introduction of Arishima to the Chinese literary world in 1919. In an essay about Arishima Takeo called "Re feng" (Hot Wind) Lu Xun recollects how two days after writing the essay "Women xianzai zeyang zuo fuqin" (How Should We Depict the Contemporary Father?) he came across Arishima Takeo's essay "Chiisaki mono e" (To the Little Ones) and discovered a number of corollaries in Arishima's essay to his own thought concerning familial roles and social responsibilities.[57]

In his essay, Lu Xun introduces Arishima Takeo as a member of the anti-naturalist White Birch School, thus, he remarks, it is not surprising that Arishima should have written an essay like "To the Little Ones," though he admits that the extent of Arishima's commitment to social reform at any cost is unique even among the Shirakaba members.[58] Lu Xun translates a two-page passage of Arishima's essay and provides a brief interpretation of the piece. He says that the essay, which is a father's heartfelt message to his children about his inability to genuinely effect social change in order to facilitate the future that they deserve, nevertheless conveys a sense of hope that his children will be able to continue the process that his generation set in motion. The essay concludes with the positive assertion that certainly the future will be characterized by a "spirit of emancipation."[59] The essay expresses a belief that social harmony is dependent on love and that all human love must be a manifestation of a child's love. This observation by Arishima, and Lu Xun's endorsement of Arishima's social thought, was to establish a pattern that would be repeated on several occasions in the years to follow. This essay established an affinity between the two writers. This was an affinity that transcended national borders in a way that Mushanonkōji's platitudes about universal love ultimately did not.

Beyond the attractions of this particular essay, Lu Xun found in Arishima's essays and works of fiction ample resonance with his own evolving socialist thought. At the heart of Arishima's thought is an unwavering faith in the transformative power of love.[60] This was a conviction shared by Lu Xun and can explain the fundamental empathy Lu Xun felt for Arishima. Moreover, one can detect in Arishima's essays the belief that given the limitations of the individual's capacity to effect change coupled with a social environment in which social amelioration is seen as subversive and potentially dangerous, one has to be willing to make personal sacrifices in order to bring about change. This concept of sacrifice was very central to Lu Xun's social thought, and it provided a common point of reference with the thought of Arishima.[61]

Along with Lu Xun's attraction to Arishima's articulation of the transformative power of love, Lu Xun was also drawn to Arishima's compelling portrayal of social inequities. Such a portrayal can be seen for example in works of fiction such as *Kankan mushi* (The Rust Chippers, 1910) which describes the plight of workers at a Russian shipyard and "Kain no matsuei" (Descendents of Cain, 1917) the evocative portrait of a couple who struggle against oppression and natural elements in rural Hokkaido and who, after enduring the vicissitudes of a painful existence, find themselves again wandering and at the mercy of fate at the story's end.[62]

Arishima Takeo, of all of the Shirakaba writers, exhibited an emotional intensity in his writing, and wrote with a directness and stylistic vigor that seemed to place him outside of the Japanese literary tradition.[63] This can be explained in part as a result of his direct exposure to Western literature while living in the United States and in part as the result of natural inclinations. On one level, Arishima seemed to appeal to Lu Xun as an Asian writer who was able to transcend the expectations of adherence to traditional East Asian literary values and conventions and could stand alongside Western writers.

Arishima Takeo and Lu Xun lived in an era in their respective country's history in which the writer was excruciatingly aware of his own limitations to effect desperately needed social reform. Both saw in humanism and universal love the only true remedy for the social malaise around them. Furthermore, both man felt that as artists they were charged with the grave responsibility of inciting their contemporaries to recognize the need for radical social reform.[64]

Along with the themes of social amelioration prominent in Arishima's mature works, Lu Xun was likewise drawn to the rugged individualism and vague eccentricities of many of Arishima's most memorable characters such as Nin'emon in "Descendants of Cain" and Sasaki Yōko in *A Certain Woman*. Arishima Takeo and Lu Xun were also alike in their decisive repudiation of naturalism and their commitment to a literature that celebrates the capacity of the individual to overcome even the most oppressive circumstances. It was Arishima, who in his essay "Geijutsu o umu tai wa ai nomi" (Only Love Can Give Birth to Art) which was translated by Lu Xun in 1926, said that art is nothing but the expression of the individuality of the artist.[65]

And yet for Arishima Takeo, unlike fellow Shirakaba members Shiga Naoya or his own brother Satomi Ton, the expression of individualism is always situated within the larger context of social tensions, and individualism is displayed precisely against an ever-shifting social diorama. This propensity on the part of Arishima helps to explain Lu Xun's attraction to what he perceived as a literature of individual struggle played out against the background of social conflict. Both Arishima Takeo and Lu Xun evinced a certain measure of discomfort with the privileges of the elite social class into which they had been born, and each felt keenly the guilt associated with their status and certain urgency about the need to abolish the very class to which he belonged.[66]

A brief examination of Arishima's novel *A Certain Woman* (1919) and Lu Xun's story "Mourning the Dead" which appeared in the collection *Nahan* (A Call to Arms, 1923) demonstrates some of the qualities and concerns shared by the two writers. *A Certain Woman* is the story of a woman awakened to modern selfhood who experiences suffering, some measure of vindication and final defeat. More specifically, in the novel Yōko, after her divorce from an ineffectual writer, on a ship bound for Seattle where she is to meet Kimura, the man to whom she is now betrothed, falls passionately in love with Kurachi, the ship's purser. She chooses not to disembark in Seattle, and the two return to Japan where Kurachi abandons his family in order to live with Yōko.

Kurachi becomes involved in criminal activities and begins to tire of Yōko. Yōko, for her part, has become terribly jealous of her lover. After she taunts him during a terrible fight, Kurachi abandons her in a fit of passion. Yōko subsequently becomes ill and is portrayed in the final scene, alone and inconsolable in a Tokyo hospital.

Lu Xun's "Mourning the Dead" (*Shangshi*) too is the story of a powerfully delineated female protagonist named Zijun, struggling against the obstacles imposed upon her by the persistent remnants of the old feudal order. In this story, the influence of Ibsen's Nora of "A Doll's House" is evident as Zijun emphatically states, "I belong to myself! No one has the right to interfere with me!"[67] The narrator Juansheng describes how he and Zijun had met and fallen in love, and how they, against convention and beneath the withering glares of family and neighbors had attempted to establish a life together. Eventually the disapproval of society, exacerbated by poverty, leads to a fissure in their relationship and to the dramatic declaration by to Zijun that he no longer loves her. Eventually, Zijun's father comes from the countryside to fetch her back, and Juansheng is left alone with a mixture of relief, emptiness and regret. In the end, Juansheng learns that Zijun has died though he never learns the cause of her death.

In the two works, Arishima and Lu Xun attempt to portray a bold new female character, a woman who challenges not only society's expectations of her but dares to defy tradition itself. In both stories, the female protagonist relentlessly and wantonly flaunts her newfound status and mocks tradition. In the case of *A Certain Woman* the protagonist's flaunting of tradition seems an extension of the character's very being. In "Mourning the Dead" on the other hand, Zijun, who is described initially as "not completely freed from the shackles of traditional morality" seems to grow into that part.[68] Ultimately, in both works the female protagonist tries to force change in those around her who are holding her in place. When that fails, each attempts to start over again. Both are denied that opportunity.

Both *A Certain Woman* and "Mourning the Dead" are products of discrete historical and social circumstances, which nevertheless exhibit striking parallels. The Chinese critic Zhang Hua insists that *A Certain Woman* be seen in the context of a society, which had experienced rapid capitalist development in conjunction with the rise of authoritarianism. Seen in that light, Satsuki Yōko's emancipation and fall into destruction reflect the specific historical realities of Meiji Japan.[69] In the May Fourth China of "Mourning the Dead" individual revolt and a woman's ability to choose her own destiny were also virtually impossible. There was no "exit" other than death.[70]

Arishima Takeo articulates in *A Certain Woman* and his other works of fiction the sense of frustration that accompanies his class status. In his essay "Sengen hitotsu" (A Manifesto) he relates that frustration to his decision to return the land of his tenants in Hokkaido. Lu admired Arishima's decision and later translated the essay. He also referred to Arishima's proclamation in a speech that he gave in April 1927 at the Huangpu Military Academy entitled "Literature in a Revolutionary Age," in which he says, "Ultimately I was attracted to his [Arishima's] assertions because they were firmly and passionately held."[71] Furthermore, like Arishima, Lu concluded that the "Fourth Estate" (i.e. the peasants) needed to produce a literature of their own, and he admired Arishima's willingness to provide economic sustenance, in the form of returning land to the tenant farmers, in order to encourage such a movement.[72] In "A Manifesto," which was published in *Kaizō* in January of 1922, Arishima spoke passionately about the responsibilities of the artist to society. He also expressed the frustration that he felt as the member of a privileged class to effect real social change.

The year 1922, in which "A Manifesto" appeared constituted something of a turning point in Arishima's career, and from then onward political writings came to constitute the bulk of his literary output.[73] What is significant about the reception of this essay in both Japan and subsequently in China is that it was accompanied by action. Soon after "A Manifesto" appeared, Arishima announced his decision to hand over his land to his tenants in the form of a communal farm in a speech entitled "Farewell to My Tenant Farmers," delivered on August 17, 1922 and later published. It was clear from the timing of this act that Arishima had been considering such a step for some time and with the publication of "A Manifesto" his resolve had been steeled.[74]

Lu Xun was truly affected by both Arishima's essay and by the act to which it gave rise. Lu Xun was later to interpret Arishima's death to his readers as the result of his frustration at his inability to effect change in a society resistant to the fundamental changes that he deemed necessary.[75]

Lu Xun was not the only writer affected by "A Manifesto." Yu Dafu, who was also an admirer of Arishima's and who understood Arishima's unique status as something of an outsider in the Japanese *bundan* also produced an essay that spoke admiringly of Arishima's resolve in producing such a bold essay and in coming to the decision to return the lands entrusted to him by his father. Like Lu Xun, Yu also focused on the implications of Arishima's essay for the emergence of a truly popular literature. The essay that Yu produced in response to "A Manifesto," "Nongmin wenyi de tichang" (Advocating a Literature by Peasants), interpreted acts like Arishima's return of the lands as the necessary first step in the creation of a truly mass art.[76]

Nevertheless, despite Lu Xun's advocacy of Arishima's thought and his bold actions in support of his beliefs, and despite his clear attraction to Arishima, Lu Xun was reluctant to embrace Arishima unreservedly as a thinker or social reformer. It was entirely in keeping with Lu Xun's character and his response to other writers and thinkers that he remained wary of fully embracing any one doctrine or credo. Everything that Lu Xun encountered of foreign literature and thought had to pass through a final filter preceding his acceptance, and that filter for Lu Xun was the needs of contemporary China.[77] Lu Xun was constantly gauging how a particular doctrine or literary work might contribute to creating a truly modern society and culture in May Fourth China. Although Lu Xun identified parallels between his position in May Fourth China and Arishima's status in the Taishō intellectual world, he was informed sufficiently about Japan to recognize telling differences as well.

Whereas Arishima was writing from the perspective of the citizen of a powerful nation that had recently won victories over its neighboring countries and had become a colonizer of those neighbors, Lu Xun was writing from the perspective of the citizen of a country that was both colonized and still clung to the vestiges of an antiquated feudal order.[78] Moreover, whereas Arishima saw the emancipation of the peasants and the provision of that class with a political voice as the most immediate social needs, Lu Xun recognized that the most profound needs in May Fourth China were to overcome feudalism and to break the bonds of colonialism.[79]

Differences in the ideological goals of the two writers were accompanied by differences in temperament. The result was differing conceptualizations of the manner in which each man thought that social reform ought to be accomplished. Although both advocated humanism and universal love as the necessary catalysts for a better, more equitable society, the means each writer advocated were different qualitatively.[80] While Arishima in "A Manifesto" advocated bold, revolutionary acts effecting social change and enfranchisement of the masses, Lu Xun preferred the pursuit of a more evolutionary approach in accord with the concepts of the Social Darwinism of Herbert Spencer.[81] Lu Xun, who was, during the late teens and early twenties, skeptical of the utility of Marxist class struggle to initiate constructive social change, clung to hope in a more evolutionary ideal grounded in love, in order to initiate real change.

Whereas Arishima Takeo dwelled on the responsibility he had been burdened with as a member of the landed gentry and struggled with the ambivalence and guilt of that position, Lu Xun proved more capable of resigning himself to the responsibilities and privileges of his station. Arishima saw his birthright as a curse; Lu Xun saw his birthright as a member of the landed gentry as an opportunity to critique his class and his privileges and furthermore seemed comfortable to act as a spokesman for his class in his advocacy of a more just, a more equitable, and a more inclusive society.[82]

Although both Arishima and Lu Xun pinned their hopes on universal love as the necessary catalyst for social change, they framed such a love in different terms. Arishima's conceptualization of love was the direct result of his experience as a Christian, and was attended by a concept of sin, which attached to his position as the representative of a privileged class. On the other hand, Lu Xun's concept of love, the result of his wide reading in Western literature and his familiarity with traditional Chinese thought, was not tempered by the same weighty sense of guilt and personal responsibility for China's suffering. An important dimension of Lu Xun's idea of love must be traced back to his well-known initial declaration concerning his decision to become a writer: he saw the expression of a universal love in literature as ultimately healing. What Lu Xun admired in Arishima Takeo's writing, and the works of the other Shirakaba writers for that matter, was the idealistic expression of universal love, which he felt could be effective in displacing the time-worn Confucian values that warped Chinese society.[83] Lu Xun was attracted to particular writers or works commensurate with the capacity he saw in them to cure the "malaise" of Chinese society.[84]

Although Lu Xun and Arishima Takeo can be seen as kindred spirits and comrades of sorts, qualitative differences in their ideological perspectives and in their dispositions distinguished the two. Lu Xun was alternately attracted and repelled by the intensity of Arishima's convictions. While Lu Xun saw mirrored in Arishima's principles his own commitment to social melioration, the revolutionary quality of Arishima's commitment and the tragic result of his grappling with the guilt that he felt at his inability to effect change no doubt frightened Lu Xun. One can see a certain irony in the fact that Lu Xun's first collection of fiction *Nahan* (A Call to Arms) with its exhortation to reform Chinese society, appeared in 1923, the same year that Arishima took his own life. Arishima was urging profound social change in an environment characterized by the brutality of the Taigyaku Jiken (High Treason Incident) and the increasingly menacing silencing of opposition voices. In such an environment, which evinced little sympathy for heterodoxy or opposition, Arishima was destined to become a victim of his own strongly held convictions. Lu Xun could witness in such a tragedy the limits of single voice "brimming with human love" and advocating social reform.[85] The suicide of Arishima Takeo was for Lu Xun, on one level, a cautionary tale.

Conclusion: The Limits of Aestheticism and the Politicization of the May Fourth Literary Community

In the late teens and early twenties the literary and aesthetic achievements of the White Birch School exerted a fascination on the May Fourth literary community, particularly on Zhou Zuoren and Lu Xun. Moreover, the Shirakaba writers who exerted the greatest appeal on May Fourth writers were those who approached literature and art as expressions of the larger goal of social reform and whose literary works were accompanied by projects of social melioration. The suicide of Arishima Takeo, one of the school's most celebrated figures and the writer who had so affected Lu Xun, was in a sense symbolic of the demise of the White Birch School's influence on the May Fourth literary world.[86]

When the White Birch Society was in vogue in China in the teens and twenties no Shirakaba member so captured the imagination or seemed to so adroitly articulate the aspirations of May Fourth writers as did Mushanokōji Saneatsu. Mushanokōji's leadership in the School, his sense of self-importance and individuality and the zealous single-mindedness of his aesthetic and ideological vision polarized readers in China the same way those very qualities did in Japan. Mushanokōji found in China both supporters and equally vocal detractors. At least initially, between 1919, the year he was introduced to Chinese readers and 1923, the year of Arishima's death, Mushanokōji's Chinese supporters far outnumbered his detractors.

Moreover, those Chinese who were drawn to Mushanokōji were not confined to writers; Mushanokōji found favor among scholars, students and revolutionaries as well. Although the source of Mushanokōji's appeal can be traced to the various factors described earlier in this chapter, what initially attracted May Fourth era Chinese to Mushanokōji was the New Village experiment in aesthetic communal living which Mushanokōji, along with several other Shirakaba members, established in Japan in 1918. The New Village had an ideological and practical appeal in the May Fourth era that touched individuals who would become leading figures in the intellectual and political life of twentieth-century China.

4
Greener Pastures: The New Village Ideal and May Fourth Intellectuals

The attraction of May Fourth writers toward the White Birch School was not confined to the school's literary or artistic achievements. Those writers among the school's members who were favored by May Fourth intellectuals were those who were perceived to be men of action, those who put into practice the ideals of the school. No manifestation of Shirakaba idealism had a more immediate and dramatic appeal than the New Village commune. The New Village (*Atarashiki mura*) was, in the context of Taishō period Japan (1912–1926), a unique experiment in communal living. As a manifestation of humanist and egalitarian ideals it appealed not only to a number of Japanese artists and intellectuals of the period, but also to members of the Chinese intellectual community who saw in the New Village Movement not only an achieved example of aesthetic, communal living but also an example of socialism in practice that could be transferred to a May Fourth era China in the throes of violent political and social change.

The New Village Movement, which was initiated in 1917 and realized in 1918, was the brainchild of Mushanokōji. Mushanokōji, while not a neglected figure in Japanese studies in the West, has certainly not received scholarly attention commensurate to the magnitude of his importance in the Taishō and early Shōwa intellectual and artistic scene. Moreover, very few of his works have been translated into English, and yet few cultural figures in Japan of the prewar period were as influential as Mushanokōji. Considering the substantial number of Chinese intellectuals of the May Fourth Era who had spent their formative years in Japan, it is not surprising that they should have become familiar with the idealism of the Shirakaba coterie or that they should have perceived in the New Village ideal an intriguing, albeit small-scale model for the society they hoped to cultivate. The emergence of the New Village experiment coincided with the New Culture Movement in China and with the ascendancy of communism among Chinese intellectuals. For Zhou Zuoren (1885–1964) who introduced the movement in China, the New Village represented the realization of socialist ideals within a clearly defined aesthetic framework.

It should be admitted that while the New Village continues to exist in Japan even today, the movement that gave rise to it never received the attention that its founders initially anticipated, and certainly the scope of its influence in China also ultimately was limited. Nevertheless, the attraction of the New Village to a certain segment of May Fourth intelligentsia was undeniable. The attempt to gauge the influence of the movement in China is especially intriguing because it provides a barometer for the influence of Japanese aesthetic and social theory in the interwar period.

The New Village Movement: In the Context of the Social Engagement of the White Birch School

The New Village Movement (*Atarashiki mura undō*) was initiated by the White Birch School but is more properly attributed to the vision of Mushanokōji. Although a number of famous cultural figures emerged from the school such as Shiga Naoya, Arishima Takeo, Yanagi Sōetsu and Satomi Ton, the group's most impassioned spokesman and arguably its most important figure was Mushanokōji whose views provided direction for the White Birch School in its early years and dictated the course for the school in the years to follow.

The enduring image of the White Birch School is that of a cohort of young aristocrats, dilettante and apolitical. While it is true that the group's members were comparatively aloof to political issues (contrast them for example with writers associated with the Proletarian Movement), there were nevertheless many facets to this complex coterie. As demonstrated in the previous chapter, certain members of the group demonstrated an abiding commitment to social ideals, and the school as a whole worked ceaselessly to transform the cultural life of Taishō period Japan through the dissemination of information about Western art and culture.[1]

After the school's initial phase, in which many of the writers had already established a reputation for disengagement from social issues, some of the members began to demonstrate an increasing social engagement. This social consciousness was expressed in a variety of ways. The engagement with social issues itself can be attributed to a variety of factors which included a growing sense of disillusionment on the part of certain members of the school to reach out and touch those beyond the pale of the limited readership for pure literature, and their failure to achieve the status of "useful citizens" which even to these young writers so consciously opposed to Meiji utilitarianism still had an attraction.[2]

The most celebrated example of a literature of social engagement among the Shirakaba writers was that of Arishima Takeo, described in Chapter 3, who began to wrestle with the question of the place of the intellectual in Taishō society earlier than his colleagues. In Arishima's case, his early and long engagement with Christianity certainly contributed to his sense of duty to serve society in some capacity.

Arishima's obsession with the question of the intellectual's responsibility to society set him apart from most other members of the school and sometimes put him at odds with Mushanokōji.[3] Nevertheless, Mushanokōji too, in response to the imperatives of the humanism that he espoused, struggled to find a means of expressing in concrete and practical terms the idealistic vision manifested in his literary works. For Mushanokōji, the solution to this disjuncture between ideology and practical application was the ideal of communal living, which was to result in the creation of the New Village in Kyushu in 1918.

The New Village was established by Mushanokōji and other members of the White Birch School at Hyūga in Miyazaki Prefecture, Kyushu in 1918 at a time when Mushanokōji had ostensibly "graduated" from the influence of Tolstoy (1828–1910), but still remained in fact attracted to Tolstoy's humanistic credo of universal love. Essays by Mushanokōji from the 1910s such as "Torusutoishugi" (Tolstoyism) and "Jindōshugi no bungaku" (Humanistic Literature) bear testimony to the strength of the appeal that the Russian thinker continued to exert on Mushanokōji during that period.[4] Mushanokōji's ideal of the New Village was based in part on Tolstoy's own attempted reforms at his family's estate, Yasnaya Polyana, including education for the peasants and reorganization of the distribution of labor. Mushanokōji wrote about the New Village before the dream was actually realized. For example, he wrote an essay called "Atarashiki mura" (The New Village) in July of 1918 in the *Osaka Mainichi Shinbun* and "Atarashiki mura ni tsuite no taiwa" (A Dialogue about the New Village) before ground was broken in Kyushu in November.[5] He wrote again about the process of obtaining the land and constructing the village in the essay entitled "Tochi" (The Land) in 1921.[6]

Mushanokōji envisioned the New Village as a place where people from a variety of backgrounds would come together in a self-sustaining community. The residents would produce all of the food that they needed and many of their other material needs and, in an egalitarian, nurturing environment there would still be ample opportunity for artistic and literary pursuits. This last point is critical to an understanding and appreciation of the New Village ideal. The village was not merely a socialist experiment in communal living; it was an aesthetic experiment as well, which presupposed individual artistic and intellectual pursuits as an integral part of life in the community. Mushanokōji started to publish the journal *Atarashiki mura* (New Village) on September 20, 1918. Soon after that he departed for the Hyūga region to solidify plans for the construction of the village.[7]

In an essay called "Atarashiki mura no dōki" (The Motivation for the New Village) describing what he had originally envisioned, Mushanokōji said the following:

> I had arrived at the feeling that all people could live a secure life. Moreover, I had the feeling that there was no way that a society wouldn't come into being in which every individual could give birth to selfhood. For that reason, even while being harangued in Osaka every day for manuscripts, I began writing about the society I imagined, and I concluded that anyone who thought to create what I had in mind should be able to carry it out. And if anyone could do it, I certainly could do it.[8]

Life in the village was intended to promote a humane life based on the fair and equitable distribution of labor and the peaceful resolution of differences. Before assessing the breadth of the appeal of the New Village Movement in May Fourth China, it should be noted that its appeal in Japan, even among those writers who one would expect to support Mushanokōji, was far from universal.

The New Village Movement, initiated with much fanfare by Mushanokōji and his supporters, met with a fairly cool reception in the Japanese literary community. There were virtually no ardent supporters from among major writers in Japan and most seemed utterly unimpressed by the movement and its goals. Even Shiga Naoya, Mushanokōji's close friend and Shirakaba colleague, did not participate in the movement. Another leading voice in the White Birch School, Arishima Takeo, was openly skeptical and critical of the movement.

In the July 1918 issue of *Chūō kōron* (Central Review) Arishima Takeo wrote a criticism of the New Village experiment called "Mushanokōji Kei e" (To Mushonokōji). In the essay, Arishima expresses approval of Mushanokōji's choice of an aesthetic communal model as a means by which society might be reformed. Nevertheless, Arishima believed that the New Village was bound to fail insofar is it would succumb to the pressures of capitalism and that the experiment itself smacked of self-indulgence.[9] Mushanokōji reacted angrily to this criticism from his old friend and charged Arishima with misrepresenting his intentions in an essay in the August 1918 issue of *Shirakaba*. Moreover, he challenged Arishima to respond to his charge that he had not properly understood the motivations for the Movement. Arishima complied with Mushanokōji's request and issued an open letter in September 1918's *Shirakaba* called "To my Readers" in which he apologized and confessed that the very attempt on the part of Mushanokōji to initiate social reform must be considered a success.[10]

Given the generally cool reception the movement had received in Japan, the enthusiasm with which it initially was received in China seemed to provide for Mushanokōji a validation of his vision and the potential for the dissemination of his ideals that he earnestly desired.

Zhou Zuoren and the Appeal of the New Village Movement

Zhou Zuoren (1885–1967) apparently had been introduced to the *Shirakaba* journal by his brother Lu Xun soon after the first number was issued in 1910, and he was well versed in Mushanokōji's particular brand of humanism by the time he visited the village in 1919.[11]

Zhou had first come to Japan in 1906 as an exchange student. While studying European literature and Classical Greek, he also read widely in both Japanese and English and took a special scholarly interest in anthropology and mythology.[12] In 1909, the same year that Lu Xun returned to China, Zhou married Hata Nobuko. From 1909 until the couple's departure for China in 1911, Zhou devoted his time to reading Japanese literature.[13] It was apparently at this time that Zhou became familiar with the White Birch School and their eponymous journal, although there is no indication that he actually met any of the Shirakaba members during that period.

Zhou had his first opportunity to revisit Japan in 1919. He traveled from Tokyo to the New Village in Kyushu and stayed there for four days from July 7 to July 11.[14] Zhou's visit to the New Village came literally in the wake of the May Fourth demonstrations. His trip was actually delayed while he tried to obtain the release of Chen Duxiu and several students from jail.[15] It was during this visit that Zhou was able to meet Mushanokōji Saneatsu, and the two were to remain in contact through the tumultuous decades that followed.[16]

Zhou's position in May Fourth literature was in some ways analogous to Mushanokōji's position in the Japanese *bundan* of the Taishō period. Although there were admittedly significant differences between the two, one of their many similarities was their position in the vanguard of the creation of a new culture and literary idiom. Unlike contemporaries who made their names as writers of fiction or poetry, Zhou and Mushanokōji were primarily cultural critics and spokesmen for the particular ideology they represented who both advocated a similar variety of humanism. Both men seemed to relish the opportunity to articulate their aesthetic vision as the appropriate course for their respective societies and both welcomed challenges from ideological adversaries. It should come as no surprise then that the two made an immediate connection when they met during Zhou's visit to the New Village in 1919.

Another quality that Zhou shared with Mushanokōji was his sense of himself as a moral agent, a kind of evangelist for enlightenment who looked at art for its didactic potential and conceived of the artist as a prophet charged with the duty of social amelioration and leadership in shaping a new society and culture. While in Japan, Zhou followed his brother Lu Xun into literature, but unlike Lu Xun and, for that matter, most of his contemporaries in the May Fourth literary world, Zhou did not simply see the Japanese language as the conduit for knowledge of the West via translations, he saw Japanese literature itself as a field worthy of scholarly attention and introduced Japanese literature to Chinese readers via essays and translations.

The most immediately important contribution made by Zhou to the understanding of Japanese literature was his essay "Riben jin sanshinian xiaoshuo zhi fada" (Developments in Japanese Fiction in the Last Thirty Years), which appeared in the journal *New Youth* in July of 1918. The essay begins with the powerful contention that Japanese civilization was not merely the "child" of Chinese civilization but was unique and worthy of study in its own right. Moreover, because the Japanese had begun to create a vernacular literature earlier than the Chinese, and had been able to develop a modern fiction, Chinese writers, he urged, should be willing to emulate the Japanese model in the creation of a new literature. After briefly tracing the development of modern fiction in Japan over the previous thirty years including the emergence of the anti-naturalist fiction represented by the White Birch School, Zhou advocated the need for a work in China akin to Tsubouchi Shōyō's (1859–1935) "*Shōsetsu no shinzui*" (Essence of the Novel, 1885) to act as a catalyst for the creation of a modern fiction in China. What is particularly interesting about this essay is the timing. It was in the following year that Zhou was able to visit Japan and meet Mushanokōji and other writers associated with the New Village Movement.[17]

Zhou Zuoren had been acquainted with Mushanokōji's work since soon after his return to China in 1911. In 1918 Zhou introduced Mushanokōji to Chinese readers in the pages of *New Youth* via Lu Xun's translation of Mushanokōji's play, "Yige qingnian de mu" (A Certain Young Man's Dream). In the essay that Zhou Zuoren wrote to accompany the translation, he praised Mushanokōji's writing for the humanism and pacifism it reflected, which transcended not only parochial concerns and distinctions but also fervent nationalism as well.[18]

Zhou's visit to the New Village the following year, an experience that he would later refer to as the "greatest joy in life,"[19] prompted a passionate response in which he expressed admiration for almost every aspect of life in the village:

> These days, even though we still dwell in the old world, in this one small corner one can glimpse something of a miracle. Already my visit has served to buoy my beliefs, and I am confident that in the future we will see the day when this movement achieves complete success ... the very air of the New Village is suffused with the completeness of love.[20]

For Zhou, however, if the village had succeeded as some kind of aesthetic utopia but failed to realize its egalitarian ideals, it would not have so moved him. What really appealed to Zhou was that this place where artistic creativity was celebrated and people of different backgrounds had opportunities to mix was a working, self-sustained community in which all members toiled for the collective good of the community.

During his four-day stay at the village, Zhou worked alongside the others, including some college students, planting beans and pulling weeds in the communal fields. At the end of the day, tired but elated, Zhou looked back on the day's activities.

> After we returned from the fields we shared some barley tea, and I had the chance to mull over what I had seen. Although physically spent, mentally I was exhilarated. I felt that in my thirty something years I was now for the first time experiencing life in a genuine way ... and had just come to an understanding of the happiness of a humane life and this was a reason for real celebration.[21]

It was this realization of the ideals of communal life in the New Village based on the values of individualism and mutual respect that appealed to Zhou. While culture and creativity were integral to the ideals of the group and important elements of life in the village, it was this imperative of working side-by-side with people from a variety of walks of life that appealed to Zhou and led to his endorsement of a similar movement in China.

Just before his departure Zhou was invited by Mushanokōji to write something to commemorate his visit. At the celebration of this brave new humanist experiment, Zhou did not turn to the words of Tolstoy or other Western advocate of humanism, with no doubt a certain irony. Rather, he turned to the source of East Asian orthodoxy, Confucius, and referred to a passage in the *Analects*:

> Confucius says, isn't *ren* [benevolence] far away? *Ren* arrives as I come to desire *ren*.
>
> Confucius says, how can it be worrisome and fearful if one finds no regret in self-reflection.[22]

One manifestation of Zhou's commitment to disseminate the ideals of the New Village Movement in China was the establishment of the *Xincun Beijing zhibu* (The Beijing New Village Support Division) in July of 1920. In May of that year an article had appeared in *Xin qingnian* (New Youth) outlining the goals of the society:

> The Support Division was conceived in February of this year. Mr. Zhou Zuoren conceived of the society, which corresponds directly to the various facets of the New Village. The objectives of the division are manifested, for instance, in the intention to travel to Hyūga to observe

conditions at the Village. The Division intends to facilitate, though not arrange, travel to the New Village. The Support Division will organize its meetings as follows: the division will meet at Zhou Zuoren's home at #1 in 8 Daowan Lane on Friday, Saturday and Sunday evenings from 1:00 until 5:00 PM.[23]

The Beijing New Village Support Division was an ambitious first step by Zhou Zuoren to determine whether or not Mushanokōji's ideal would have currency among Chinese intellectuals or whether, indeed, the ideal that Mushanokōji struggled to realize in Japan might not be more easily realized in May Fourth China than in Taishō Japan.

Cultivating New Ground: The New Village Movement in China

Zhou's visit to the New Village in Japan left him convinced that it was his duty to launch a similar *Xincun yundong* (New Village Movement) in China. He resolved to introduce a movement based on what he himself had experienced in Japan as a first step in creating the type of humanistic socialism that he felt was ultimately necessary in China. It is intriguing to note that both Mushanokōji and Zhou saw the creation of nonviolent communes of this type as both necessary and imminent. Zhou adopted from Mushanokōji the habit of referring to the New Village Movement as a "necessary current" and as a "future revolution."[24] Mushanokōji himself, in considering the likelihood of the success of the New Village ideal said, "No, this is no mere fancy. Even allowing that what I am talking about might not be plausible right now, it will be realizable in the not-too-distant future. This is my belief."[25]

Zhou attempted to disseminate information about the New Village in a series of essays and speeches in 1919 and 1920.[26] Zhou's message about the New Village was aimed not only at other intellectuals but also at students, workers and communists — to anyone who might have an interest in the social revolution he had in mind. Reactions to Zhou's message were mixed, as one might expect from the ideological maelstrom in China of the period.

Mushanokōji Saneatsu was not yet a well-known figure among May Fourth intellectuals when Zhou acquainted Chinese readers with the New Village Movement. The decade to follow would see a number of Mushanokōji's works translated into Chinese. Along with Mushanokōji's play about the haiku poet Issa translated by Zhou alluded to earlier and Lu Xun's translation of the play "A Certain Young Man's Dream," a number of Mushanokōji's works were translated in quick succession in the early 1920s including "Atarashiki mura" (New Village) and "Hito no seikatsu" (Human Life) among others.[27] Moreover, according to the Chinese scholar Wang Jinhou, two of Zhou's essays about the New Village, "Riben de xincun" (Japan's New Village) and "Fang Riben xincun ji" (A Record of a Visit to Japan's New Village) were included in a contemporary Chinese junior high school textbook.[28]

Most intriguing of all, from the perspective of this study, Mushanokōji himself contributed a letter, which appeared on December 1919 in *New Youth* called "Yu Shina weizhi de pengyou" (A Letter to Chinese Friends I Do Not Yet Know). In the letter, Mushanokōji, who had not yet visited China, urges young Chinese intellectuals to accept humanistic values and nonviolent methods in the creation of a new society. A brief appendix to the letter by the editor Chen Duxiu makes an intriguing connection between the message contained in Mushankōji's letter and a similar message to Chinese readers from Leo Tolstoy some years earlier.

> I remember Tolstoy also sending a similar letter to his Chinese friends some years ago. In that letter he urged us not to abandon farming, not to envy the West its material wealth, not to blindly worship constitutional government, and not to adopt violent resistance. Chinese at that time did not pay heed to his worthy message. I only hope that today's youth do not sneer at Mushanokōji's teachings as we did on that earlier occasion.[29]

Such a letter and the association with Tolstoy suggest that Mushanokōji had strong advocates in the Chinese intellectual community who were sympathetic to the goals of the New Village Movement. Among those who expressed an initial interest in the movement were some like Chen Duxiu, involved in the founding of the Chinese Communist Party.

The New Village and Its Impact on the Fledgling Chinese Communist Party

The communists who expressed interest in what Zhou had to say about the New Village Movement included early leaders of the Party such as Chen and Li Dazhao (1888–1927), but also emerging student leaders such as Mao Zedong and Zhou Enlai. Part of the appeal to the established generation of intellectuals embracing communism may have had to do with what one commentator characterizes as the special relationship that Zhou had with Li Dazhao but this does not explain the appeal of Zhou's vision of the New Village to Mao, Zhou Enlai and the other young student-age communist leaders.[30]

The December 1919 issue of *Hunan jiaoyu yuekan* (Hunan Education Monthly) included a brief description of Mao Zedong's visit to Zhou Zuoren in Beijing to talk about the New Village Movement. On one level, it was the visit on the part of the young communist Mao to an admired scholar and intellectual figure. In his diary from a later date reminiscing about that visit, Zhou noted that at the time Mao's visit did not garner much outside attention and it was only later, in retrospect, that anything was made of the meeting.[31]

In 1920 Zhou Zuoren delivered a lecture to a group of university students in Tianjin entitled "Xincun de jingshen" (Spirit of the New Village). It was a lecture that attracted representatives from a number of student groups, including some who were to later play significant roles in the Communist Party. Among the students in attendance that evening was a young Zhou Enlai who later told the Japanese scholar Ozaki Hideki that he had attended that lecture and enthusiastically listened to the ideals of the New Village. The lecture would later be transcribed and published in *New Youth*. In the speech Zhou Zuoren had the following to say:

> The basis of his [Mushanokōji's] thought is not to be found in a particular school of economics, nor can it be situated in a certain faction of socialism. It is simply the benign expression of an awakening of conscience. His [Mushanokōji's] greatest contributions are moral and spiritual.[32]

In the following year, Zhou Enlai went to France where he founded the Chinese Communist Party Support Society.[33]

Like Zhou Enlai, Mao Zedong also had received the influence of the ideals of Mushanokōji's New Village through the vision of Zhou Zuoren. In the December 1919 issue of *Hunan Education Monthly* alluded to earlier, Mao submitted an article entitled "Xuesheng zhi gongzuo" (The Duty of Students) in which he introduced the values and practices of the New Village as an exemplary model in socialist living to his fellow students. He expressed admiration for the fact that the village, while grounded in idealism, nevertheless functioned as a community unto itself. Moreover, Mao was drawn to the utilitarianism of the movement and urged that socialist students in Hunan consider adopting the New Village daily schedule of eight hours of sleep, four hours of recreation, four hours of self-study, four hours of classes and four hours of manual labor.[34]

Ultimately, the young communists rejected Zhou Zuoren's vision of the New Village Movement as too idealistic (*lixiang de*) and not suited to the dire social and political exigencies of China of the time. Nevertheless, it is interesting to note the intriguing irony of young communist leaders enthusiastically embracing the socialist model of this Japanese man of letters, a vision that had met with a rather cold reception in Japan, even from among many from whom Mushanokōji expected support.

In China also, it was from established writers that the most severe criticism of the New Village Movement came, and it was ultimately this resistance, more than anything else, that accounted for the failure of the movement to take hold in China. Ironically, one of the most vociferous opponents of Zhou's attempts to encourage the New Village Movement was his elder brother Lu Xun, who was critical of the movement for many of the same reasons as the communists. In a piece by Lu Xun called "Toufa de gushi" (A Story About Hair) one of the characters satirizes a movement like the New Village Movement. "You speak of revolution? Where are the weapons? Where is the work and study? Where are the factories?" the character asks.[35]

An even more contentious and influential opponent appeared in the form of Hu Shi, who took several opportunities to question the potential efficacy of the New Village Movement as Zhou envisioned it, including in a public speech dating from 1920. In the speech, Hu Shi uses a passage from Mencius in order to accuse Zhou and his proposed movement from encouraging escape from the responsibilities of society. Hu further portrayed the New Village Movement as merely a modern version of the old Daoist tradition of escape from political life to a life of reclusion, which was ultimately an asocial act rather than the social revolution Zhou portrayed it to be.[36]

The ideological differences that emerged between Zhou and his critics suggest that Zhou's humanist concept of the responsibility and the moral imperatives of the individual were different from many of his contemporaries who envisioned the individual's fundamental and ultimate responsibilities as being to the state rather than the realization of individual goals. Hu Shi portrayed this dichotomy as one between society articulated as the *da wo* (greater self) and the subordinated individual as the *xiao wo* (small self).[37] Furthermore, Hu argued that Zhou (and, by extension, presumably Mushanokōji) was mistaken in positing the individual as the starting point for a social revolution. Such a revolution, Hu argued, could only start from society and take place within the existing social framework, and not outside of it.[38]

These were only the most vocal and influential of a number of opponents to Zhou's vision of the New Village who saw this ideal as naïve and facile given China's circumstances, and thus it is not surprising that this vision failed to be realized in the manner that he had hoped.

The Legacy of the New Village Movement in China

Any attempt to assess the legacy of the New Village Movement in China must begin with the works of Zhou Zuoren himself. The humanism and idealism embodied in China's failed New Village Movement found expression in all of Zhou's important literary treatises of the 1920s. In essays such as "Ren de wenxue" (Humane Literature), "Pingmin de wenxue" (Popular Literature), and "Ziji de yuandi" (Our Own Garden, 1923), Zhou advocates an art that serves life and that expresses the individuality of the writer but also guides society. In the literature that Zhou advocated, the writer is a moral exemplar who employs literature as a tool to reshape and redefine China. All literature, according to these aesthetic standards, is grounded in the experiences of the individual, as is apparent in this oft-quoted passage from "Humane Literature": "The Humanitarianism that I have in mind therefore starts with man, the individual. To be able to discuss humaneness, love of humanity, one must first acquire the qualifications of man and stand in the position of man."[39]

What appealed about the New Village Movement to Zhou was precisely the connection that was made in the village between artistic production and daily work. The communal and egalitarian values embodied in village life and individual artistic production would coexist in a symbiotic relationship and the individual's concerns would merge with those of the village. This was not simply wishful thinking on the part of Zhou Zuoren, this is what he experienced during his brief visit to the New Village in Japan. If Zhou's writing about the ideals of village life sometimes amounted to a kind of humanistic evangelism and suffered from overly effusive enthusiasm for the possibilities of village life, that can be attributed to the fact that, like Mushanokōji, Zhou believed in the ideals and efficacy of the village with an almost religious zeal. Furthermore, he saw in the creation and proliferation in China of such villages, a possible panacea for the political and social chaos of contemporary China.

Finally, one dimension of the legacy of the New Village Movement is that this ideal appealed, at least momentarily, to May Fourth era figures as varied as Zhou Zuoren and Li Dazhao, Tian Han and Chen Duxiu, Guo Moruo and even Zhou Enlai and Mao Zedong. The spirit of the movement, if not the movement itself, was welcomed by those who wanted desperately to believe that the inexorable political and social changes of the era could be achieved without bloodshed but with mutual understanding.

5
The Art of Wanderlust: Hayashi Fumiko's Encounters with China

Hayashi Fumiko (1903–1951) made an art of wandering. Along with her more celebrated sojourns to Paris and Moscow, Hayashi also visited Shanghai on several occasions during visits to China in the 1930s and became acquainted with Chinese writers during her visits there. Hayashi was well respected among Chinese writers, which was due in part to the powerful portrayal in her fiction of social inequities and the sympathy her works elicited for the downtrodden and displaced. Moreover, Hayashi's works invariably portrayed a tough female character, freed from the shackles of tradition, which appealed to Chinese writers seeking to portray the modern woman. Hayashi's early work was not easily characterized as belonging to any of the specific schools or movements of the period. Writers of pure literature initially dismissed her as a proletarian writer. Proletarian writers derided her *Diary of a Vagabond* as an example of "runpen bungaku" (hobo literature), borrowing the Marxist designation for the poor class of itinerant workers. Despite the initial critical lambasting she received, Hayashi's works, particularly *Diary of a Vagabond*, were well received by the reading public, and critical accolades eventually followed.

Hayashi Fumiko was a self-described wanderer, and much of her early writing was born of the experience of wandering, and describes the experience of the itinerant artist. Creativity and the peripatetic experience merge in Hayashi's finest works of fiction such as *Hōrōki* (Diary of a Vagabond) and *Onna no nikki* (A Woman's Diary). Hayashi's birth and childhood prepared her for a life on the road. The child of itinerants, Hayashi quickly became accustomed to moving from place to place, and much of her formative years were spent shuttling between one temporary home and another. It was the only lifestyle that she knew and she describes it with remarkable candor to a contemporary audience for whom such a life of wandering held a fascination. She became the voice for a class of destitute itinerants whose lives were virtually unarticulated prior to her dramatic debut.

Born to the Road

Hayashi Fumiko's roaming and the literary works that reflected that experience are best appreciated as part of the great tradition of travel literature in Japan, that stretches from the *Tosa nikki* (Tosa Diary) to the popular *Otoko wa tsurai* (It's Tough Being a Man) film series. In keeping with that venerable tradition, Hayashi's protagonists celebrate the urge to travel as a need that is at the very core of the human experience, in much the same way that the speaker in Matsuo Bashō's classic *Oku no hosomichi* (Narrow Road to the Deep North) describes the urge to take to the road as a primordial and ultimately ontological need. Moreover, like so many of the great traveling personae in Japanese literary history, Hayashi's protagonists take to the road alone; there may be innumerable encounters with others along the way, but ultimately the journey must be conducted alone.[1]

Because the characters portrayed in Hayashi's work tend to be socially marginalized and politically powerless, her early literature was characterized, perhaps unfairly as *runpen bungaku*. It was a characterization that served to restrict her artistically, and Hayashi chafed under that that categorization. Moreover, such an association left her vulnerable to attack from increasingly vigilant and arbitrary authorities in the 1930s.[2]

The literature of wandering that characterizes Hayashi's early mature style in the interwar period was accompanied, not surprisingly, by actual travels by Hayashi both within Japan and beyond. These travels, in turn, served as the inspiration, either directly or indirectly, for further works. Thus, in Hayashi's oeuvre, the solitary act of travel and the solitary act of writing coexist in symbiotic fashion, with one nurturing and sustaining the other. The writings took a variety of forms, including both traditional literary forms and distinctive, idiosyncratic contemporary interpretations of traditional forms.

Travel abroad was made possible by the popular acclaim and accompanying financial benefits that accrued following the commercial success of *Hōrōki* (Diary of a Vagabond, 1930). As a consequence of that success, Hayashi was able to travel in the 1930s to such important cultural centers as Paris, London and Moscow. However, during that decade, there was no place that Hayashi visited as frequently as China. The experience of travel in China, to various places and in an array of official and unofficial capacities allowed Hayashi to perceive herself as capable of heightened responses in a variety of settings.

While Hayashi Fumiko's five visits to China in the 1930s influenced her own later literary output, her writing also had an impact on the contemporary Chinese literary world. Hayashi's early works were known to Chinese readers proficient in Japanese soon after their publication in the early 1930s, although *Diary of a Vagabond* only became available in its entirety in Chinese translation in 1937. Hayashi also had the chance to meet directly with members of the

Shanghai literary community during her 1932 visit to China. Her works appealed to Chinese readers both as realized examples of the socialist realism to which the Chinese leftist writers aspired and as a dynamic representation of female protagonists challenging traditional mores and rising above the traditionally circumscribed roles.

Hayashi Fumiko's *Diary of a Vagabond* does not satisfy the criteria of socialist realism according to the standard Soviet definition. If socialist realism is to be described in the conventional sense as a teleologically oriented style, the purpose of which is the promotion of socialism and its goals, then Hayashi's work clearly falls short of the mark. If, however, one is willing to broaden that definition to describe a literary approach defined by its uncompromising portrayal of social inequities and class struggle, then it is small wonder that leftist writers in both Japan and China should see in Hayashi's work an achieved example of socialist realist fiction of the highest order.

Kurahara Korehito (1902–1991), who visited Russia in the 1920s and returned to Japan as one of the most respected spokesman for proletarian literature, did not characterize Hayashi's work as an example of socialist realism. According to Kurahara in his essay "Saikin no puroretaria bungaku to shinsakka" (Recent Proletarian Literature and New Authors, 1928), a writer such is Kobayashi Takiji is clearly a writer working within the socialist realist aesthetic framework.[3] What Hayashi's literature lacks as a work of socialist realism, in Kurahara's estimation, is a sense of the indissoluble ties between art and political consciousness. Moreover, Kurahara in his essay "Puroretaria rearizumu e no michi" (The Path to Proletarian Realism, 1928) states emphatically that a consciousness of class is the *sine qua non* of all proletarian literature and the class struggle must be enacted in the text for it to meet the standard of socialist realism.[4]

In fact, it is the striking portrayal of the struggle between social classes and the sexes in *Diary of a Vagabond* with its unsettling descriptions of the impoverished underclass in Taishō Japan that clearly places Hayashi's maiden work within the parameters of socialist realist fiction, contemporary critics' protestations notwithstanding. Hayashi's stark representation of prewar Japan's dark underbelly and particularly the obstacles confronting the urban woman, were as powerful and accomplished an example of socialist realism as any work produced by a proletarian writer.

Hayashi Fumiko's achievement in *Diary of a Vagabond* most closely parallels the achievement of May Fourth era Chinese writer Ding Ling (1904–1986), who was at the same time producing a body of literature in China, which portrayed female characters who challenged tradition while searching for new patterns of living and new modes of self expression in modern urban China. It is one of the unfortunate twists of fate of the period that these two writers, whose debut works bore so much in common and whose writings were so well received in the other's literary community, never had the opportunity to meet. Unlike so many of her May Forth contemporaries, Ding Ling never had the opportunity to study in Japan, although she had once planned to do precisely that. Moreover, unlike so many of her contemporaries considered in this study, Hayashi Fumiko first visited China several years after the truly focal years of Sino-Japanese literary interaction in the late twenties, and was only able to first visit when mounting tensions between the two countries made positive interactions between writers of the two literary communities increasingly difficult. What little intercourse took place in the late thirties was state-sponsored and propagandistic.

Nevertheless, during her brief 1932 visit, Hayashi, who was already known to Chinese writers, made a powerful impression on the writers she met, and she had the chance to meet with Lu Xun, the one writer whom all Japanese writers were particularly anxious to meet.

Westward to the "Paris of the East": Hayashi Fumiko's Interactions with the Shanghai Literary Community

Hayashi Fumiko's travels abroad imbued her later writings with a worldliness and depth that came from viewing the self against the backdrop of the foreign and the novel. Commentators on Hayashi's work have commented on the significance of the experience of foreign travel on her writing, and it was a boon that Hayashi herself recognized. For Hayashi, travel abroad was the next logical progression from her various domestic travels. One commentator says, "Whenever she had the wherewithal, travel had always been for Fumiko something close to a predilection, but she was now able to go beyond that and travel abroad. It was a leap that was so like Fumiko."[5]

Foreign travel offered Hayashi perspectives on Japanese society and her place in it that she would not have possessed had she never been abroad. Hayashi traveled abroad over one dozen times between 1930 and 1943. These experiences abroad became important material for travelogues and fiction.[6] Hayashi often spoke about her travels in Europe and the impact that they had on her personally and professionally; she was less wont to talk about the significance of her travels in China during the 1930s in terms of her development as an artist. Yet China was the place she visited most often during that period and her visits there affected her in several ways that the other countries she visited did not.

China, first of all, offered a physical proximity and a rich tradition of travel literature by literary predecessors that was known and appreciated by all modern Japanese writers. Thus, as with Tanizaki, Satō Haruo, and the other Japanese writers treated in this study, the journey to China was for Hayashi a journey to the cultural homeland. As writers reveled in the exoticism of China, they also found comfort in the familiar forms and expressions of a culture that had always provided a touchstone and barometer for Japan's cultural achievements.

Furthermore, whereas Hayashi was able to live in relative anonymity in Paris and London, in Shanghai she found that she was a known quantity, a writer recognized and admired by the community of leftist writers who dominated the Shanghai literary scene in the 1930s. This attention from a foreign readership bestowed on her work an added legitimacy and gave her the confidence that comes with international recognition.

Hayashi Fumiko's first trip abroad was her 1930 trip to Taiwan. Hayashi was invited to visit Taiwan in January 1930 along with other women writers to participate in a series of lectures and readings by the Taiwan General Command.[7] This party of writers gave a series of lectures in several Taiwanese cities and had opportunities to visit major tourist attractions. The immediate works that resulted from this trip were "Taiwan no subuniiru" (Souvenir from Taiwan, 1930) and "Taiwan fūkei" (Taiwanese Landscape, 1930).[8] The success of this trip and Hayashi's recognition of her ability to negotiate in a foreign setting emboldened her to plan the more ambitious trips that soon followed.

In August 1930, Hayashi traveled to mainland China. She traveled throughout Manchuria, then to Shanghai, Harbin, Jinzhou, Qingdao, Nanjing, Hangzhou and Suzhou.[9] In all, Hayashi visited many of the main points of cultural interest that were seen as obligatory destinations for Japanese literary travelers to China. Susanna Fessler suggests that it was this grand tour of China, and not the more celebrated journey to Europe the following year, that was the immediate payoff for the success of *Diary of a Vagabond*.[10] While in Shanghai, Hayashi was able to establish personal connections that would serve her in her next visit in 1932.

Hayashi Fumiko's trip to Europe, which lasted from October 1931 to June 1932, turned out to be the most celebrated and oft-cited travel experience in her career. And yet, it can be argued that the final destination on this tour, Shanghai, had as profound an effect on Hayashi's career as the more celebrated sojourns in Paris and London. Hayashi was able to finance her trip abroad due to the success of *Diary of a Vagabond,* published in book form by Kaizōsha, which brought a measure of financial success and the subsequent wherewithal to fund her travels to Europe.[11]

In 1931, Hayashi set off alone toward Paris on the Trans-Siberian Railway. It appears that initially Hayashi may have followed an artist named Sotoyama to Paris. While in Paris, Hayashi met a number of artists, writers and thinkers pursuing their professions in the most culturally dynamic city in the world. From Paris, Hayashi sent back miscellaneous writings detailing her visits to the theater, opera, concerts, and museums. It was a stimulating environment in which Hayashi flourished. According to later revelations, it also seems that the sojourn in Paris included an affair with the archeologist, Morimoto Rokuji (1903–1936).[12]

Hayashi then visited London for two months at the beginning of 1932. When she returned to Paris, the feverish pace of her lifestyle seems to have caught up with her. She was physically exhausted and malnourished, with insufficient funds for the return trip to Japan.[13]

Hayashi sent a telegram to Kaizōsha president, Yamamoto Sanehiko (1885–1952) asking for help, and he wired the tickets for her return trip to her in Marseilles.[14] The ship she boarded, the *Harunamaru,* stopped in both Naples and Shanghai before returning to Japan, and it was during this visit to Shanghai that Hayashi was able to spend several weeks interacting with Chinese writers in Shanghai before arriving back in Japan on June 16, 1932.[15]

During this visit Hayashi was able to meet Lu Xun for the second time. She had apparently met him briefly in 1929, during one of Lu Xun's visits to Japan. This second meeting with Lu Xun in Shanghai left Hayashi with a strong impression of the writer and resulted in several essays about Lu Xun. Before her return, Lu Xun presented Hayashi with a placard on which he had composed a Chinese poem entitled "Xiayi shan" (Mount Xiayi).[16] In a published diary from 1933, Hayashi writes about those qualities that she admires not only about Lu Xun but also about China:

> June 17: I recently received a copy of *Lu Xun's Selected Works.* I first met Lu Xun in the autumn of 1929 and again in 1932 on my return from Europe when he was living a simple lifestyle. I found the stories "My Hometown," "A Comedy of Ducks" and "The True Story of Ah Q" in that collection particularly moving. Lu Xun is, moreover, a truly prolific poet. China is a country with a literary tradition that is splendid to the point of envy. I went off and wrote Lu Xun a long letter.[17]

Hayashi's 1932 visit coincided with the ascendancy of the League of Leftist Writers, and she was welcomed by Lu Xun and other league members who admired the candid portrayal of the disenfranchised class of workers and vagrants in her representative works. The members of the league were at that time engaged in a critical debate about the form a socialist realist body of literature should take.[18] Hayashi's *Diary of Vagabond* and works of fiction by Miyamoto Yuriko and other contemporary Japanese writers provided an appropriate model, which unselfconsciously portrayed class struggle and social inequalities. While not directly involved in the Proletarian Movement in Japan, Hayashi's work seemed to be a more aesthetically accomplished example of socialist realist fiction than many of the movement's writers.

While leftist writers were debating the definition and form of this new socialist realist literature, they continued to engage in other debates initiated during the May Fourth period. Among the most significant debates involving writers was the status of women in the new society and the representation of women in the new literature and art. In the May Fourth period the search for a new subjectivity was carried out in terms of defining the role of the "new woman."[19] Chinese writers, male and female, struggled to produce works that represented the new woman and her concerns. Thus, Hayashi Fumiko's powerful protagonists, struggling against authority, social mores and abusive relationships, and yet thriving against all odds, were admired by the Chinese literary community as realistic representations of the new woman.

When Hayashi Fumiko next visited China in the late thirties, her politics had changed and she approached the experience from a different perspective. The schism that had opened between Chinese and Japanese writers in the latter half of the 1930s and the changed status of their relations is the subject for the final chapter in this book, but Hayashi Fumiko's transformation from a writer sympathetic to the goals of Chinese leftist writers to an enthusiastic supporter of Japanese imperialist efforts was a common response among Japanese writers of that era.

Nevertheless, Hayashi Fumiko's encounters with writers in Shanghai during the 1932 visit constituted an intriguing episode in relations between the literary communities, and this positive interaction represents a critical period in her career. The visit affected Hayashi's own sense of confidence as a writer along with her perspectives on travel and the self. Moreover, the popularity of her fiction provided Chinese writers with a mode of socialist realist fiction from the perspective of an emancipated, strong female character at the very time that the League of Leftist Writers was contesting the form and direction that this new body of literature should take.

Just Out of Reach: Imagining the New Woman in Hayashi Fumiko's *Diary of a Vagabond* and Ding Ling's *Miss Sophie's Diary*

Hayashi Fumiko was among the Japanese women writers in the Taishō and early Shōwa periods whose works reflected feminist concerns and who dared to represent a new woman whose lifestyle and values was a direct challenge to the traditional image of women endorsed by the state. In May Fourth China, Ding Ling was among a small cohort of women writers who similarly challenged traditional assumptions about the social status of women and sought to voice the concerns and aspirations of a new class of educated, urban women. The respective debut pieces of the two writers, Hayashi Fumiko's *Diary of a Vagabond* and Ding Ling's *Miss Sophie's Diary*, demonstrate a number of interesting parallels in terms of both style and content. It is also rather telling that the writers and their works were well received when translated and introduced into the other's community. It is one of the unfortunate omissions of this rich period of constructive interactions between the two literary communities that these two writers who potentially had much to share with one another, never had the opportunity to meet.

Ding Ling (1907–1986) was a leading voice in the May Fourth era whose illustrious career extended beyond even the trials of the Cultural Revolution. Ding Ling was an important contributor to May Fourth era literature and remained an imposing and influential figure in China's literary world until her death. During the years under consideration in this study Ding Ling was active in Shanghai where she suffered as much as any writer for her association with the burgeoning Communist Party. Like many of the other Chinese writers studied here, including the members of the Creation Society, Ding Ling's writing evolved from aesthetics associated with the New Culture Movement to a literature dedicated to supporting the Chinese Communist Party.

Ding Ling arrived in Shanghai in 1921 at the age of seventeen. She had conflicts with her aunt and uncle, with whom she was living, due to her progressive and, in their eyes, decadent lifestyle. In 1923 she went to study at Shanghai University, but decided to leave after only one year. In 1924, Ding moved to Beijing, which she felt would be a more comfortable place to live and write than Shanghai. She had hoped to study in France but eventually was forced to abandon the idea due to strong resistance from her family.[20]

It was in Beijing that Ding met Hu Yepin (1904–1931), whose death would constitute a source of personal tragedy in the decade to come. Beijing was also the place in which Ding Ling was to make her remarkable debut as a writer with *Shafei nüshi de riji* (Miss Sophie's Diary) in 1927. The fourteen stories produced by Ding between 1927 and 1929 depict lone young women who are sensitive and intelligent and alienated from a society which refuses to recognize or respond to their needs.[21] When *Miss Sophie's Diary* appeared in 1927 it had the effect, according to the contemporary critic Yi Zhen, of a "bombshell" lobbed on a "deadly quiet literary scene."[22] Contemporary readers found the first-person meditations on life and romance written in the form of a diary fascinating, and it is certain that part of the contemporary interest in the narrative was due to the fact that both author and protagonist were female.[23]

Miss Sophie's Diary presents the meditations of a young woman about romance, life, illness and the desire for emancipation. In scattered diary entries written between December 24 and March 28, Sophie, who is suffering from tuberculosis, responds to changes in her life and tries to control her own destiny while she wrestles with the tides of romance and tries to decide between two suitors, Ling Jinshi and Yun. Written candidly in the voice of a young woman railing against traditional concepts of morality, the illness that the speaker is suffering only serves to compound the urgency and vulnerability of her situation. The consumptive Sophie's own fate is sealed, when after wrestling with the decision for a long time she moves into a damp room in order to be closer to her beloved Ling Jinshi.[24]

While in Beijing and just prior to her successful literary debut, Ding and Hu had planned to pursue studies in Japan. Toward that end, Ding had begun to study Japanese with the writer Ma Xuefeng, who was studying Japanese at Beijing University.[25] Unfortunately, the two were unable to fulfill their dream of study in Japan. Nevertheless, Ding's fascination with her senior Ma, whom she professed to admire deeply, while her relationship with Hu deepened, is cited as the immediate source of inspiration for the love triangle depicted in *Miss Sophie's Diary*.[26]

In 1928, as young writers felt the literary tide shifting from Beijing to Shanghai, Hu and Ding decided to return to Shanghai. In March of 1930, Hu and Ding joined the League of Leftist Writers which had recently been organized and included a number of the leading writers of the age.[27] Soon after the move to Shanghai, Ding gave birth to a son, but the couple's newfound parental bliss was short lived. On January 17, 1931, Hu Yepin and four other leftist writers, along with nineteen other Communists were rounded up by the Guomindang police and summarily executed.[28] After recovering from the shock of the tragedy and while facing the prospects of having to carry on alone, Ding rededicated herself in her efforts in support of the leftist cause. Ding thereafter acted as the editor of the League of Leftist Writers' literary periodical, *Beidou* (Big Dipper).[29]

At approximately the same time that Ding Ling was coming into prominence as an important new feminist voice in May Fourth China, Hayashi Fumiko was embarking on her own literary career. Interestingly, just as Ding Ling broke onto the literary scene with a debut work of fiction written in a woman's voice in the form of a diary, Hayashi produced a work remarkably similar in form. Just as *Miss Sophie's Diary* had taken the May Fourth literary scene by storm, Hayashi's *Diary of a Vagabond*, which was serialized in *Nyonin geijutsu* (Women's Arts) between October 1928 and October 1930, created a stir in the Japanese literary world before being published in book form by Kaizōsha in 1930.[30]

Diary of a Vagabond describes the life of an itinerant woman who, faced with myriad trials, perseveres on the basis of ambition and determination. It also portrays the emancipating power of literature itself. Despite the various obstacles arrayed against her, the protagonist continues to write, and it is literature along with a true hunger for life that allows her to survive misery and poverty and to rise in the world. Although there are intimations of the protagonist's struggles with despair, what finally remains from the work is a strong sense of optimism and will to survive.

While *Diary of a Vagabond* received an immediate and enthusiastic response from the reading public, its critical reception was initially more tepid. The 600,000 copies of *Diary of a Vagabond* that sold in the first two years after publication catapulted Hayashi into immediate fame. The presentation of a woman clinging tenaciously to her dreams and surviving with optimism despite the obstacles arrayed against her had a strong appeal to a contemporary readership. The work elicited genuine sympathy from its readers.[31]

Initially, Diary of a Vagabond was dismissed by many critics of pure literature, with its characterization as a piece of runpen bungaku which smacked of the world of thieves, vagabonds, and other dispossessed individuals.[32] The Diary was published at the peak of the ascendancy of proletarian literature in the Japanese literary world, and because its subject matter dealt with the life of a marginalized member of society, many readers perceived the Diary as a piece of leftist literature that was intended to describe the plight of the proletariat. Hayashi, for her part, denounced any specific connections to the Proletarian Movement, or to any political ideology for that matter.[33]

Critics in subsequent periods were able to recognize the fundamental qualities that distinguish Diary of a Vagabond from the ideologically hidebound works associated with proletarian literature. Isogai Hideo, in considering these differences, unequivocally states:

> What she [Hayashi] constructed was not some superficial ideal but rather the desperate wish for self-preservation, and what was ultimately liberated was her character itself. The difference between this work [i.e. Diary of a Vagabond] and typical works of proletarian literature lay in precisely that fact. Moreover, it can be said that the reason that this work continues to live is due precisely to that feature of the work.[34]

In fact, in Diary of a Vagabond, when the writer refers to her association with proletarian literature and to the act of writing, she tends to mock the ideological absolutism and dogmatism of the movement. In ridiculing the movement's faith in imminent class revolution, she says: "Where exactly blew the winds of revolution? You Japanese radicals certainly knew my clever words. I wondered exactly what kind of fairy tales the socialists were inventing."[35]

Part of the immediacy and power of both Hayashi's Diary of a Vagabond and Ding Ling's Miss Sophie's Diary is the product of the diary form in which both works were written. It is first and foremost in terms of the form and parallels between the utilization of the fictional diary that the two works are truly comparable. The diary presents an air of verity that invites the reader to approach the narrative as the genuine record of lived events. Moreover, the form revolves around the act of voyeurism as the reader views the record, which ostensibly was meant only for the eyes of the one who wrote it. The voice is the internalized voice of self-revelation and self-reckoning, and the reader becomes the willing participant in the act of eavesdropping.[36]

The reflexive act of diary writing possesses certain qualities that appealed to both Japanese and Chinese writers of the new vernacular fiction searching for a flexible mode of self-expression. Diary writing itself is an act of self-reflection and understanding. In both *Miss Sophie's Diary* and *Diary of a Vagabond* the diarist's voice we overhear is at once the writer, subject and reader of the text.[37] Moreover, the diary was a particularly apt form for women writers in both traditions in the period under discussion. Women writers were able to utilize the immediacy of the diary form in order to address intimate subjects and to adopt a bold tone in a form that permitted the exposition of issues affecting the modern woman.

Despite the diary form's suitability as a tool for expressing modern concerns and debating contemporary issues, the form also possessed by that period a substantial lineage in both literary traditions. According to Joan Ericson, Hayashi Fumiko's *Diary of a Vagabond* belongs to a lineage of literary diaries that can be traced back to Heian period female diarists.[38] In particular, Ericson sees *Diary of a Vagabond* as belonging to a tradition of diaries by women about relationships that deals with mistreatment of women by men that can be traced back to *Kagero Nikki* (Diary of Gossamer Years), the Heian period classic which takes as its theme mistreatment and neglect of a woman by a self-satisfied man.[39]

Like traditional Heian Diaries, *Diary of a Vagabond* as a record of events is fragmented and contains poetry at critical moments in the narrative.[40] Moreover, the narrative is disjointed, and although it is essentially a chronological record of events, it tends to proceed in a herky-jerky fashion, focusing on certain events and moments, while glossing over other large swaths of time. This is a characteristic that Hayashi's work shares with *Miss Sophie's Diary*, and in both narratives this very quality of irregularity serves to underscore the verisimilitude of a narrative which ought to be read as the private meditations of a woman struggling with a variety of challenges while embracing the promise of an uncertain future. As readers, we play witness as the diarist interrogates herself in the pages of the diary. For example, in *Miss Sophie's Diary,* as the "implied reader" of her own diary, Sophie's "neurotic self-dramatization" and ambivalence toward romance and her position on the margins of society, merge in the act of diary writing.[41] Likewise, in *Diary of a Vagabond* the diary allows for development of a unique voice which is at once allied to the voice of the eternal traveler from the Japanese literary tradition and is also the voice of the emancipated woman, unfettered from tradition and seeking a niche in a society struggling to define a role for the new woman.

The diary as a narrative form in its directness and self-reflexivity allowed both Ding and Hayashi to develop a unique feminist voice to challenge the dominant patriarchal voice. These two writers' ability to intentionally subvert and reconstruct the norms associated with the diary form allowed them to create a narrative voice suited to the task of articulating feminist concerns.[42] Both

Hayashi and Ding Ling were attempting to handle the dilemma of articulating a woman's perspective in a "sociocultural space" in which the dominant voice was very much patriarchal.[43] This dilemma of finding ones own voice within a society determined to silence such a voice is reflected in the narratives themselves. In *Miss Sophie's Diary* Sophie's attitude toward herself and toward writing reflects the dilemma of wanting to reject the male-centered discourse about gender and yet finding "no alternative fully satisfying within a largely male-centered language."[44]

Although it is true that one should not expect a complete isomorphism between women's literature and men's literature or of the narrative voice used to convey those narratives, one must recognize the achievement of Ding and Hayashi in developing a voice that both subverts and transcends the voice of male discourse used to articulate women's experience. Nakamura Mitsuo (1911–1988) praised the style of Hayashi Fumiko's prose for the vigor and directness of expression that goes beyond the traditional expectations of literature by women. These qualities of style are related directly to the diary form itself. For example, in *Diary of a Vagabond*, in describing her response to discovering the infidelity of her lover, the diarist says, "I began to shake like a sick dog. Shit! This wasn't the way it was supposed to be. Today I again roamed the pavement like a stray."[45]

In *Miss Sophie's Diary* also the diary form allows Ding Ling to explore a new feminist subjectivity that was decidedly different from that articulated by male writers of the May Fourth period. In *Miss Sophie's Diary,* female desire and the experience of romance are not the excuse for subjective effusions, but rather the occasion for "tough moral questioning."[46] The reader witnesses with morbid fascination as Sophie moves inexorably further into romance, and closer to death, as she debates the morality that forces her to confine her struggle to the pages of the diary. The entry for January 1 states, "I know well that in this society I'm forbidden to take what I need to gratify my desires and frustrations."[47] Using the diary form, Ding Ling was able to extend the range of Chinese literary expression to areas of experience that it had never encompassed before, in the process revealing the sensibilities of the modern young woman to an emerging generation.[48]

Just as Hayashi's *Diary of a Vagabond* and Ding Ling's *Miss Sophie's Diary* are strikingly similar in terms of their mutual utilization of the diary form to express the feminist voice, likewise the two works parallel one another in terms of their realistic presentation of a character who embodies qualities of the "new woman." Both works explore the consciousness of a woman who is struggling with tradition while attempting to attain a goal — romantic, personal, artistic — that remains just out of reach. All literary representations of women in China and Japan from the interwar period can be seen as responses to the challenge presented by the representation of Nora in Henrik Ibsen's *A Doll's House*. Both *Miss Sophie's Diary* and *Diary of a Vagabond* present a woman attempting, like Nora, to break free from the bonds of tradition and attain a happiness that remains elusive.

In Japan, the redefinition of women's social position and of the woman artist began in the Meiji period (1868–1912). The success of Shimamura Hōgetsu's production of *A Doll's House* in 1911 was simply one important milestone in a process that led to the redefinition of women's social status and led to the rejection of the *ryōsai kenbo* (good wife, wise mother) Confucian ethical model.[49] Women who had been largely denied a political and literary voice in Japan in the Tokugawa Period (1600–1868), arose to express feminist concerns in a variety of fora, including Hiratsuka Raicho's *Seitō* (Blue Stocking), the eponymous journal of the movement which sought to change the status of women in the early modern period. Actual changes for women were admittedly slow, but by the 1920s, transformations in education for women and an increase in discretionary income for women led to the growth of a women's market in the publishing industry and the emergence of women's journals which were accompanied by rapid growth in the literacy rate among women.[50] Among the women writers of note who emerged in the Meiji Period are Higuchi Ichiyō (1872–1896) and Yosano Akiko (1868–1942).

A number of journals arose in the Taishō period to cater to the growing interest in literature by and about women. Some of the journals that appeared during this era included *Fujin kōron* (Ladies' Review, founded 1916), *Fujin kurabu* (Ladies' Club, founded 1920), and *Shufu no tomo* (Housewive's Friend, founded 1920).[51] The journal *Nyonin geijutsu* (Women's Arts) in which *Diary of a Vagabond* was first serialized, also originates from this period. These women's journals opened up new possibilities for publishing and income for women writers and allowed writers like Hayashi to establish literary careers.

Part of the initial appeal of *Diary of a Vagabond* for contemporary readers was the presentation of a new variety of woman. Not the well-heeled elite "modern girl" but rather a tough-as-nails, determined woman of the working class who clung tenaciously to life "like a weed" and offered a realistic portrait of a woman that shook up the literary establishment. The genius of *Diary of a Vagabond* was Hayashi's ability to work within the tradition of female diarists while subverting that tradition by presenting the reader with a female voice that expresses thoroughly modern feminist concerns, and challenges conventional values concerning romance and women's position in society. Challenging conventional concepts of morality, the diarist says, "I shuddered merely at the thought of roughing it in the wilds on my own. But having a man support me would be ten times harder. Even my friends laughed at me derisively."[52]

The model of an independent woman, depending on her wits, resourcefulness, and pure strength of character, coupled with the uncompromising colloquial style of the diary can account for the popular reception of *Diary of a Vagabond*. However, it is Hayashi's adeptness at manipulating the traditional diary form and her successful creation of a thoroughly new variety of female protagonist that resulted in the work's ultimate critical success. The work's inclusion in Kaizōsha's series *Shin'ei bungaku sōsho* (A Collection of New Literature) and the invitation extended to Hayashi to participate in 1930 lecture tour in Taiwan by important new women's literary voices, suggests the impact of the *Diary* and the considerable status that she had achieved in this maiden work.

In May Fourth era China, the construction of women's literature and the characterization of the new woman in literature was part of the larger project of the New Culture Movement. Ding Ling's portrait of a "modern girl" which "stunned her generation" must be seen in the context of the reconceptualization of women's social status that was taking place in the 1920s among urban intellectual elite in China.[53] During this early phase of Ding Ling's career, when she produced the stories while in Beijing including *Miss Sophie's Diary* upon which her early reputation rested, she was most concerned with feminist issues and was wrestling with questions pertaining to female sexuality and a woman's status in the new China.[54] In this early fiction, Ding Ling used Western ideology as a "fulcrum" to dislodge the Confucian heritage.[55] In May Fourth China, feminist concerns for universal suffrage and equal legal rights for women were subsumed into the larger revolutionary dogma and cultural reform.[56]

Sophie's most fundamental question in the *Diary*, "What is love?" reflects the struggle of the liberated Chinese woman attempting to reconcile the contradictory claims of political emancipation and conventional practices and values that continued to repress women. Ding Ling directly challenged those values in the *Diary*: "Why shouldn't you embrace your lover's body? Why repress that part of your love? How can they be so preoccupied with all the details before they've even slept together! I won't believe that love is so logical and scientific."[57]

Ding Ling, along with other May Fourth era women writers such as Bing Xin (1900–1999) and Xiao Hong (1911–1942), attempted in her fiction to challenge traditional assumptions about women and call attention to women's issues while also presenting models of the new women. In the period between 1925 and 1935, leftist critics theorized "literature" in such a way as to exclude a category of *funü wenxue* (women's literature).[58] Against this backdrop, after 1925, literature is "seemingly affirmed but also challenged."[59]

Part of the importance attached to *Miss Sophie's Diary* and the reason for its initial popularity was that it was perceived as accurately portraying the psychology of a woman in love.[60] In particular, Ding Ling is characterized as a feminist writer during this period due to her representation of the consciousness of a woman in love.[61]

In Qian Qianwu's 1931 essay entitled "Ding Ling nüshi" (Miss Ding Ling), the critic credits Ding Ling with developing the "stance of the 'modern girl' " that was, by that time, the normative depiction of the new woman in Chinese literature.[62] Chinese writers were shifting from modernist and aesthetic concerns toward a more consciously revolutionary literature. In the 1930s, Ding Ling and other women writers were criticized by contemporary critics precisely for those qualities, which were used to earmark them as women writers. Among the qualities raised for criticism were extreme emotionalism, decadence, lack of social awareness, and the emphasis on individual psychology.[63] It is particularly ironic insofar as this era of criticism coincides with the ascendancy of the League of Leftist Writers and Ding's own distancing from the propensities of her early fiction toward political engagement and revolutionary themes. This move away from specifically feminist and aesthetic concerns by Ding Ling moreover coincides with Hayashi Fumiko's first visits to China and the beginning of the decade in which her career also was to take a decidedly political turn.

Inexorably Apart: Hayashi Fumiko's Movement away from the Chinese Literary Community

A number of reasons can be cited to explain why Hayashi Fumiko and Ding Ling never met and why Hayashi, a writer clearly influenced by her travels in China and well received by the Chinese literary community should, in the latter half of the 1930s, have so consciously distanced herself from that community of writers. There was a political shift on both sides: Hayashi to the right; Ding and the Shanghai literary community to the left. The separation also reflects a survival mechanism, the need to survive at all costs, that was a prominent quality both of Hayashi's characters and of Hayashi herself.

The discussion of this unavoidable separation must nevertheless begin with a discussion of politics. The League of Leftist Writers to which Ding Ling belonged was formed in Shanghai in 1930. In the late 1920s many May Fourth writers moved away from the aesthetic concerns of their earlier romantic phase toward the creation of a revolutionary literature of socialist realism. This shift, which was articulated in dramatic fashion in Cheng Fangwu's 1926 essay, "Cong wenxue geming dao geming wenxue" (From Literary Revolution to Revolutionary Literature) was actually the result of a variety of factors that culminated in the formation of the League of Leftist Writers in Shanghai in 1930. The league, which was formed under the auspices of the Communist Party, was originally comprised of members of the Creation Society and Sun Society, but eventually expanded to include virtually every writer of note in the Shanghai literary scene.[64]

Surprisingly, it was in the late 1920s and early 1930s, when communism was at its lowest ebb and nationalism was on the rise that these leftist writers attempted to create a literature that would reflect the "proletarian spirit."[65] Many of the Sun Society and Creation Society members belonged to the Chinese Communist Party prior to forming the league and were associated with the

Cultural Party Branch in Shanghai. Thus, the league was, from the beginning, well organized and disciplined.[66] One of the most important early decisions of the league was to invite Lu Xun to join. Party members realized that the participation of this revered writer was of critical importance in establishing the legitimacy of the league.[67] Lu Xun did join the league and his participation helped lure other writers, such as Hu Yepin and Ding Ling, from Beijing to Shanghai in order to join the league.

Ding Ling's participation in the league had barely begun when Hu and other leftist writers were arrested and ultimately executed by the Guomindang. Rather than drive her away from political involvement, the tragedy seemed only to steel her resolve, and the thirties mark the era of Ding Ling's greatest political activity.[68] As an artist, this marks a transitional period for Ding Ling. Ding underwent a radical transformation in the early thirties from being a writer of introspective fiction, with *Miss Sophie's Diary* as the primary example, to becoming politically radical and a proponent of revolutionary literature.[69] Thus, by the time that Hayashi arrived in Shanghai in 1932, Ding Ling had already moved away from the consciously feminist concerns of her early fiction.

All of the writers associated with the League of Leftist Writers can be said to have experienced similar transformations. In Ding Ling's case the tragedy she experienced may have intensified the change. Revolutionary activities served in one real sense as a refuge from grief. Moreover, the subjectivity and feminine consciousness of the early fiction seems to have been exhausted so that by the early thirties Ding was moving away from those romantic concerns toward revolutionary commitment.[70] Ding, at the time the target of criticism for the subjectivity of her early fiction, may have been reluctant to associate with a Japanese writer celebrated for the same articulation of the consciousness of the new woman.

From the early thirties onward, when Ding embraced the Communist cause, politics became the conspicuous and defining feature of her writing. Moreover, Ding continued to write even as political upheavals and ideological shifts made publication nearly impossible.[71] Under such circumstances, it was understandably difficult for Chinese writers to meet with visiting writers from Japan, even if they so desired. Leftist writers, as Hu Yepin's case clearly demonstrated, were confronted with genuine dangers as they attempted to persevere in their literary and revolutionary activities. Ding Ling, in fact, was arrested by the Guomindang police in 1933 and was presumed executed before being released.[72]

As Ding Ling was becoming more deeply committed to political activism, Hayashi Fumiko remained largely aloof from political issues, reluctant to become affiliated with any particular ideology. Hayashi always considered herself apolitical and scrupulously avoided becoming involved in ideological debates in the early thirties.[73] Nevertheless, it was an age in which state censorship and repression of leftist artists was increasingly frequent and draconian as evidenced by the incarceration and murder of Kobayashi Takiji in 1933. Hayashi herself was arrested and retained for nine days in 1933 for having subscribed to the Communist Party newspaper *Akahata* (Red Flag). Hayashi's actual interest and involvement in the party seem to have been slight. In fact, Hayashi was among the few writers presumed to be sympathetic to socialism who was not forced to write a *tenkō* (recanting) of her earlier association with socialism, suggesting that the authorities too did not consider her connections with socialism to be particularly deeply rooted.[74]

Nevertheless, in the late 1930s Hayashi, who had hitherto proudly proclaimed her apolitical stance and mistrust of particular political ideologies was drawn into propaganda on behalf of the militarists. In 1936, Hayashi went to China to meet her husband. She was to return to Shanghai, Nanjing and other Chinese cities in the years to follow as part of the *Pen butai* (Pen Squadron) in order to write reports of the war efforts for the newspapers back in Japan.[75]

Thus, Hayashi Fumiko and Ding Ling, who were closely allied aesthetically and ideologically during the late twenties and early thirties, began to move irrevocably apart in the latter half of the decade. In 1937, when Hayashi first returned to China as a correspondent associated with the *Pen butai*, Ding Ling had already fled to the communist stronghold at Yenan in Shaanxi Province and was firmly involved in anti-Japanese activities there.[76] Ironically and sadly, just as Ding Ling and Hayashi Fumiko had moved irreconcilably apart and became involved in fervently patriotic activities, the first complete translations of their works began to appear in the other's language.

Ding Ling had been introduced to Japanese readers in 1930. Her name was mentioned along with brief biographical notes in an article called "Daihyō shin Chūgoku no josei sakkagun" (A Group of Representative New Women Writers in China) which appeared on November 30, 1930 in *Nichinichi Shinbun*.[77] An entire article was devoted to Ding in the August 1933 issue of *Kaizō* about her incarceration, supposed death, and her subsequent release and reemergence to prominence.[78] What these early essays have in common is that the focus on Ding Ling as a figure of intrigue and as a victim, rather than on the literary works themselves. The first Japanese translation of Ding Ling's literary works was the translation of her story "Shui" (Water) in the October 1935 issue of *Nippon hyōron*, the theme of which was *mondai shōsetsu* (problem fiction).[79] This was followed by translations of other stories including "Songzi" (Pine) in *Mita bungaku* in October 1937 and *Muqin* (Mother) in 1938 as the seventh volume in the series entitled *Dalu wenxue congshu* (Compendium of Continental Literature). It was this, the first book-length Japanese translation of Ding Ling's work, which also included *Miss Sophie's Diary*.[80]

The admiration of Hayashi Fumiko in May Fourth China as an important feminist voice in Japan is best seen in the context of the reception of other *joryū sakka* in May Fourth era China. Hayashi was one of a number of Japanese women writers whose works conveyed the presence of a social conscience and a sensitivity to women's issues that appealed to contemporary Chinese readers. Other respected women writers included Hirabayashi Taiko, Miyamoto Yuriko and Uno Chiyo, among others. However, it was in fact the generation of Japanese women writers that preceded these writers which first influenced May Fourth writers. This generation of pioneer feminists included Higuchi Ichiyō, Yosano Akiko, and Tamura Toshiko, who were known to Chinese writers through the essays of Lu Xun and Zhou Zuoren, and two of them, Tamura and Yosano, came to China after they were already established writers. These latter writers were both vocal critics of the vestiges of feudalism and patriarchalism, and this too captured the attention of May Fourth intellectuals.[81]

Yosano Akiko (1878–1942) was recognized in China as one of the pioneers of modern Japanese poetry whose *waka* collection *Midaregami* (Tangled Hair, 1901) and her *shintaishi* (new style verse) served to establish a new modern poetic idiom for women in Japan in much the same way that Higuchi Ichiyō had established a new standard in fiction. Yosano's poems were included among a collection of *shintaishi* in translations by Zhuo Zuoren that appeared in *Chenbao* (Morning News) on October 16, 1920.[82] Yosano had the opportunity to travel to northern China and Manchuria and continued into Mongolia in 1928 at the invitation of the South Manchurian Railroad. In describing her motivation to visit China in the piece that she later produced relating her experiences during her trip, she stated that she was hoping to contribute to the understanding of the Chinese people in order to strengthen relations between the two nations. The result was an essay that Joshua Fogel described as the "highpoint" of the genre of travel writing about China in the modern era by writers in which Yosano meticulously and sensitively describes the particulars of the daily lives of the many people she encounters during her journey.[83]

Tamura Toshiko (1884–1945) whose main literary output had been completed prior to her years abroad in Canada and the United States from 1918 to 1936 was first introduced to Chinese readers in Zhou's essay "Developments in Japanese Fiction in the Last Thirty Years." However, real interactions between Tamura and the Chinese literary community took place during the final years of her life, which she spent in China, first in Beijing and then in Shanghai from 1942 until her death in 1945. In Shanghai she edited a magazine called *Nüsheng* (Woman's Voice, Japanese *Josei*) which was produced in Chinese and aimed at an audience of well-heeled urban young women.[84] Tamura and the publishers of *Nüsheng* meticulously avoided including anything that could be used for propaganda purposes and concentrated instead on fashionable articles about

Shanghai's vibrant urban culture. Tamura employed a bevy of talented young women writers and translators, and she herself wrote an editorial column each month under the Chinese name Zuo Junzhi.[85]

During this period, until her death by cerebral hemorrhage in 1945, Tamura became acquainted with a number of May Fourth writers through the offices of Uchiyama Kanzō and befriended the Creationist writer Tao Jingsun, spending many of her final days with Tao's family.[86] Ironically and painfully for Tamura, her influence on Chinese writers like Tao who had become familiar with her work as students in Japan may have been stronger than it was on young Japanese writers whom she met in China who apparently often took exception to receiving unsolicited advice from a writer whose heyday in the Japanese literary world had occurred before they were born.[87] In the absence of any immediate family, it was Uchiyama Kanzō who served as the leader for Tamura's funeral committee and conveyed the news of her death to the literary community back in Tokyo.[88]

Hayashi, whose early works had been widely available to Chinese readers in the original Japanese, was well known among the many Chinese writers who had studied in Japan and whose excellent Japanese skills impressed her when she met them in 1932 as they had impressed Tanizaki Junichirō and Satō Haruo during their visits in the late twenties. However, the first complete Chinese translation of Hayashi's *Diary of a Vagabond* came in 1937, just as she became involved in the *Pen butai* in China and coincided almost exactly with the period of Ding Ling's first translations into Japanese.[89] This translation was enthusiastically received as was a later translation of the *Diary* in 1956.[90] Hayashi Fumiko, whose wanderings had brought her to China so often in the interwar period, was influenced by Chinese writers just as her work inspired them. Her writing and the trajectory of her career from aesthetics and feminist concerns in the 1930s mirrors that of her Chinese contemporary Ding Ling. The distance separating Hayashi and Ding seems to be symbolic of the rift between the two literary communities themselves as they moved away from the idealistic promise of the late twenties, the golden age of interaction between the two literary communities, to a period of separation and hostility in which writers were compelled to cut ties with writers across the sea and stand in service of the homeland.

6
Satō Haruo's "Ajia no ko" and Yu Dafu's Response: Literature, Friendship and Nationalism

In the March 1938 issue of *Nippon hyōron* there appeared an essay by Mushanokōji Saneatsu about Zhou Zuoren. In the essay, Zhou is praised as a refined man of peace, espousing the same Tolstoyan creed of nonviolence adhered to by Mushanokōji himself. Despite the enmity between the two warring nations, Mushanokōji expressed his intent to remain loyal to a friend with whom he felt a strong personal and intellectual, if not political, kinship. Unabashedly propagandistic, Mushanokōji's essay nevertheless casts relations between the two literary communities in a positive light.[1]

Given the generally sympathetic tone of Mushanokōji's essay, the inclusion in the same issue of *Nippon hyōron* of Satō Haruo's (1892–1964) "Ajia no ko" (Children of Asia), an inflammatory story which provides an unflattering portrayal of events in the lives of Yu Dafu (1896–1945) and Guo Moruo (1892–1978), was bitterly ironic and underscored the unsettled state of relations between the Japanese and Chinese literary communities during the 1930s. Yu, in particular, took exception to his portrayal in the story and gave vent to his ire in an essay called "Riben de wenshi yu changfu" (Japanese Literary Men and Whores). The essay was more than a simple criticism of Satō's story, it was also a formal declaration of the termination of a literary association and friendship that spanned nearly fifteen years. The relationship between the two writers was further complicated by the matter of literary influence — specifically the influence of Satō's self-referential fiction on Yu Dafu during his formative years as a writer. It is impossible to gauge with any accuracy the nature of the two writers' relationship during those years, but it apparently took the form, at least initially, of a relationship between the established *bundan* figure Satō and the emerging young writer, Yu.

Yu acknowledged genuine admiration for Satō's work on several occasions. This admiration preceded the first meeting between the two and was to dictate the way the two writers were to relate to one another thereafter.[2]

The Dilemma of Influence: Satō's *Rural Melancholy* and Yu's "Sinking"

Satō Haruo's *Den'en no yū'utsu* (Rural Melancholy), published in book form in 1919 via the Shinchōsha publishing house, is a work based on the author's experiences from several years earlier. *Rural Melancholy* describes the author/protagonist's escape with his wife from the grime and frantic pace of the capital to a lonely old house out in the country where he hopes his frazzled nerves and his strained relations with his wife will be healed by the nurturing influence of the countryside. The protagonist and his wife arrive at their new rustic home "on the outskirts of the Musashino Plain" with two dogs and a cat and set about the business of clearing the overgrown garden and making the old dilapidated house livable. The protagonist takes special pride in a cluster of rosebushes that he discovers in a corner of the garden and resolves to restore them to their former vitality.

After a brief period of hopefulness and contentment a shift in the mood of the work is signaled by a long rainy spell that confines the two inside the house with their flea-ridden dogs and introduces the dreariness and melancholy that are to characterize the latter part of the story. The protagonist's delicate sensibilities are further tested by several hallucinations that he experiences during this period along with incidents that smack of the supernatural. His wife too, who had begun to tire of rustic life, flees to Tokyo and only reluctantly returns to the country home late in the narrative. In the end, the protagonist, already on the verge of a nervous breakdown, is shocked to find that the roses, which his wife has wantonly cut in order to make a bouquet, have been thoroughly destroyed by bugs. In the final scene the husband is found wandering around the garden in a daze muttering the first line of William Blake's poem, "O Rose! Thou art sick!"

Yu Dafu's (1896–1945) "Chenlun" (Sinking), referring here to the story which also served as the title piece for Yu's 1921 debut collection of stories, is a personal narrative based on the author's experiences from several years earlier. Like Satō's *Rural Melancholy*, "Sinking" describes a young protagonist's alienation from his immediate social milieu and his mental and emotional decline in a hostile environment. The story, written in the third person, is divided into eight parts and tells of a young Chinese exchange student's experiences in Japan. In the first part, the sensitive young protagonist walks through a deserted field reading aloud Wordsworth's poem *The Solitary Reaper* and is moved to tears by the beauty of the lyric and his association with the emotions of the speaker of the poem. As the narrative develops, the protagonist's sexual frustrations begin to take on a central importance and are exacerbated by his inability to communicate his feelings of attraction to the daughter of the owner of the boarding house where he is living. The reader begins to understand these feelings of frustration as symptoms of much deeper feelings of loneliness and paranoia that plague the young man. He feels himself ignored by women, despised by the Japanese public, disdained by his fellow exchange students and generally betrayed by his homeland. His attempts to ease this great loneliness through poetry and masturbation lead him only into deeper despair. In the end, convinced of the futility of continued attempts at combating his loneliness, he commits suicide by throwing himself into the sea, all the while imploring China to change.

Even an initial description of the two works suggests some of the similarities they share. Nevertheless, there are also some striking differences between the two works as well.[3] Whereas Satō's novel portrays the protagonist's journey to the countryside in aesthetic terms, with the young artist questing after a quiet, inspirational setting in which to revitalize his artistic output, "Sinking" portrays the loneliness and the alienation of the young artist not in such aesthetic terms but rather in bold, physical terms. Yu portrays a character in search not only of understanding and recognition as an artist but also in quest of sexual and emotional fulfillment. The cause for the demise of Yu's protagonist proceeds from this sexual frustration rather than from the simple failure to be recognized as an artist. By contrast, in Satō's *Rural Melancholy,* sex plays virtually no role in the protagonist's emotional collapse.[4]

It is, however, in the degree to which the action in *Rural Melancholy* is closed off from social and political concerns that it differs most markedly from "Sinking." Insofar as *Rural Melancholy* can be said to be a fairly representative *shishōsetsu,* the world of the text is a private one and the protagonist exists, as it were, in a vacuum, immured from all concerns that transcend the parameters of his highly aesthetic, almost hermetic existence. "Sinking," on the other hand, was to become the model for similar works of fiction by Creation Society members that were to follow. The socio-political orientation of "Sinking" was to become not merely a trademark of Yu Dafu's personal narratives but set the tone in fact for other such *shishōsetsu*-like fiction that appeared in the pages of Creation Society journals. Why this engagement with society, which is largely absent in the Japanese *shishōsetsu* of the Taishō period, emerged in the Chinese model is not so simply answered, nevertheless its existence in "Sinking" and elsewhere gave the Chinese *shishōsetsu* a markedly different flavor from its Japanese antecedents. The following passage from the conclusion of *Sinking,* in which the protagonist is standing on the shore and contemplating suicide, points to the work's political orientation.

> "Beneath that one twinkling star, there lies my homeland. There lies my birthplace. Beneath that star I passed eighteen years, but now it seems I will never again set eyes on my hometown." While walking he uttered to

himself this lament of deep suffering. Walking a little more he looked up again at that lone star and tears began to fall like the soft patter of rain. He was only vaguely aware of the scenery around him. Wiping the tears away, he got to his feet, and heaving a deep sigh he muttered, "Homeland, O my homeland. My death will be on your head! Hurry up and prosper! Hurry up and become strong! Still countless of your sons and daughters are suffering!"[5]

It was the success of "Sinking" that inspired the other Creationists to follow suit and produce similar stories based on experiences in Japan. It was while living in Japan that the Creationists began to read the various Japanese anti-naturalist literary journals such as *Waseda Bungaku* and *Shirakaba* and were exposed to the personal narrative of the *shishōsetsu* variety. One of the salient features of the *shishōsetsu*, what might in fact be called its defining characteristic, is its portrayal of a protagonist separated from society.[6] In such narratives, social concerns and political events seldom intrude on the generally inward-looking narrative. Given such criteria it is perhaps surprising that in the Chinese case such a form should have been embraced.

Nevertheless, in the hands of the Creationists, the *shishōsetsu* form was transformed into a tool for social and political critique. The Japanese *shishōsetsu* was able to transcend in its plot many of the complexities and contradictions that inclusion of political and societal concerns would have implied, whereas Chinese writers literally had nowhere to hide from their responsibilities to their society.[7]

Ironically, this tendency among the Creationists toward patriotic literature can in part be interpreted as a natural response to having lived and studied abroad. One commentator in fact suggests that had not Yu and the other members lived in Japan, they would not have produced literature with this political strain.[8] Yu himself suggested that it was while living in Japan as a young student that he first considered China's place in the world and began to concern himself with the political fate of his homeland.[9] Put another way, the experience of living abroad in a country in which respect for that country's material and social development was tempered by his disgust toward its role as an ideological and military menace, Yu and the other Creationists were forced not only to look inward but to look outward at political and social realities as well. Mulling over China's ills while portraying the self became a recurrent theme in Chinese personal fiction during the 1920s. In the early personal narratives of the Creation Society this "national consciousness" becomes a propensity that exerts itself in a variety of ways.[10]

It is interesting to note that in the 1930s, a full decade after the Creationists saw in the *shishōsetsu* form the potential for political and social critique, Japanese writers began to produce works that exhibited uncannily similar tendencies.

One sees in the *shishōsetsu* of certain Japanese socialist writers in the years leading up to the war a similar conscious construction of a social milieu in which to frame the actions of the protagonist-cum-author. Moreover, there is a like portrayal of a political consciousness that parallels that of the representative Creationist stories of the twenties, but which is conspicuously absent from the Japanese *shishōsetsu* of the Taishō period.

In the 1930s, Ishikawa Jun (1899–1987) produced *shishōsetsu* such as *Hinkyū mondō* (Dialogue on Poverty, 1935), *Fugen* (Bodhisattva), for which he won the Akutagawa Prize in 1936, and *Marusu no uta* (Song of Mars, 1938), a brilliantly ironic antiwar story, which was banned by the military authorities for fomenting antimilitary thought. With the other members of the Buraiha coterie, Ishikawa continued to produce self-referential fiction in the postwar period that challenged social mores and the moral authority of the state in the same manner that the Creationists had in the fiction they produced first in Japan and later in Shanghai through their various publications in the 1920s.

In much the same way as Ishikawa, Takami Jun (1907–1965), a writer who was originally attracted to the anti-naturalist, "pure literature" of the White Birch School, was drawn increasingly to the political left and saw in self-referential fiction the potential for political critique. His novel *Kokyū wasureubeki* (Should Auld Acquaintance Be Forgot, 1935), which was short-listed for the Akutagawa Prize, describes the personal agony that the protagonist, in fact a thinly veiled portrait of the author, felt in his forced recanting of Marxism and of his association with the Communist Party. The utilization of the *shishōsetsu* form to challenge political power and the social status quo was also apparent in Takami's novel *Ikanaru hoshi no moto ni* (Under What Star, 1939–1940) which describes the struggles that Takami faced as a writer who bore the stigma of a leftist affiliation during the war era.

Likewise, Nakano Shigeharu (1902–1979), a writer known primarily as a poet and critic associated with the Proletarian Movement, also produced a work of fiction which challenged the very conceptualization of the *shishōsetsu* form. His story, "Shōsetsu no kakenu shōsetsuka" (A Novelist Who Cannot Write Novels), which appeared in the January 1936 issue of *Kaizō,* challenged the boundaries between fiction and nonfiction while portraying the challenges faced by a leftist writer in an authoritarian state on the verge of war. His work suggests not only the innovations of the Japanese *shishōsetsu* novelist Kasai Zenzō (1887–1928) but also the politicization of the genre that characterizes Yu Dafu's fiction in the 1920s and 1930s.

Ultimately, Yu Dafu's "Sinking," contains all of the most important elements of the *shishōsetsu*. As with *Rural Melancholy,* "Sinking" draws on the author's lived experience in order to sketch out the increasingly severe neurosis of a young artist cut off from society and his attempts to construct an artistic alternative to a world in which he feels unequipped to dwell. The sense of alienation in "Sinking" is made more complete by the young student's sexual frustrations and sense of solitude in a hostile foreign land. Perhaps it is natural that the *shishōsetsu* in China should have been thus interpreted. Young Chinese writers repatriated from Japan had a sharpened sense of the urgent need for their homeland to modernize. Thus the protagonist in "Sinking" is never cut off completely from his social surroundings. That "Sinking" otherwise does in fact bear all of the characteristic trademarks of the typical *shishōsetsu* is revealed in comparison with as distinguished an example of the genre as Satō Haruo's *Rural Melancholy.*

A Literary Friendship

Yu first expressed his respect for Satō Haruo's writing in a brief essay entitled "Haishang tongxin" (Correspondence from the Sea) in the *Creation Weekly* in October of 1923. In the essay, Yu professed a genuine preference for Satō among contemporary Japanese writers while admitting that there were many writers better known and more highly lauded in China than Satō Haruo.[11] The two writers were apparently introduced in 1922 by Tian Han (1898–1979) who was already acquainted with Satō. Satō, who visited Taiwan in 1920, had a well-documented affection for classical Chinese literature and was familiar with several young Chinese writers and intellectuals.[12]

Yu, no doubt, also felt a certain debt of gratitude to Satō whose literary works had served as an inspiration and touchstone for his own early efforts. In 1927, when Satō Haruo, his wife and niece came to visit Shanghai, Yu made a determined effort to guide the Satōs to various sites of cultural interest. Both writers were, by that time, relatively influential figures in their respective literary communities and this visit marked the high point of their friendship.

Some years later, at the behest of the scholar Itō Toramaru, Satō Haruo's niece, Chieko, wrote of the 1927 visit to China and her memories of Yu Dafu. According to her account, although the Satōs were entertained by a number of Chinese writers, it was Yu Dafu who gave them the warmest welcome and spent the most time showing them around both Shanghai and Hangzhou.[13] Moreover, she recounts how Yu changed his schedule to be their guide when Tian Han canceled a commitment to take them to Nanjing due to political unrest. Knowing their desire to visit culturally significant sites, he took them to Hangzhou and the West Lake. Toward the end of the Satōs' visit, Yu was late for an appointed meal with the Satōs. They later discovered that he was detained by the authorities and he had to slip beneath their surveillance in order to see them one last time before their departure.[14]

Following the pattern established in earlier visits by Akutagawa and Tanizaki, the Satōs stayed at the same hotel where Akutagawa had stayed during a visit several years earlier.¹⁵ It was through Uchiyama Kanzō's intercession that Satō was able to reacquaint himself with Yu Dafu and Tian Han and to meet other intellectuals including Hu Shi (1891–1962) for the first time. By the time the Satōs returned to Japan after nearly a month in China, Haruo had strengthened his ties with the Chinese literary community, and a conventional literary acquaintance with Yu Dafu had ripened into a genuine friendship.

Thereafter, the two writers continued to exchange letters periodically as evidenced by a letter sent by Yu to Satō the following year. The warmth and familiarity of the letter suggest a continuation of the bond that had developed between the two men the previous year. In the letter Yu, who was still in virtual hiding in a Shanghai suburb, expressed misgivings about the state of Chinese society. Moreover, he implored Satō to contact Mushanokōji Saneatsu on his behalf, and expressed regrets about not being able to send Satō books as intended.¹⁶ Yu was to visit Japan soon after that but, according to this letter, this journey was in jeopardy due to the general unrest in China.

In 1927 and 1928, when the relationship between Yu Dafu and Satō Haruo was at its closest, Yu was a rising literary star in China and Satō was already an established writer in the Japanese *bundan*. At the time, Yu was not only involved with the Creation Society but was also teaching at the Shanghai College of Law and had begun to edit a monthly magazine with Lu Xun (1881–1936) called *Benliu* (Surging Current). After the Creation Society was forced to suspend publication activities in February 1929, Yu's association with Lu Xun led to the formation of the League of Leftist Writers in 1930.¹⁷

During these years, the ambivalence toward Japan that Yu had always harbored — Japan the exemplar of modernization and bastion of a rich traditional culture juxtaposed with Japan the imperialist aggressor — became particularly acute. Yu arrived in Japan in 1913 at the age of seventeen, and through his involvement in Chinese student groups in Japan, became increasingly critical of Japanese imperialism while admiring Japan's economic progress.¹⁸ As the intensity of Japanese imperialism in Asia increased during the 1930s, so did Yu Dafu's anti-imperialist activities. Yu's knowledge of Japanese economics and society was a boon to the League of Leftist Writers, and his role in the league soon jeopardized the generally good reputation he enjoyed in Japan. Although his early works of fiction had been praised in Japan, his anti-imperialist writings of the early thirties were soon banned.¹⁹

Drawing Ideological Lines

Although the focus of Yu's writing shifted in the late twenties along with his contemporaries from "literary revolution" to "revolutionary literature," several of his collections from this period exhibited qualities observable in his earlier fiction. These collections, which included *Guoqu* (The Past), are comprised of both essays and the self-referential literature, which brought Yu much of his early success.

While Yu was becoming more and more involved in anti-Japanese activities, Satō Haruo, whose early writings demonstrate no overt political predilections, became caught up in the political fervor of the era. For Satō, as for Mushanokōji and a number of other established writers of the day, that meant allying himself with the writers and intellectuals who supported Japan's increasingly imperialistic aggression.

In conformity with the cultural climate of Japan in the thirties, Satō's literary production during this era bore testimony to a repudiation of his earlier modernist and *shishōsetsu* style narratives and a move toward works consciously steeped in traditional culture. Satō's prose from the thirties and forties tended toward fictional celebrations of Japan's mythic past alongside politically charged essays supportive of Japan's militarism and the creation of a unified Asian cultural sphere centered in Japan and emanating outward to the rest of Asia.

Without any declaration of enmity on the part of either man, Satō and Yu had begun to move irrevocably apart in the early 1930s. Both writers who, at least in the mind of Satō, had occupied unique, unequivocal positions in their respective literary communities, proved in the end to be fairly typical writers of their age, firmly entrenched behind the ideological partitions that separated the two countries in the years leading up to the war. Seen in this way, the works written by both men during the thirties can be conceived of as the logical conclusion to their professional and personal relationships.

"Ajia no ko" (Children of Asia) which appeared in the October 1938 issue of *Nippon hyōron* was originally intended as a film script.[20] Although Satō never explicitly stated that he was using Yu Dafu and Guo Moruo as models for his fictional characters, even a casual acquaintance with the biographies of the two writers makes it clear that Yu and Guo were the immediate inspiration for these characters.

The story opens with a "theme song" which evidently was meant to be played while the credits rolled at the beginning of the film. The lyrics describe how Asia has been "awakened" from a long stormy night to face the light of a new day dawning in the East. The protagonist, Zhumou (i.e. Guo Moruo) is the son of a wealthy family in Hangzhou who has come to study medicine in Kagoshima. There he becomes the object of the attentions of a number of the young nurses at the hospital in which he is serving as an intern. He eventually becomes captivated by a nurse named Yasuda Aiko, a modern, practical-minded young woman with whom he shares an interest in socialism and contemporary poetry. The two eventually marry, against the wishes of their families. After the birth of their second child, Zhu is coaxed by his old friend Zheng (i.e. Yu Dafu) to take part in his homeland's political struggles. Eventually, he returns to China where he participates in the Communists' conflicts against the Northern Warlords and Jiang Jieshi's (Chiang Kai-shek) Republican forces. There he meets a young woman with whom he has a brief affair. Zhu is forced to flee to Japan and is reunited with his family after several key Communist losses.

The next section treats a period in Zhu's life approximately ten years after the preceding events. Zhu is forty-five and his sons are now twenty and twenty-three. While he is in his study reading with increasing concern about the escalating instability in China, Zheng, who has also come back to Japan, comes to call. Zheng reminds Zhu of the importance of his status in China as a successful man of letters and, as the logical successor to Lu Xun as a leading light in the Chinese literary world, implores him to return again to China with him in order to contribute to forging a new society. The two go out for a stroll and talk long into the night about the state of China and its future. In the end, Zhu becomes convinced that he must return to China.

In the interim, the authorities come to visit Zhu's home and warn his wife to report any suspicious activities involving her husband. Several days later, Zhu takes his boys aside and tells them to look after one another and their mother since he will soon be going away for a while. He describes the sense of duty that he feels toward China and swears them to secrecy before bidding them farewell. Before leaving, he writes a long explanatory letter to his wife. While he is on the ferry from Kobe to Shanghai, his sons disclose to their mother the content of the previous night's conversation with their father. Soon after that, the boys hear malicious rumors about their father at school, and their mother goes to the police station to volunteer information about her husband's disappearance.

The third and final section describes Zhu's life back in China. Jiang Jieshi is back in power and friends of Zhu warn him that there is a warrant out for his arrest. Zhu avoids incarceration by promising, despite pangs of conscience, to produce anti-Japanese propaganda for the Republican government. It is a bleak period in Zhu's life in which he feels betrayed by his friend Zheng for convincing him to return to China and guilty about his relationship with the young woman during his previous stay in China.

Through these experiences, Zhu begins to believe that the Communist creed, which hitherto had sustained him, might not be worthy of his undying devotion. He sends a letter to the Japanese army in Northern China in the hope that he yet may be able to fulfill the dream that he and his wife had long cherished of building a clinic for the needy. Moreover, he sends a letter to his wife and sons back in Japan requesting that they come and live with him in China. His wife, Aiko, is overjoyed by the prospect of being reunited with her husband and of the possibility of finally realizing their shared dream. The two sons begin to study Chinese at night in the hope that they can open a school for Japanese language and culture near their parents' clinic.

Excited about the idea of toiling beside her husband in the north of China, Aiko returns to her parental home in Tōhoku to request money from her older brother for their travel fees. Reluctantly, and still bearing a grudge against his sister for marrying Zhu in opposition to her parents' wishes, the older brother gives Aiko the requested money.

Zhu and his family are reunited in dramatic fashion at the port of Kobe where he and Aiko had celebrated their honeymoon many years earlier. The ship on which they cross to China is decorated with Japanese flags in celebration of the anniversary of a Japanese naval victory. In the end, the family arrives in the northern village in which they are to live and work. A new hospital has already been built for Zhu and his wife by Japanese residents of the area, and another Japanese-style building is under construction to house the boys' Japanese language and culture school.[21]

Nippon hyōron, originally called *Keizai ōrai,* was initially an important vehicle for contemporary literature and included works by such major writers as Kōda Rohan (1867–1947) and Tokuda Shusei (1871–1943). Insofar as it was not primarily a literary magazine, its readership was considerably larger than contemporary periodicals devoted solely to new literary works. After a temporary suspension of publication, *Nippon hyōron* recommenced publication in 1935 with a more pronounced emphasis on political writing, and those works of fiction that were included possessed, like Satō's story, a decidedly political bent.[22]

Yu Dafu's Reaction

It is unclear when Yu first read Satō's story, but apparently it was not long after publication. That he had not anticipated Satō producing such a piece, so evidently using him and Guo Moruo as models, can be surmised from the essay that he wrote in response to "Children of Asia." Yu's rejoinder, "Riben de wenshi yu changfu" (Japanese Literary Men and Whores), appeared soon afterward in 1938. Yu's essay begins with a strong general denunciation of Japan's intelligentsia for having been deceived by the military. Furthermore, he regrets having in his youth attributed to Japanese intellectuals a sensitivity and high-mindedness which, in retrospect, they clearly do not possess. He further indicts the Japanese government and its imperialistic policies, which he castigates as utterly hypocritical, likening the Japanese government to a "dressed-up monkey."[23]

Yu then identifies the immediate cause of his diatribe against Japanese intellectuals. After introducing Satō's story and describing the characters and plot of "Children of Asia," Yu criticizes Satō's story for not being properly grounded in fact and for so twisting actual incidents so as to create a fiction that invites misunderstanding. Yu confesses that he believes that he and Guo have been reduced in the story to mere caricatures to be used in the service of propaganda. In the story, he asserts, the male Chinese characters are portrayed as weak-willed and conniving and, whereas the Japanese woman Aiko is portrayed as virtuous and self-effacing, the Chinese woman with whom the protagonist Zhu has an affair is not developed in any sense and appears merely as a whore who attempts to separate the protagonist from his virtuous Japanese wife.[24]

The remainder of the essay denounces Satō, who Yu now considers a traitor and who, despite his avowed love of Chinese culture and his association with the Chinese literary community, took advantage of those friendships to slander the Chinese. Yu qualifies his criticism of Satō by stating that for every writer like Satō, cheapening himself by producing propagandistic literature, there were writers like Shimazaki Tōson (1872–1943) and Shiga Naoya (1883–1971) who held true to their art, remaining above the political fray, and were thus worthy of praise.

The bitterness of Yu's essay reflects his wounded pride and sense of betrayal. It seems likely that much of the disappointment conveyed by Yu was the result of the fact that the story in question was written by none other than Yu's friend Satō Haruo. However, Yu's criticism of the story on the basis that it was a twisting of events in his life and that of Guo Moruo seems, in retrospect, somewhat ironic given that Yu so masterfully handled the contemporary *shishōsetsu* form, and so imaginatively recast incidents in his own life and those of his friends in his most successful stories such as "Sinking."

With the appearance of Satō's "Children of Asia" and Yu's rejoinder, "Japanese Literary Men and Whores," the relationship between the two men effectively came to an end. The depth of acrimony on both sides made reconciliation during the war virtually impossible and, regrettably, Yu's life was not to outlast the war. Fundamental ideological differences became painfully apparent in these two works and led to the dissolution of a relationship which had endured for over ten years. The last few encounters between Yu and Satō, in 1936 when Yu called on Satō in Japan and in 1938 when Satō met Yu and Guo during a Japanese government-sponsored trip to China, do not reveal any overt animosity between the men. However, Satō's visit, in which he came representing the magazine *Kaizō* and during which Guo and Yu were summoned to provide information about Lu Xun, reveals the degree to which friendship had been reduced to the exigencies of political posturing.

After the rupture of relations with Yu Dafu, Satō Haruo became more deeply involved in politics and cultural activities related to Japan's increasing imperialism in Asia. Starting in 1936, Satō acted as the Chair of the Literature Department at Bunka University. In September of the following year, along with Hayashi Fusao (1903–1975), he established the New Japanese Culture Society and was instrumental in the production of the magazine *Shin Nippon* (New Japan), which was to become the organ for the society.

Conclusion

The relationship between Yu Dafu and Satō Haruo represented the kind of productive, amicable interaction that some of the writers in the Chinese and Japanese literary communities endeavored to create and sustain in the twenties and early thirties. As late as 1937, during the Yomiuri symposium held in Taiwan alluded to earlier, Yu Dafu repeatedly stressed his conviction that both China and Japan would benefit from literary projects that bridged the gap between the two countries and applauded recent Japanese literary works that drew from Chinese cultural sources. In a very real sense, the rupture of relations between Yu and Satō signaled the demise of opportunities for such constructive contact between the two literary communities.

In the years following the war, Satō returned to a more personal and, consequently, less political literature and produced some of his most remarkable collections of poems including the collection *Saku no kusabue* (The Reed Flute of Saku, 1946) and his translation of Chinese poems, *Gyokuteki fu* (Poems of the Jade Flute, 1948). In the latter collection in particular, Satō seemed to be attempting to reestablish his earlier ties with Chinese literature while reconnecting his own creative works with, what had been until the military period, the touchstone for his creative work.

Ironically, this rejuvenated interest in Chinese literature on the part of Satō came too late to have any effect on his relationships with specific writers in the Chinese literary community. Perhaps the schism that had opened between the communities during the thirties would have been too broad to bridge by this point anyway, but the tragic murder of Yu Dafu, Satō's closest link to the Chinese literary scene, spelled the demise of such possibilities.

The contact between the two literary groups during the 1920s, centered in Uchiyama Kanzō's bookshop in Shanghai, was undermined by the nationalism and militarism of the thirties. On the personal level, friendships between writers like Yu and Satō were crushed beneath the juggernaut of ideological orthodoxy. Yu, whose writing had been praised by the Japanese literary community, became a victim of increasing polarization along national and political lines. Moreover, the breaking off of relations between Yu and Satō, and Yu's death in 1945, came to symbolize in a broader sense the demise of intimacy and fellowship between Chinese and Japanese writers in the interwar period.

7
Return to the Brush: The Polarization of the Chinese and Japanese Literary Communities in the 1930s

The vigorous exchange between the Chinese and Japanese literary communities in the interwar period portrayed in this study was destined not to last. As early as 1930, in fact, these relations showed signs of strain. The exacting convergence of factors that made this interaction possible in the 1920s had begun to bend beneath the weight of political and ideological differences. Several events served to signal the increasing deterioration of relations between the two communities, and the writers examined in this study came to a variety of fates as a result of this polarization.

Among the factors that conspired in the latter part of the interwar period to signal a new era of fissured relations between the communities were the formation of the League of Leftist Writers in China, The death of Lu Xun in 1936, the activities of the Pen Butai (Pen Squadron) among Japanese writers in the late thirties and the closing of Uchiyama Shudian. By the time of the murder of Yu Dafu in Sumatra by the Japanese military police in 1945 the period of interaction had long passed.

Some of the issues identified in this chapter as signifiers of a breakdown in Sino-Japanese relations may appear more symbolic than substantive, such as the death of Lu Xun. Others, such as the formation of the League of Leftist Writers and the activities of the Pen Squadron among Japanese writers have a more obvious causal relationship to the breakdown in relations that is the subject of this chapter. Nevertheless, all of these factors constitute verifiable markers in the deterioration in relations between the two literary communities.

The official end of the period under discussion was the outbreak of violence and the beginning of war between the two nations. On July 8, 1937 the Japanese garrison in North China held a field exercise outside of Beijing near the Marco Polo Bridge. The Japanese demanded to enter the city of Wanping in order to conduct a search for an allegedly missing Japanese soldier. When refused entry by the Chinese garrison leader the Japanese army bombarded and occupied the city, thus beginning an undeclared war and effectively closing this dynamic chapter in intercultural relations between the two nations.[1]

The League of Leftist Writers

The single most important manifestation of the politicization of the Chinese literary community in the latter half of the interwar period was the establishment of the League of Leftist Writers (Zuoyi zuojia lianmeng) in Shanghai in 1930.[2] The existence of the league, in which many established Chinese writers of the period participated, profoundly affected relations between the Chinese and Japanese literary communities. The decision to establish the league not only underscored the fissure between artists faithful to the Guomindang and those sympathetic to the Communist Party, it also signaled the beginning of an era of increased political engagement of writers in which even those writers who had theretofore assiduously avoided political affiliations were forced to disclose their political orientation or risk being ostracized.

The League of Leftist Writers was formed in 1930 under the auspices of the Chinese Communist Party (CCP). Originally, the league was comprised of members of the Creation Society and the Sun Society, but was expanded eventually to include an increasing number of writers with leftist sympathies.[3] The mission of the league, simply stated, was to promote proletarian literature.[4]

Ironically, the league can be seen as the culmination of efforts that dated back to 1927, when the Guomindang was on the rise and communism at its nadir. Communist leaders at the time recognized the need to create a literature reflecting "proletarian spirit."[5] In the late 1920s literature was seen as one of the few areas of intellectual life in China in which the struggling Chinese Communist Party (CCP) still conceivably could exert influence.[6] Those leftist writers who rushed to support the communist cause via literature were eager to join the ranks of the league when it was formed in 1930.

At the time of the founding of the League of Leftist Writers in 1930, Shanghai was a highly politicized and divided city, and was moreover the center of both CCP and the Guomindang activities.[7] Shanghai during the thirties continued the tradition of political engagement that had been the hallmark of the Shanghai *wentan* in the twenties, but the politics of Shanghai writers in the thirties had become more polarized and radical, reflecting economic as well as cultural developments.[8] Shanghai, moreover, had a somewhat ambiguous relationship with national politics because the city was often perceived and portrayed as "foreign" — the product of imperialism and disconnected from the rest of China politically and culturally.[9]

The League of Leftist Writers was inaugurated on March 2, 1930 in Shanghai. At the inauguration ceremony Lu Xun gave the keynote address before an audience of about fifty people. Branches of the league were also established in other cities including Beijing, Guangzhou, Nanjing and even Tokyo.[10] Ultimately, nearly three hundred writers officially joined or were associated with the league, a number representing a substantial proportion of writers active in China in the early thirties.[11]

Several events conspired to make the league increasingly radical soon after its inception, to the extent that league members began to condemn such moderate voices as those of Hu Qiuyuan and Su Wen.[12] Military events which contributed to this radicalization included the invasion of Shenyan (Mukden) by the Japanese in September of 1931 and the subsequent occupation of Northeastern China, followed by the punitive bombardment of Shanghai on February 28, 1932. Thus, national salvation and emancipation from Japanese occupation became ever more critical issues among league writers.[13]

However, the move away from moderation to the radical left by the league was precipitated not by Japanese imperialism but rather by the challenge of the Guomindang. Under the slogan "Nationalist Literature" Guomindang leaders established in 1930 the journal *Qianfeng yuebao* (Vanguard Monthly) which contained an essay that expressed a direct challenge to the League of Leftist Writers entitled "Minzhuzhuyi wenyi yundong xuanyan" (A Declaration by the Nationalist Literature Movement).[14] However, the single event which steeled the will of the league's members was the murder of five young communist writers by the Guomindang in 1931. As described in Chapter 5, this incident had a particularly profound impact on league member Ding Ling.

Ding Ling's decisive step into the political arena had been the move to Shanghai in 1928 and entry into the League of Leftist writers in 1930. Ding and Hu Yepin arrived in Shanghai in 1928 at a time when many young writers felt the political tide shifting toward the left.[15] Rather than becoming demoralized by the execution of her husband, Ding Ling rather found a renewed sense of purpose and urgency. In fact, after Hu's death Ding became an even more active figure in the league.[16] In Ding Ling's case, tragedy was recast in literary form on several occasions including in the much anthologized story "Mouye" (A Certain Night) published in June 1932, sixteen months after Hu's death.[17]

For Ding Ling, the act of remembering and indeed recreating this tragic event apparently made the event more immediate and paradoxically more distant; it reopened the wound but ultimately had a cathartic effect. As Yi-tsi Feuerwerker has said of Ding Ling's perspective on the role of the writer and the significance of literature, the aesthetic transformation proved ultimately healing. For Ding Ling, in writing about the events of that fateful night as with writing about other significant turning points in her life, "… writing comes as a restorative, a reaffirmation. She writes to let herself — and she finds now she can — face life and go on living."[18]

During this period Ding Ling, as with many other young leftist writers, demonstrated some disillusionment with literature's capacity to effect lasting political and social change. If total revolution, in the accepted Soviet view, was the only real solution, would literature, which appealed to only a small literate minority in China, have any real effect on the ability to achieve revolution? Ding Ling during the 1930s continued to wrestle with the question of the writer's place in society and determined at times to subordinate literature to political action. Nevertheless, she always returned to literature as the one honest means that she had at her disposal to ignite the revolution that she now felt was destined to occur. From this period, when Ding suffered loss and found solace in the revolutionary activities of the League of Leftist Writers, and even after her incarceration and presumed death in 1933, politics remained a conspicuous theme in her writing, and Ding continued to write even as political change limited what she could write.[19]

For Lu Xun, leadership in the league and his increasingly close association with the Chinese Communist Party were the logical conclusion of ideological developments that had begun twenty years earlier in Japan.[20] At least at the beginning, Lu Xun seemed content to serve as the spokesman and apologist for the League as the CCP sought to legitimize the league by engaging a figure of Lu Xun's stature. Lu Xun eschewed involvement in more radical elements of the league's activities and contributed instead to the league via his editorial efforts of its publications along with Rou Shi, Feng Xuewen and Qu Qiubai. The most important organs for the league's thought were *Wenyi yanjiu* (Literary Research) issued first in February 1930 and *Mengya* (The Sprout) from January to May, 1930.[21] Most significant were Lu Xun's contributions to *Qianshao* (Outpost) and its successor *Wenxue daobao* (Literary Guide), which contained league documents but also Lu Xun's heartfelt denunciations of Guomindang terror, including memorials by Lu Xun and others to their five martyred colleagues. Lu Xun wrote four essays commemorating his slain colleagues, suggesting in one of these that this sacrifice had allowed the five to become true "revolutionary writers."[22]

The extent to which the league influenced the course of China in the thirties and affected the literary production of Lu Xun can be surmised from the fact that between 1930 and 1932 virtually all that Lu Xun published appeared initially in the league's various periodicals and addressed issues related to the new literature and the obligations of the writer.[23] As with other league writers, after the murder of the five writers associated with the league in February in 1931, the tone of Lu Xun's writing changed radically. He now spoke more candidly about the capacity of proletarian literature to facilitate the "sacred goal" of a classless society.[24]

By way of contrast, Yu Dafu, who was one of the founders of the League of Leftist Writers and who was seen as one of the members most instrumental in defining the goals of the league, soon fell out of favor with its leadership. As a graduate of Tokyo Imperial University's Economics Department, Yu was regarded as someone who could potentially contribute a great deal of useful information about Japan to the league.[25] Nevertheless, Yu Dafu's penchant for going his own way and for producing the provocative and occasionally ill-advised statement, resulted in a split with his colleagues in the league. At the Fourth Convention of the League of Leftist Writers in January of 1930, presided over by fellow Creationist Zheng Boqi, Yu Dafu was expelled from the league for having proclaimed in English to the poet Xu Zhimo, "I am a writer, not a fighter," thus revealing a squeamishness for revolutionary activity that was apparently unacceptable to the league's other leaders.[26]

Ultimately, the League of Leftist Writers, which pulled together a wide range of writers under its radical political banner, forever changed Chinese writers' perceptions of their role in creating a new revolutionary culture. For Yu Dafu, Ding Ling and Lu Xun it colored their relations with Japanese writers thereafter and resulted in a new guardedness in their interactions with the Japanese literary community. In fact, the league lasted for only three years due to internal pressures pulling the members apart along with the increasing vigilance of the Guomindang authorities. Nevertheless, despite the brevity of its existence, the league left the political landscape for Chinese writers utterly changed, and in its wake possibilities for positive interactions with Japanese writers of the kind that had taken place in the 1920s were seriously compromised.

A Link Broken: The Death of Lu Xun and Its Significance for Sino-Japanese Literary Relations

Lu Xun's association with the League of Leftist Writers in the early 1930s had a profound effect on his perception of himself as an artist and also contributed to the manner in which he was perceived by the Chinese literary community. From Lu Xun's leadership of the league in 1930 until his death in 1936, he was the most revered figure in the Chinese literary world. He was by far the most popular Chinese writer among Japanese writers and readers and it was Lu Xun who every Japanese writer visiting China wanted to meet. Thus, Lu Xun's death in 1936 had an impact on Sino-Japanese literary relations that was as substantive as it was symbolic, and his death can be seen as the true end of this era of positive Sino-Japanese literary relations.

In the final days of Lu Xun's life he remained active as a writer of poetry and essays and as an artist working in the woodblock print medium. In the latter capacity he met frequently with colleagues and protégés and produced an impressive body of new work. Increasingly, Uchiyama's bookstore became the true center of Lu's aesthetic universe during those years. Therefore, a discussion of Lu Xun's death and its significance necessitates a return to Uchiyama's bookstore.

Lu Xun used his position of cultural authority during his final years to challenge younger writers and intellectuals to constantly interrogate themselves and to be willing to reinvent their roles as writers. For his part, Lu Xun, the man of letters, relentlessly scrutinized his own position and sought to reconcile his status as a writer with his responsibilities as a leading leftist thinker. Thus, Lu Xun's death resulted in a vacuum, involving as it did the loss of an important voice and model for an emerging generation of politically engaged writers and artists. Ultimately, as W. J. F. Jenner argues, Lu Xun's death in 1936 had a greater impact on China than that of any other figure in the nationalist era with the exception of Sun Yatsen.[27]

Between the years of his involvement with the League of Leftist Writers and his death in 1936, Lu Xun remained active in a variety of aesthetic and intellectual undertakings, which included writing, woodblock printmaking, teaching, public speaking and political activities. This range of activities served, on one level, to keep him preoccupied from thoughts of his own deteriorating health, which could be traced to tuberculosis and to bronchial asthma compounded by years of chain smoking.[28] Lu Xun had long been fatalistic about his own life and seemed resigned to accept his fate, whatever it might be, even after the murder in broad daylight of his friend and associate Yang Quan and the abduction and reported murder of Ding Ling in 1933.[29] While Lu did not actually court death, he understood that a responsible artist living in an age of political turmoil and social instability was obliged to accept the proximity of personal tragedy and death.

Among the activities that most occupied Lu Xun during his final days was the production of woodblock prints accompanied by his association with other, younger artists working in that medium. It was a medium in which Lu Xun excelled and in which he became increasingly engrossed in the 1930s.[30] As with many other cultural activities in which Lu Xun was involved, discussions between woodblock print artists and the exhibitions themselves often took place in the second floor of Uchiyama's bookstore, which continued to be a true cultural center and the focal point of Lu Xun's artistic endeavors. It was also the place where he was most likely to be found by those wishing to meet with China's greatest living literary luminary.

Lu Xun remained, during the final years of his life, prolific in terms of literary production as well. His literary activities were extensive and involved a number of collaborative efforts with fellow writers. Lu Xun had always been a serious translator of foreign literature, both Western and Japanese, and he became during those years the editor of a journal of translated literature called *Yiwen* (Translated Literature). In fact, on the very day that he died, Lu Xun was able to see the most recent installment of his translation of Nicolai Gogol's *Dead Souls*.[31]

Lu Xun also wrote a number of essays during the final months of his life that were intended to be incorporated into several book-length and serial projects which he had undertaken either individually or in conjunction with other writers.[32] It is ironic that Lu Xun should have been so prolific during his final days and that his literary activities should have reached such a frenetic pace during the final months of his life. This increase in literary output can be attributed to his increased awareness of the gravity of his illness and the recognition that his remaining days were limited.[33] Lu Xun, who as a young man had conceived of his literary works as somehow related to the healing processes of his medical studies, now may have envisioned the potential of this flurry of literary activity to revitalize a body racked with pain.

Among the other literary projects that Lu Xun was working on at the time of his death in 1936 were a collection of reminiscences and miscellaneous personal essays along with Feng Xuefeng, which would have contained such works as "My First Teacher" and "Death."[34] He also intended, according to a letter to Cao Jinghua dated May 23, 1936, to write a long essay in order to roundly critique what he perceived to be the corrupt literary politics of his day, which caused him and so many other writers of conscience to suffer.[35]

Lu Xun had also, the year before, written the preface for a collection of observations on contemporary Chinese society by Uchiyama Kanzō entitled *Chūgoku no shitai o kataru* (Talking about the State of China). Lu Xun enthusiastically agreed to write the preface, thereby providing immediate credibility to Uchiyama's work for potential readers. In his preface, Lu Xun introduces Uchiyama to readers, both Chinese and Japanese, who might not be familiar with him:

> The author of this work has for more than twenty years lived in China and has traveled to a variety of places in China where he has encountered people of all classes. Thus, when reading these reminiscences it might be easy to mistakenly believe that this is someone who has always lived in China.[36]

Lu Xun seemed in his later years to revel in the attention lavished on him by foreign writers visiting Shanghai who invariably sought to meet him. More often than not Lu Xun was amenable to such meetings which he seemed to see as an opportunity to act as a cultural ambassador and an apologist for contemporary China to the outside. Among the foreign writers who visited him during this period was George Bernard Shaw. The celebrated 1933 meeting had been arranged via the offices of Kaizō's Yamamoto Sanehiko, who called upon Uchiyama to act as the intermediary.[37]

However, in terms of Sino-Japanese literary relations an even more significant visit was that of Mushanokōji Saneatsu in 1936. Mushanōkoji's ties to the Zhou brothers extended all the way back to their translation of his works in the late teens and twenties, and their association with Mushanokōji via the New Village commune. Yet, though Mushnokōji had welcomed Zhou Zuoren to the New Village in Kyushu and subsequently had met him a number of times, Mushanokōji had never met Lu Xun. Now in 1936, in the last year of Lu Xun's life, Mushanokōji at last had the chance to meet the great writer and cultural giant who had translated his play seventeen years earlier.

In May of 1936, Mushanokōji visited his older brother, who was then working at the Japanese embassy in Germany. On the way back he passed through Shanghai and used that opportunity to visit Uchiyama's bookstore. In keeping with past conventions, it was Uchiyama who arranged this meeting between the two noted writers. In his 1940 travelogue "Kohan no gashō" (The Art Dealer on the Lakeshore) Mushanokōji describes that meeting:

> With Hirayama Hiroshi of the *Shan Nippō* newspaper I first went to call on the proprietor of the Uchiyama Bookstore. After it was reported to Lu Xun that I had arrived, he came immediately to meet me. There was no coldness on his part. He was in high spirits and appeared quite happy to meet me.[38]

The two writers talked about Chinese drama, and their easy conversation moved to a consideration of Western architecture. Eventually their discussion turned to reminiscences of Mushanokōji's play, *The Dream of a Certain Young Man* that Lu Xun had translated all those years earlier, and which, according to Lu Xun and to the delight of Mushanokōji, was still selling. About this encounter with Lu Xun and his own feelings about the chance to interact with China's literary luminary during the final year of his life, Mushanokōji went on to say in the above quoted essay, "Lu Xun was maybe one or two years my senior, but he made me feel like a peer. Or, rather I should say that I felt I matured a year or two simply by being in his presence."[39]

By eschewing any discussion of politics, the two writers, who were just then engrossed with their colleagues in their respective literary communities in very contentious issues regarding the relations between their two nations, were able to gingerly negotiate the high ground of culture and scrupulously avoid the tension that would have inevitably accompanied discussions of politics. Although Lu Xun could not speak freely about politics with Mushanokōji, he could speak openly with Uchiyama Kanzō about such matters. Uchiyama, in fact, was one of the few Japanese with whom Lu Xun felt comfortable discussing the rapidly deteriorating political relations between China and Japan. On the very last day before he died, Lu Xun met with Uchiyama to discuss the disintegrating relations between the two nations, and expressed the desire for China to become stronger militarily in order to foster better relations between the two nations.[40] This level of candor is not something that could have been achieved between Lu Xun and Mushanokōji or virtually any other Japanese with whom Lu Xun was associated.

Lu Xun's last days were characterized by the same ambiguous feelings toward Japan that he had exhibited since his student days in Japan. Like many of the Chinese writers treated in this study, Lu Xun had spent his formative years in Japan and had a deep, visceral affection for Japan which, although shaken by subsequent events in Japan never was eradicated completely. Japan meant a great deal to Lu Xun, and like many of his contemporaries he held up Japan to his protégés as a country that China should emulate in the construction of a modern culture.[41]

Moreover, Lu Xun, along with Uchiyama Kanzō, had relationships with a number of Japanese during his years in Shanghai and often sought solace in their company. He associated with Japanese from many walks of life including some, such as bankers, tourists and businessmen, with whom he probably would not have associated had they been Chinese.[42] It seems that in the company of Uchiyama and other Japanese acquaintances, conversing in Japanese, Lu Xun was at ease and able to resist the temptation to descend into petty squabbles concerning politics and literary factions which often occurred when in the company of other Chinese.[43] One is left to wonder what role Lu Xun might have played along with his friend Uchiyama in sustaining positive relations between the two literary communities had he survived beyond the outbreak of war between China and Japan.

It was evident that Lu Xun relished the attention given him by the Japanese literary world. He understood that his work was taken seriously in Japan and the Japanese *bundan* was willing to countenance his genius separately from his political leanings. The literary establishment in Japan was not threatened by Lu Xun as his Chinese colleagues sometimes appeared to be, nor did his sometimes acerbic personality or political convictions drive Japanese readers away as they did with his Chinese readership.[44]

In Japan, the death of Lu Xun was a major news story, and for those who knew him, his passing came as a great blow insofar as they recognized that his loss would have a profound impact on cultural relations between the two countries. Masuda Wataru, for example, a friend of Lu Xun and translator of his work, found the news difficult to accept, having just received a letter from Lu Xun two days earlier. Chinese writers in Japan at the time of Lu Xun's death such as Xiao Hong and Guo Moruo also grieved for the loss and felt even further alienated from their homeland.

It is interesting to note that even in death Lu Xun's friendship with Uchiyama Kanzō and his ambiguous relationship with Japan continued. It is somehow appropriate that Lu Xun's funeral committee should include Uchiyama and yet that the ceremony itself should be marred by anti-Japanese demonstrations. Japanese invasion was imminent, and with the ensuing war, stockpiles of good will accumulated between the two literary communities were quickly depleted as writers on both sides were forced to make choices about political orientation and modes of engagement. None of these choices permitted reconciliation or engagement with the enemy.

Fateful Choices: Writers' Activities during the War

The events of July 7, 1937 brought to tragic completion the deterioration of Sino-Japanese literary relations signaled in symbolic fashion by the passing of Lu Xun. A brief overview of the activities of the writers treated in this study will demonstrate the range of choices available to Chinese and Japanese writers during the war. By the time that war broke out on that day in 1937, of course, any opportunity for continued healthy interaction had already been exhausted, and the actual outbreak of declared war is best seen as merely the crystallization of factors that had been gaining momentum throughout the interwar period.

Writers were forced, in sometimes dramatic and even violent fashion, to make hard choices vis-à-vis their relation to the other country. Guo Moruo, for instance, cofounder of the Creation Society and leading May Fourth literary voice, felt compelled by Japan's declaration of war on China to abandon his Japanese wife and children and return to China. Shortly after Japan's declaration of war and the fall of Beijing, Guo slipped out of his Tokyo home one evening wearing nothing but a summer kimono and *geta* on his feet. He then surreptitiously boarded a train bound for Kobe where he met a friend who provided him with a change of clothes and passage to China.[45]

For their part, Japanese writers were also forced to write under circumstances that were, by the late thirties, excruciatingly oppressive. Rigid authoritarianism did not permit them to maintain the freedoms of movement and expression that they enjoyed in the 1920s. Writers consequently responded in a plethora of ways, but their reactions fit more-or-less neatly into three distinct categories: resistance to authority, withdrawal from public life and from literary production, or acquiescence to imperialism and collaboration with the military authorities. A brief examination of the writers considered in this study reflects the range of reactions to the increasing pressures exerted by the Japanese military authorities, which demanded nothing less than total compliance and collaboration.

Discussion of the activities and stances of the Japanese writers touched upon in this study must begin with Uchiyama Kanzō whose bookstore remained the final bastion of Japanese and Chinese literary interaction and whose unflagging support of Lu Xun in his last days, despite increasing dangers, was an act of grace that constituted the last truly noble act between the two literary communities.

Uchiyama Kanzō possessed a quality shared by many of the Chinese and Japanese writers of his generation — an innate capacity to negotiate political exigencies and to shift with the ever-changing political landscape in order to survive. Beyond that, Uchiyama, who stood at the epicenter of this web of literary relations, possessed an uncanny ability to extricate himself and those around him from potentially threatening situations. This ability allowed Uchiyama to save Lu Xun and his family at a time when the writer was being pursued by the Guomindang authorities, and it helped him on several occasions during the war years.

Lu Xun's death was not only an event which effectively marked the cession of relations between the two literary communities, it was also a great personal blow for Uchiyama who characterized the period in which he was acquainted with Lu Xun from 1927 to 1936 as the happiest time of his life. Not long after Lu Xun's death, fighting again became fierce in Shanghai in August of 1936 inhibiting the range of cultural activities at Uchiyama's shop. For Uchiyama this disruption coincided with the deterioration of his wife Miki's heart condition. This merging of unfortunate events led to Uchiyama's decision in 1937 to return to Kyoto with his wife in order to receive treatment and convalesce.[46] The two lived at his wife's home in Uji city in Kyoto, and she appeared to benefit from the treatment. By this point in the war foreigners and those who had recently returned from abroad were treated with suspicion. After Uchiyama spoke at a few local schools about contemporary Chinese society he was brought in by the police for questioning.[47] During the second interrogation session he was incarcerated for four days, leading him to decide to return to Shanghai.[48]

Uchiyama was invited in February of the following year to participate in a speaking tour in Northern China by the Welfare Division of the South Manchurian Railroad Company. He agreed to participate in this tour in which he would be speaking to audiences of Japanese living in each of those cities once he was assured that he would only be asked about his personal observations of China.[49] He traveled alone, after sending his ailing wife and family back to Kyoto. His speaking tour included a number of venues, large and small, and covered eighteen cities in one month.[50] For Uchiyama not only was it physically exhausting insofar as he had to contend with the brutal Manchurian winter, but he also had to negotiate the political complexities that he had sought so meticulously to avoid. In Dalian, for example, the final engagement on the tour, he found himself giving a two-hour presentation in front of fewer than fifteen people in a hall that could easily have held an audience of several hundred. Uchiyama later discovered that when his engagement had originally been discussed by the local Japanese authorities, someone had objected to his coming, accusing him of being a member of the Chinese Communist Party. Even though no proof had been submitted by the accuser, the accusation itself had been enough to cast a pall on his lecture.[51] After briefly returning to Kyoto, he and his family returned to Shanghai after an absence of nearly ten months.

In 1941, Uchiyama again used his connections and his charisma to help a friend out of trouble. In December of 1941, Lu Xun's widow, Xu Guangping, who was living with her son on Joffre Boulevard in Shanghai's French Concession, was arrested and incarcerated in an early morning raid of individuals deemed "suspicious" by the authorities. Uchiyama was able to broker her release only after introducing her as the widow of Lu Xun and describing her ongoing work to consolidate his literary legacy and assuring the authorities that he would assume the responsibility of watching over her and her son.[52]

The subsequent war years continued to bring a succession of hardships to Uchiyama who sought to maintain some semblance of normalcy at the bookstore and endeavored to remain the mediator between the two literary communities that he had been for the past two decades. At the war's end in 1945, Uchiyama was one of twenty-five Japanese community leaders chosen via special election to lead in the evacuation and repatriation of Japanese living in and around Shanghai.[53] These representatives had to deal with issues ranging from feeding the substantial numbers of refugees during the evacuation process to providing shelter for the refugees and their possessions while in transit. During the daily meetings of the representatives at the Japanese Club, Uchiyama took a decisive role in the discussions.[54] He also spoke to the returning Japanese and urged them in choosing a path of recovery to follow the example of Switzerland as a nation embracing pacifism and neutrality.[55]

Uchiyama was not among those repatriated in 1945, instead choosing to stay behind in his beloved Shanghai. Nevertheless, Uchiyama could not avoid the political unrest that continued to plague Shanghai as political lines became more firmly drawn. On October 23, 1945, by order of the Guomindang government, the doors and windows of Uchiyama's bookstore were sealed shut. When Uchiyama and some of his employees went to investigate they found one bathroom window open. They slipped inside in order to recover the most valuable books. When some of the employees began to retrieve books from among the second tier items, having already removed the most valuable works, Uchiyama stopped them saying, "Let's stop there. I don't want the Chinese authorities to say that there were no good books in Uchiyama's store."[56]

Uchiyama lasted a few more years in Shanghai but was eventually forced, along with his family and many of the others who had aided in the repatriation of Japanese citizens in 1945, to return to Japan by order of the Guomindang authorities in December of 1947. Machine gun wielding soldiers entered Uchiyama's home on December 6 and told Uchiyama and his family that they were to leave on a designated ship the following day for Japan. Following those orders, Uchiyama and his family prepared their possessions and were unceremoniously evacuated the following day. Many of Uchiyama's Chinese friends and associates were unaware of his forced repatriation until long after the ship had left. Uchiyama Kanzō continued to write about Shanghai, the writers with whom he was associated, and that golden age of literary interaction until his death.

Unlike Uchiyama Kanzō, who quietly but steadfastly opposed the Japanese occupation and exploitation of China, Tanizaki Jun'ichirō chose to vanish during the war years, to submerge himself into the depths of classicism and art-for-art's sake aestheticism from which he could avoid direct involvement in the militarism expected of Japanese writer and artists. Tanizaki's activities and his stance during the war can be seen as the culmination of the author's retreat into the realm of tradition and the exoticism of the East embodied in the Kansai region that had begun with his move to that region ten years earlier. Tanizaki, in fact, had compared the appeal of Kansai to that of China in his essay "Tokyo o omou" (Thinking of Tokyo, 1934):

> What was more, seeing the region for the first time in ten years — I had not walked on Kansai soil since the end of Meiji — I realized that the good features of the ancient East, which one runs across in Peking [Beijing], Nanking [Nanjing], Kiangsu [Jiangsu], or Chekiang [Zhejiang], could still be found around the old capital cities of Japan as well.[57]

For Tanizaki Jun'ichirō, this retreat to Western Japan was at once a retreat into a highly charged aesthetic realm as well as a sojourn to a place far from Tokyo where he could afford to disengage himself from the mounting responsibilities and expectations as an artist. After publishing the charming novel, *Neko to Shōzō to futari no onna* (A Cat, Shōzō and the Two Women, 1936), Tanizaki concentrated on only two large literary projects for the remainder of the war years, apparently biding his time and hoping to remain unobtrusive to the authorities who expected from established writers a certain measure of cooperation and participation in propoganda.[58]

The first major undertaking by Tanizaki during this period was a translation into modern standard Japanese of *The Tale of Genji*. It was a project that he had long considered, and the timing of the project would demand total immersion and commitment on his part that would allow him to truly concentrate on those labors to the exclusion of activities related to the war effort. Tanizaki began the translation in 1935 at the invitation of the editor of *Chūō kōron* (Central Review). He worked with a scholar of classical Japanese on the more thorny textual issues, and the translation appeared in twenty-six installments between 1939 and 1941.[59]

In this translation of *Genji*, the first of three that Tanizaki was eventually to complete, he made an important textual decision in order to appease the censors. He decided to expunge all mention of Prince Genji's illicit affair with Fujitsubo, the consort of his father, the aging emperor. Tanizaki was compelled to submit drafts of each section of his translation to the rightist scholar Yamada Yoshio.[60] Rather than be forced to rewrite passages that had been expurgated by the censors, Tanizaki apparently thought it more prudent to take the initiative to make those deletions himself. This cuckolding of his father by Genji is an extremely critical narrative incident in terms of the development of the story, but Tanizaki readily removed what one critic referred to as the "spinal cord" of the work in order to avoid censorship due to the unflattering portrayal of the imperial institution.[61]

Despite these concessions to the censors, Tanizaki seemed to find the act of translating *Genji* very satisfying. These accommodations to the censors allowed Tanizaki to retreat into an aesthetic realm largely removed from the military which he abhorred.[62] The translation was accomplished while he was living with his third wife and her two sisters in the Hanshin suburb of Sumiyoshi. He built around him a "distinctive world of taste and sensibility" at odds with the drab utilitarianism of the war. This rarified and exotic world of Kansai refinement was to be the setting of the work of fiction that was to occupy his energy for the remainder of the war years, *Sasameyuki* (The Makioka Sisters).

Tanizaki began to write *The Makioka Sisters* in 1942, and the first episodes appeared in *Chūō kōron* in January and March of 1943. However, in place of the next installment of the work in *Chūō kōron*, there appeared a notice explaining that publication of further installments would cease due to national interests "during a time of emergency."[63] The work was banned not because of the presence of an anti-militarist or subversive ideology but rather because of its evident nostalgia for the past and its indifference to Japan's "sacred mission" in Asia that were expected of all works during this period.[64]

Unlike Tanizaki's experience with the translation of *Genji*, in which he compromised his translation to appease the authorities, in the case of *The Makioka Sisters*, Tanizaki did not submit to the demands of the censors. Rather than compromise his work in order to be able to resume publication, Tanizaki chose to continue to work on it discretely and published it privately (the first of three volumes was published privately in 1944).[65] He had no guarantee that the novel would ever be publishable commercially, but he continued to work on the manuscript and carry it with him even as the Allied bombing increased and his family fled first to Atami and later to the small town of Tsuyama in Okayama Prefecture.[66] Tanizaki's persistence and unwillingness to cooperate with the militarists were rewarded only after the war when *The Makioka Sisters* became a best seller in 1948, winning both the *Mainichi* and *Asahi* cultural prizes.[67]

In his own way and on his own terms Tanizaki Jun'ichirō protested the direction that Japan's military government was leading the country by withdrawing into an aesthetic realm that was disconnected from the demands of a country attempting to justify its imperialist ventures. As with Uchiyama Kanzō, Tanizaki made attempts to appease and comply with authorities, but he did not contribute to the militarist efforts. The other three Japanese writers included in this study, Hayashi Fumiko, Mushanokōji Saneatsu and Satō Haruo, all participated, with some greater or lesser degree of apparent jingoistic zeal in Japan's propaganda machine in support of Japan's actions on the continent.

Hayashi Fumiko had a chameleon-like capacity for adapting to new circumstances that confounded writers of lesser resolve. Although associated with the Japanese Communist Party, and despite having been arrested and detained for nine days for having subscribed to the Communist Party newspaper *Akahata* (Red Flag), Hayashi never truly embraced leftist politics.[68] In fact, Hayashi was one of the few Japanese writers associated with the left who was not coerced into performing a *tenkō* renouncing her connection to socialism. Hayashi's indifference to politics and her propensity to go her own way made her embracing of right wing politics in the late thirties all the more puzzling.

In 1937, soon after the China Incident, Hayashi Fumiko became involved in the war effort. In that year, Hayashi was one of only two women writers among a group of twenty-two popular writers chosen by the Ministry of Education to go to the front and write back to readers at home.[69] The members of the Pen Squadron were to provide stimulating accounts of the bravery of Japanese soldiers at the front in order to fan the flames of patriotism in the homeland.

As a member of the Pen Squadron and a correspondent for the *Mainichi Shinbun*, Hayashi observed Japanese military action in China and Southeast Asia from December 1937 until the summer of 1943.[70] It is ironic to note that in 1937, just at the moment that Hayashi was embracing the Japanese patriotic cause and preparing to go to China to chronicle and celebrate Japanese atrocities against the Chinese, the first of two Chinese translations of *Hōrōki* (Diary of a Vagabond) appeared.[71]

Hayashi took pride in the fact that as a correspondent for the *Mainichi Shinbun* she was the first Japanese women in Nanjing after the fall of that city and raced to beat her rival Yoshiya Nobuko in order to be the first Japanese woman journalist in the city of Hangzhou after its capitulation to Japanese troops.[72] After serving in China, Hayashi was sent to Southeast Asia where she observed fighting in Java, Borneo and what is now Vietnam. When in Vietnam, Hayashi stayed in the highland city of Dalat, which later provided some material for her ambitious postwar novel, *Ukigumo* (Drifting Clouds, 1951).[73]

While in China and Southeast Asia, Hayashi wrote stirring accounts of Japanese victories against its enemies the intent of which was to excite the sympathies and raise the morale of the populace. Hayashi's condemnation of the wanton behavior of Western soldiers while at war juxtaposed with her praise for the sacrifices of ordinary Japanese soldiers during these campaigns served to echo crude stereotypes. In this sense, Hayashi's writing stood in stark contrast to such writers as Ishikawa Tatsuzō (1905–1985), whose *Ikite iru heitai* (Living soldiers, 1938) included graphic depictions of the brutality of Japanese soldiers in Nanjing including the massacre of civilians, or the skepticism contained in Ibuse Masuji's *Hana no machi* (City of Flowers, 1942), which treated the Japanese military's extensive utilization of collaborators in Singapore to support Japanese military ventures there and to root out dissenters at any cost.[74]

Hayashi returned to Japan in early summer 1943, adopted a child and traveled around with him to various hot springs resorts in the mountains throughout the duration of the fighting.[75] As soon as the war ended Hayashi resumed her literary activities and her first serialized novel which appeared in the *Mainichi Shinbun* in 1946 was about the issue of Japanese war widows and the hardships that they were forced to endure.[76] The appearance of this novel critical of militarists soon after the war's end suggests that Hayashi never truly embraced the war effort nor felt comfortable with her role in sustaining the fevered pitch of Japanese propaganda. Hayashi was the ultimate survivor, who had been accustomed since her youth of skillfully adapting to whatever particular set of circumstances in which she found herself. She apparently found it easier to simply embrace her role as propagandist than to fight against the authorities and lose her audience and forfeit her ability to write. As soon as it seemed feasible to relinquish her duties to the militarist authorities, she returned to Japan, and in keeping with her personality, never looked back.

Like Hayashi, Mushanokōji Saneatsu, whose youthful credo of humanism and pacifism was so at odds with the rigid Meiji ethical code, became an enthusiastic propagandist and apologist for the Japanese military during the war years. Mushanokōji, who had interpreted Tolstoy's pacifist message for eager audiences both in Japan and China, abandoned those principles in deference to Japan's imperialist project. It was Mushanokōji's wont to ferociously embrace and tirelessly champion particular causes and ideologies with a single-mindedness and tenacity that left no room for compromise and often had the effect of disenchanting friends and even the most ardent among his supporters.

In Mushanokōji's acceptance of the paradigm of the Greater East Asian Co-prosperity Sphere and his enthusiastic support of Japan's invasion of its neighbors he was simply exhibiting the same traits that had made him such a charismatic and popular figure among Chinese intellectuals during the May Fourth period. However, the universal love that Mushanokōji advocated during the teens and twenties was reduced, during the war years, to a pan-Asianism with Japan in a position of leadership. In one of the essays included in the collection, "Daitōa sensō shikan" (Private Views on the Great East Asian War) Mushanokōji wrote excitedly about the possibilities generated by Japan's attack on Pearl Harbor and the Japanese military advances on the continent, "Now is a time when I can gladly die: this is literally a holy age. I was certainly born at a fortunate time!"[77] Although Mushanokōji did not join the Pen Squadron, he nevertheless contributed to wartime propaganda through a steady barrage of inflammatory radio broadcasts and articles fulminating against the Allies and urging steadfast support of the war effort by ordinary Japanese. With the same naiveté that Mushanokōji had exhibited in the New Village experiment, he now accepted, uncritically, the purposes of Japan's "sacred war."[78] Mushanokōji also participated in and took a leading role in the Greater East Asian Writer's Union and attended their meetings in Tokyo and Nanjing.[79]

As the end of the war drew near and Japan's demise became clear, Mushanokōji left Tokyo and evacuated his family to Akita Prefecture. When the war ended, Mushanokōji was tried and convicted as a category G war criminal in July 1946 for having made public statements on behalf of the militarist government.[80] Although his war criminal status was not rescinded until August 1951, as soon as the war ended Mushanokōji embraced the cause of postwar democracy with the same apparent enthusiasm with which he had embraced Japan's militarism during the war. He also expressed remorse for his role in the war effort. In an autobiographical work called *Jibun no aruita michi* (The Road I Have Walked) he said, "When I look back now, it was foolish to write such books and to cooperate with the militarists. I feel ashamed of myself."[81]

The case of Satō Haruo's capitulation and collaboration to the militarists is more problematic than that of either Hayashi Fumiko, whose powerful survival mechanism allowed her to adapt to the exigencies of even the most trying circumstances, or Mushanokōji Saneatsu, who so readily and enthusiastically embraced causes that he considered somehow "sacred." Satō Haruo, the great aesthete and modernist, in many ways as fiercely independent and inclined to flaunt authority as Tanizaki Junichirō, seemed more likely in the thirties to choose Tanizaki's path of retreat into aestheticism than enthusiastic cooperation with the militarists. Nevertheless, to the shock and chagrin of his acquaintances in the Chinese literary community, it was the latter path that he chose.

From 1938, the year in which "Ajia no ko" appeared, Satō entered the service in the Japanese Navy in the Creative Writer's Division. During his term of enlistment, not only did Satō write reports of the war, but other facets of his literary output were also influenced by his newly acquired role, and he produced several collections of patriotic poems. Toward the end of the war, Satō Haruo attempted to find Yu Dafu in Singapore via the offices of *Kaizō*, perhaps suggesting a desire on Satō's part to salvage his friendship with Yu and to broach a reconciliation. Such an attempt was rendered futile by Yu's tragic death in Sumatra, and one is left to speculate about the ramifications that reconciliation between the two men might have had on the cultural relations between the two communities. Although in the postwar period Japanese writers such as Takeda Taijun (1912–1976) and Inoue Yasushi (1907–1996) continued to travel to China and produce fiction set in China or concerned with Chinese history, the two literary communities never again attained the same proximity that had been achieved in the interwar period.

Chinese writers, like their Japanese counterparts, were forced to choose political and ideological sides with the outbreak of war and the breakdown in relations between the two literary communities. The civil strife in China throughout the war years complicated their reaction to the Japanese threat. Nevertheless, all of the Chinese writers treated in this study resisted the Japanese threat either subtly, as in the case of Zhou Zuoren or more fiercely, as in the cases of Guo Moruo and Ding Ling. Finally, Yu Dafu was the one writer from among those considered in this study to become a true casualty to the fractured relations between the two literary communities.

Guo Moruo's escape from Japan and abandonment of his Japanese wife and children described earlier marked his dramatic return to the Chinese literary scene and to the realm of political engagement. The year prior to the outbreak of war and of Guo's return to China, Guo had welcomed his old friend Yu Dafu into his Tokyo home. In November of 1936, Yu suddenly appeared at the door of Guo's home, calling out to his old friend in his familiar fashion that Guo remembered from the earliest days of the Creation Society in Japan.[82] During his visit to Japan, Yu spoke at a variety of schools and organizations in Tokyo and attended an event in his honor hosted by Kaizō Publishing. Nevertheless, critical changes were underway in both China and Japan that were making such visits increasingly difficult, and would soon render such interactions impossible.[83]

After Guo's flight from Japan in 1937 following the outbreak of war, he arrived in Shanghai to a warm welcome from members of the literary community. In Shanghai Guo was met by fellow former Creationist and eminent member of the Communist Party Pan Hannian (1906–1977). Pan helped to arrange for lodging for Guo in Shanghai's French Concession.[84] While in Shanghai, Guo learned that his wife and oldest son had spent a month in jail and had been tortured there after his escape and that all of his manuscripts had been confiscated from his Tokyo home. When Guo asked the Chinese Embassy in Japan to intercede on his behalf so that his wife and children could join him in China, his request was denied.[85]

The tragedy of separation from his family seemed to galvanize Guo's commitment to the Communist Party and to his anti-Japanese activities. Guo went South to Guangzhou and later to Wuhan where he accepted an appointment to the Third Bureau in the Political Affairs Ministry and placed in charge of propaganda.[86] He continued to serve in that capacity and remained one of the most vociferous and vocal opponents of Japanese imperialism throughout the war.

Like Guo, Ding Ling too, after suffering the loss of her husband Hu Yepin at the hands of Guomindang in 1930 and after being kidnapped and presumed dead in 1933 only to reappear, emerged rejuvenated and became one of the leading literary voices in the late thirties. Throughout the war period not only did Ding Ling's literary output continue unabated, but she also occupied several important roles within the CCP. The tribulations of the early thirties convinced Ding Ling to redouble her efforts on behalf of the Party. Ding was active in the League of Leftist Writers and edited *Beidou*. In 1937, she joined the Communist leaders in Yenan where she participated in the war of resistance against Japan.[87] In the same year, Ding was appointed corps leader of the Xibei War Zone Service Corps, thereby becoming more involved in revolutionary activities.[88]

It is ironic that in the late thirties, just as Hayashi Fumiko was being translated into Chinese, Ding Ling's work was being translated into Japanese. The literary communities had moved inexorably apart, but interest in literary works produced by the other community remained strong. Translations of a number of Ding Ling's short stories appeared in translation in large circulation journals in the late thirties, and *Miss Sophie's Diary* in the first book-length translation of Ding's work by Amizaki Hideo in 1938 as part of the *Tairiku bungaku sōsho* (Compendium of Continental Literature) series.[89]

In May of 1938, Ding began to serve as an editor of *Jiefang ribao* (Liberation Daily), and in June of that year she produced her best known story from that phase of her career, *Wo zai Xiacun de shihou* (When I Was at Xia Village) which appeared in *Zhongguo wenhua* (Chinese Culture).[90] Starting in May of 1942 Ding participated in the Forum on Art and Literature, part of the Zhengfeng Movement in Yenan in which communist artists and writers, under the guidance of Mao Zedong proclaimed that all art, though it should serve political ends, should not be mere propaganda. Ding continued to publish in the *Liberation Daily*, where her contributions won the praise of communist leaders, including Mao.[91] At the end of the year, Ding left Yenan to go to the Northeast where she continued her literary and anti-Japanese activities throughout the war.[92]

Guo Moruo's and Ding Ling's activities during the war evidenced a clear position of resistance to Japanese imperialism. The case of Zhou Zuoren was more complex and problematic. The question of Zhou Zuoren's collaboration with the Japanese during the war continues, as Lu Yan argues in *Re-understanding Japan*, to remain a "divisive and much-debated issue."[93] At the end of July in 1937, a mere three weeks after the Marco Polo Bridge incident, Beijing fell into Japanese hands, and by December the occupying army formed a provisional government. Zhou, given the opportunity to flee to southern China along with a number of intellectuals, chose to remain in Beijing at the home that he now called *Kuzhu zhai* (Living-in-bitterness studio). Despite entreaties from colleagues and from the general public to flee while he had the opportunity, Zhou decided to remain in Beijing, explaining in the pages of the journal *Yuzhou feng* (Cosmic Wind) that he had to stay there in order to protect and sustain his large family with its many dependents.[94]

As Zhou was a writer and prominent intellectual figure who enjoyed a great deal of prestige in China in that era, many people took exception to his decision not to flee occupied Beijing and demonstrate solidarity with the anti-Japanese sentiments of the intellectual community.[95] The Chinese intellectual community directed even stronger disapproval at Zhou for his next decision. In 1938 news of Zhou's participation in a cultural forum in occupied Beijing sponsored by the *Osaka Mainichi Shinbun* was publicized among Chinese writers. Eighteen of them, including Yu Dafu, were so incensed that they publicly admonished Zhou in an open letter, calling him a "great traitor to the nation." Although Zhou undoubtedly chafed beneath those charges, he remained steadfastly in Beijing. While residing at the Living-in-bitterness studio, Zhou worked on a translation of Greek mythology and accepted a visiting professorship at Yenching University that allowed him to lecture a few hours each week.[96]

On New Year's Day morning in 1939 an incident occurred that severely affected Zhou. Two men broke into Zhou's home and attempted to assassinate the writer. In the process, several people were injured, including Zhou who was grazed by a bullet, and a rickshaw puller who later died from his wounds.[97] Although the perpetrators were never caught and the motives for the assassination attempt remained a puzzle, Zhou himself secretly suspected the Japanese and saw it as a final warning from the occupiers to cooperate or risk reprisal.[98] A mere twelve days later, Zhou reluctantly accepted an appointment as curator of Beijing University Library, and in 1941 Zhou became a member of Wang Jingwei's (1883–1944) puppet regime's North Chinese Political Committee.[99]

This collaboration with the puppet regime and with the occupying Japanese authorities served to confirm the dire assumptions of many of Zhou's former colleagues. In his official capacity, Zhou visited Tokyo in 1943 and called upon his old friend Mushanokōji Saneatsu with whom he had developed such strong bonds at the New Village decades earlier (see Photo 4, p. 154). When the war ended Zhou was arrested, tried for treason, and given a ten-year sentence.[100] In subsequent years, the perception of Zhou was as a collaborator and traitor who betrayed his country in order to serve the Japanese. In August of 1966, members of the Red Guard broke into his Beijing residence and made him their prisoner. He died under appalling conditions in May of 1967 at the age of 82.[101]

In the 1980s memoirs of those closest to Zhou during the occupation period revealed that he only accepted the position in the Ministry of Education after being persuaded to by both the Communists and the Guomindang in order to thwart the ascendancy of Miao Bin, a candidate for that same position who was an active leader of the Japanese propaganda organization, the New People Society.[102] Zhou apparently felt that by filling that position himself he could prevent Miao Bin from further indoctrination of young Chinese. Until his death, Zhou vehemently denied ever betraying his nation.[103]

Between 1940 and 1943, Zhou Zuoren produced a series of essays about Confucianism in which he subtly conveyed his opposition to the Japanese occupation.[104] It may seem ironic that Zhou, the great iconoclast of the May Fourth period, should turn to Confucian values in order to protest the ideological claims of the propagandist New People Movement. In fact, his was a clarion call toward a truer Confucian value system, stripped of ideological trappings, which in turn echoed the humanitarian and communal values of the New Village Movement that had once enthralled him. Although he was taken to task for what seemed his criticism of the Japanese "New Order" by members of the Literature Patriotic Association (Bungaku hōkokukai) including Kataoka Teppei (1894–1944), he found many other defenders among the Japanese including members of the White Birch School such as Mushanokōji Saneatsu and Nagayo Yoshirō, who offered letters of support.[105] Although Zhou's collaboration with the Japanese authorities remains a contentious issue, it is clear that in his own way he sought to combat Japanese imperialism while remaining true to his ideological roots.

Yu Dafu, whose tragic fate so paradoxically came to symbolize the demise of relations between the two literary communities, sought during the final decade of his life to oppose Japanese imperialism, while clinging to the vestiges of that failing relationship. Yu's attempt to balance his attachment to Japan with his outspoken opposition to Japanese imperialism was in many ways more puzzling and difficult to explain even than Zhou Zuoren's complicity with the Japanese. The intricacies involved in maintaining that stance led to flight, exile, and eventually to death.

In 1936, Yu visited Japan. It was during that visit that he called on his old friend Guo Moruo, in the encounter described earlier. During the 1936 visit, Yu and Guo were invited to attend a gathering in Tokyo of writers that was attended by, among others, Hayashi Fumiko whom Yu had met in the early 1930s in Shanghai (see Photo 5, p. 155). It was also during this visit that he became reacquainted with Satō Haruo. While Yu's anti-imperialist position was evident in his role as co-founder of the League of Leftist Writers, in no way did it signal his complete disassociation from colleagues in Japan. Yu had been invited by the *Yomiuri shimbun* to participate in a symposium concerning contemporary Chinese literature which was held in Taipei the month following Yu's sojourn in Japan.[106] The event took place at the Taiwan Railway Hotel, and each day's activities was recorded in the *Taiwan shiminbao* newspaper, a co-sponsor of the event, from

December 24 until December 29.¹⁰⁷ In the introduction of Yu Dafu on the first day of the event, he was described as a leading light in Chinese literature, second only to Lu Xun in stature. The ostensible goal of the symposium was to discuss contemporary literary trends in both China and Japan while avoiding political questions. Other participants in the symposium included writers and literary critics from both countries along with representatives from both the *Asahi shimbun* and *Mainichi shimbun* newspapers.

The intention of eschewing political issues was quickly abandoned on the first day when a participant named Huang Deshi suggested that whereas literature formerly was equated with values, it could now be equated with politics. Yu expressed agreement with Huang's observation and then introduced the topic of protectionist literature with recent examples of leftist literature by Mao Dun (1896–1981) and Lao She (1899–1978).¹⁰⁸

During the following day's discussion, asked whether he perceived any contradiction between writing literature and serving in the government, Yu replied that he did not believe any such contradiction existed and that literature written in a political vacuum, at a remove from society and its problems, was poor literature. But when reminded by Huang Deshi that in the preface of his collection *The Past* Yu had written that all great literature was no more than the record of the individual writer's experience, Yu made no attempt to rescind his earlier statement but, on the contrary, reiterated his belief that all of his stories were expressions of himself.

On the final day, Yu reexamined some of the parallels between the two literary worlds and stressed the need for a positive dialogue between writers on both sides. He continued by citing some of the foreign influences on his own writing which included, by his reckoning, the nineteenth-century Russian novel and Japanese literature of the teens and twenties to which he was exposed as a student in Japan. He closed his remarks by stating that the protectionist literature that was flourishing in Chinese literature of the day should not be seen as anti-Japanese but as anti-Imperialist.¹⁰⁹

Yu Dafu would have his last opportunity to visit Japan in 1937, as recounted by Guo Moruo in an essay from that year. Thereafter, Satō Haruo visited China on two occasions, for two weeks in May of 1937 and for about a month in 1938. The May trip was sponsored by the Japanese government and was spent in northern China, whereas in the September journey he visited Shanghai and Hangzhou.¹¹⁰ It was during this same year, 1938, that Satō's "Ajia no ko" appeared. Yu, meanwhile, left Shanghai at the end of 1938 and fled to Singapore.

In 1939, Yu wrote an essay in which he assessed contemporary Japanese writers in regard to their stance toward China before and after the invasion. In the essay, entitled "Riben de qinlue zhanzheng yu zuojia" (The Japanese War of Invasion and Writers), Yu divided contemporary Japanese writers into three types.

The first type was composed of aesthetes who remained true to their art-for-art's sake approach and avoided engagement in political issues, such as Shiga Naoya and Tanizaki Junichirō. The second type were leftist writers, many of whom, Yu regretfully informs his readers, have "converted" to the right. The third category was composed of writers associated with the right wing from the beginning who willfully served the militarists.[111] According to Yu's classification, both Satō Haruo and Hayashi Fumiko fell into the second class of writers.[112] His essay ends on this final prophetically ironic note:

> We are not far from the advent of a new age. However, in order to reach that age we must first eliminate these cultural executioners, so that in the future we can support in our neighboring country the return to an environment promoting justice and peace which will in turn give birth to a new literary community with a truly global vision.[113]

In the 1940s Yu's anti-imperialist stance, articulated in typically uncompromising fashion in his increasingly frequent essays, placed him in a precarious position with the Japanese authorities. Yu was forced to flee. He arrived in Singapore in 1939 and soon assumed the position of editor of the *Xingzhou ribao* (Singapore Daily).[114] While in Singapore, Yu became even more ardently committed to the anti-Japanese propaganda campaign and found in Singapore's overseas Chinese community a variety of outlets for his passionate denunciations of Japanese imperialism. Beside his writings, which regularly appeared in the *Singapore Daily* and other venues, Yu served in the Overseas Chinese Relief Fund and acted as editor for the *Huaqiao zhoubao* (Overseas Chinese Weekly), a journal dedicated to anti-Japanese propaganda.[115]

During the war, another Japanese writer with whom Yu was acquainted, Ibuse Masuji (1898–1993) was sent to Singapore as a correspondent for the newspaper *Shōnan taimuzu* (Shōnan Times). Ibuse had learned that Yu had fled Shanghai and that he was somewhere in Singapore. Ibuse recounted that at around the time that Singapore fell to Japan in February of 1942 Satō Haruo had visited Yamamoto Sanehiko of Kaizō to enlist his aid in tracking down Yu Dafu.[116] Yamamoto had personal ties with a number of Chinese writers and, also sensing that Yu was in imminent danger, gathered together some of his Chinese employees at Kaizōsha's Singapore office and had them help to search for Yu.

On February 14, 1942, Yu fled a besieged Singapore with eighteen other prominent Chinese intellectuals and, after several close calls with the Japanese, arrived in the city of Padang on southern Sumatra.[117] Taking residence in the vicinity of Padang in the coastal town of Bukit Tinggi, Yu adopted the alias Zhao Lian and, posing as a local businessman, started a rice wine distillery with one of his associates. The Zhaoyi Distillery, as it was called, produced several wines sold under the names "First Love" and "Taibai", which were popular with the Japanese troops garrisoned in the area.[118]

Due to Yu's presence at the distillery and through his various interactions with local politicians and businessmen, his proficiency in Japanese eventually became known to the military leadership. After various protestations, in the latter part of 1942 Yu eventually was coerced by the local Japanese authorities into helping with the interrogation of Chinese suspects. In keeping with Yu's lifelong capacity to successfully negotiate difficult and dangerous situations, it is telling to note that as a translator he would intentionally mistranslate suspects' statements in order to reduce their culpability and then go out carousing with the Japanese interrogators after the day's sessions were complete.[119]

In 1943, Yu was relieved of his duties as an interpreter for the Japanese authorities on the basis of medical certification that he was suffering from tuberculosis provided by a doctor whom he had bribed.[120] In September of 1943 Yu Dafu, who was now 48, married a local woman who bore him a son. In early 1944 Bukit Tinggi became the headquarters for the Japanese forces in the Sumatra region, and surveillance of potential threats to Japanese sovereignty in the region became more intense. Toward that end, the Japanese authorities employed a Chinese spy named Hong Genpei whose sole responsibility was to help round up anti-Japanese leaders who had fled after the fall of Singapore. Hong quickly identified the businessman Zhao Lian as the prominent writer and anti-Japanese activist Yu Dafu.[121]

On the evening of August 29, 1945, nearly two weeks after the war had ended, Yu gathered together with various other prominent overseas Chinese leaders to discuss, among other issues, matters pertaining to repatriation of Chinese refugees in the region and details of a parade to welcome the Allied forces into the town.[122] During the meeting a local young man came and called Yu away. Yu Dafu, whose wife was to give birth to their second child the following day, went off with the young man and was never seen again. Hu Yuzhi, a fellow writer and friend of Yu who was with him during those final days, reported his disappearance to the authorities.[123]

By the time of Yu's disappearance and probable death the period of constructive intercourse between the two literary communities was long over, a half remembered dream of a better age. Yu's death was the death knell of that relationship, the tragic coda to a lost era.

Return to the Brush 153

Photo 1 Uchiyama Bookstore on Sichuan Road. By permission of Uchiyama Magaki, president of Uchiyama Shoten, Tokyo.

Photo 2 Lu Xun (left) and Uchiyama Kanzō, Shanghai, 1933. By permission of the Lu Xun Museum in Shanghai.

154 *Beyond Brushtalk*

Photo 3 Tanizaki Jun'ichirō in Shanghai, 1926. Front row, first from left, Tian Han; third from left, Tanizaki Jun'ichirō; far right, Tang Lin. Back row, fourth from left, Ouyang Yuqian. Source: Itō Toramaru et. al, *Tian Han zai Riben*. Beijing: Renmin wenxue chubanshe, 1997.

Photo 4 Zhou Zuoren (left) and Mushanokōji Saneatsu in Japan, 1943. Source: Imai Nobuo, ed., *Shinchō Nihon bungaku arubamu: Mushanokōji Saneatsu*, vol. 10. Tokyo: Shinchōsha, 1984.

Photo 5 Yu Dafu in Japan, 1936. Front row, second from left, Hayashi Fumiko; third from left, Yu Dafu; fourth from left, Guo Moruo. Source: Yu Yun, *Wo de fuqin Yu Dafu*. Taipei: Lanting shudian, 1986.

Photo 6 Tian Han in Tokyo, 1927. From left, Satō Haruo, Mushanokōji Saneatsu, Tian Han, Lei Zhen. Source: Itō Toramaru et. al, *Tian Han zai Riben*. Beijing: Renmin wenxue chubanshe, 1997.

Epilogue: Dream of a Dream

> Drunken tyranny rules the world
> And some men change their tune.
> After the havoc of the storm
> Trees and flowers are bare.
> From "Thorns cover the plain"[1]
> By Lu Xun

The period treated in this study was the age of Taishō Democracy and post-May Fourth idealism; it was an age in which anything seemed possible. There was a naiveté and innocence to the age that provided fertile ground for these literary relations. For this degree of interaction to be possible, writers had to be willing to turn a blind eye to the increasingly dire nature of relations between the two nations. May Fourth writers had been among the vanguard of revolutionary social and cultural change in China and were excruciatingly aware of the increasing menace of Japanese imperialism. Japanese writers, for their part were forced to ply their craft against an increasingly fragmented social backdrop. The thirties brought a worldliness and uncompromising jingoism that made this conciliatory position less and less tenable for both sides.

In 1919 none of the writers treated in this study, Chinese or Japanese, would have dared to imagine the bloody conflict between the two countries that lay ahead. They chose instead to believe in the possibilities of constructive engagement. Each writer sought, through interaction with the other literary community and through the search for aesthetic common ground, an antidote for conflict and a resolution of troubling political and ideological differences. What united all writers, Chinese and Japanese, in this study regardless of political stance or the level of the dedication to national interests was a fierce desire to survive in an age of political tumult. Moreover, all of the subjects of this study were, first and foremost, writers who clung to a sense of mission to contribute to the creation of a new literature. In the search for a modern vernacular literature they eagerly cast aside ancient prejudices and inherited hierarchies and sought and found real common ground with writers from across the sea. They were willing to transcend the burden of tradition as embodied in the writing brush and in classical Chinese prose in order to communicate directly.

In the 1920s, writers from both literary communities had succeeded in overcoming the restrictions of brushtalk and were meeting for rich and varied cultural exchange. Much of the exchange, appropriately, took place in Shanghai, East Asia's most international city, and the hub of that interchange was Uchiyama Kanzō's Shanghai bookshop. Parallels, thematic and formal, emerged between such writers as Ding Ling and Hayashi Fumiko and between older more established writers such as Lu Xun and Arishima Takeo. More significantly, friendly exchanges developed between such sets of writers as Yu Dafu and Satō Haruo, Zhou Zuoren and Mushanokōji Saneatsu, and Tian Han and Tanizaki Jun'ichirō. At the epicenter of this complex web of interrelations stood the friendship between Uchiyama Kanzō and Lu Xun, a friendship tested and steeled in the fires of political intrigue and personal loss, a friendship which bound the communities together even as the irrevocable rift between them widened in the thirties, a friendship which only ended with Lu Xun's death in 1936 on the eve of the catastrophic war that would finally spell the end of those relations.

Ideological Polarization and Literary Disengagement

By the late thirties, writers could no longer pretend, even temporarily, that it was possible to disentangle cultural interchange from the complexities of politics. What Yu Dafu said at the end of the decade, when the two countries were already at war, could easily be applied to the relationship between the two communities in the 1930s. Yu had fled to Malaya from Shanghai along with other Chinese artists and writers where they formed a vibrant intellectual and artistic community. In speaking of the obligations of the artist toward society and nation, Yu had the following to say, "There should be no dividing line between politicians, the military and the intellectuals."[2]

The level of intercourse achieved by the Chinese and Japanese literary communities during the interwar period seems particularly remarkable when one considers the nearly complete breakdown of relations between the two communities that followed. In fact, there remained some notable examples of interaction between Chinese and Japanese writers during the war and even in the postwar period. For example, Kaji Wataru (1903–1982), who had been a friend of Lu Xun's in Shanghai during Lu Xun's final years, maintained a lively exchange with Hu Feng (1902–1985), a literary critic and protégé of Lu Xun's who produced the literary journal *Qiyue* (July) between 1937 and 1941. In maintaining such an exchange, the two writers seemed to be carrying on in the spirit of Lu Xun and Uchiyama Kanzō. Examples can also be cited of exchanges between Chinese and Japanese writers in Manchuria during the war. Moreover, there were several highly politicized visits by older established Chinese writers like Guo Moruo to Japan in the 1950s. Nevertheless, the period of truly vital interaction between the two communities must be said to have ended in 1937. It was not until the 1980s that writers from the two communities began once again to seek out writers from the other community and commenced, tentatively at first, to re-establish relations with writers across the East Sea.

A milestone in the rapprochement between the two literary communities in recent years was the lecture delivered by Ōe Kenzaburō (1935–) upon receiving the Nobel Prize for Literature in 1994. In his lecture entitled "Aimaina Nihon no watashi" (Japan, the Ambiguous and Myself), after describing how he had been influenced as a young man by the courage of his mentor, the French literary scholar Watanabe Kazuo, to stand up to authority, Ōe describes the kinship that he feels with other East Asian writers including Chinese and Korean writers in a "fraternity" of like-minded artists. He concludes by sharing concerns about the fate of Chinese literary colleagues in the unsettled climate of Post-Tiananmen Square Incident China.[3]

As social change swept across China in the late 1980s and early 1990s and Chinese writers gained access to foreign literature that had been denied them in the Maoist and immediate post-Mao era, young writers began to look for models on which to fashion a new literature. Just as Chinese writers had looked to the Japanese "pure literature" of Akutagawa and Tanizaki in the 1920s and 1930s for direction, they now found themselves looking at Post-Modernist works such as Yoshimoto Banana's (1964–) *Kitchin* (Kitchen, 1987) and Murakami Haruki's *Hitsuji o meguru bōken* (Wild Sheep Chase, 1982) in order to give expression to the frustrating complexities and apparent irrationality of postmodern existence.[4] The scholar Xing Lingjun suggests that in the cultural milieu of China in the 1990s writers were particularly receptive to the literary style of Murakami Haruki (1949–), and his novel *Noruwei no mori* (Norwegian Wood, 1987) was held out as an achieved model of Neorealism (*Xinxieshizhuyi*). Furthermore, Xing proposes that Murakami has continued to influence the direction of Chinese literature in the past two decades.[5]

Currently, Japanese readers are as familiar with contemporary Chinese writers as Chinese readers are with Japanese writers, and the translation of contemporary literary works in both countries takes place at an unprecedented pace. Mo Yan (1955–), whose highly acclaimed novel *Hong gaoliang* (Red Sorghum, 1987) was awarded the 17th annual Fukuoka Asian Literature Prize in 2006, is as popular and critically acclaimed in Japan as he is in the West, and films based on his novels including *Red Sorghum,* which was awarded a prize at the Berlin Film Festival in 1988, are similarly highly regarded. Gao Xingjian (1940–), author of *Ling shan* (Ghost Mountain, 1989) and *Yige ren de shengjing* (One Man's Bible, 1998) and recipient of the 2000 Nobel Prize for Literature, is an author as widely known and respected in Japan for his courageous activities in exile as for his literary achievements.

The mutual interest expressed by Chinese and Japanese writers in recent years and the ready availability of translations of contemporary authors from the other country certainly hearkens back to the mutual interest in the other literary community of the interwar period, but what is conspicuously absent today is the level of interaction between the two literary communities and the shared sense of the existence of a unique East Asian fraternity of writers that existed in the interwar period, Ōe Kenzaburo's noble sentiments notwithstanding.[6]

The era of cultural interaction between China and Japan that is the subject of this book, though short-lived, is nevertheless noteworthy for several reasons. Writers in the two communities were forced to look beyond the borders of their aesthetic realm and to observe questions, both artistic and political, from the perspective of the other. Moreover, ultimately as much as Japanese and Chinese writers evinced affinities for Western writers and literary schools, they were never able to forge such connections with communities of writers in the West.

Furthermore, literary relations in this period were part of the larger web of Sino-Japanese interrelations which were cultural, economic, and, of course, political. Politicians as diverse as Konoe Fumimaro, Sun Yat-sen, and Katsura Taro (1848–1913) all, at one time or another, enlisted the "same culture, same race" argument in regard to Sino-Japanese relations for political purposes. In intellectual circles, periodicals such as *Heichao* (Black Tide), an organ for discussion of Sino-Japanese relations published in Shanghai starting in 1919, and educational institutions such as Dongya dongwen shuyuan (East Asia Common Culture Academy) in Shanghai, demonstrated the relative importance attached to understanding the other. It was in this environment that writers from both sides of the divide courageously sought out one another and communicated shared objectives.

Chinese writers in the interwar period often knew Japan intimately from their years of study there. A writer such as Tian Han, who had spent much of his youth in Japan and had been weaned on the values of Japanese literature, was able to move easily between the two literary communities (see Photo 6, p. 155). Confident in their knowledge of Japan, the Japanese language and of contemporary Japanese literature, they boldly courted the Japanese literary community and forged relations that served as a catalyst for a number of important changes in a recently established *baihua* literature. On the other hand, those Japanese writers who ventured to China during the interwar period were justifiably awed by the welcome they received from their Chinese counterparts and by the depth of knowledge about Japanese literature on the part of the Chinese writers whom they encountered. Many Japanese writers arrived in China with limited expectations and left China firm believers in the possibility of the power of literary exchange. The feelings of respect that developed were mutual, and the interest in counterparts in the other literary community was reciprocated. Japanese writers came to recognize the existence of a vibrant community of young, dynamic writers in the Chinese literary community who were poised to provide leadership in a vigorous new era of literary efflorescence.

May Fourth Chinese writers found through their familiarity with Japan a fully realized contemporary culture and society, which provided a fitting paradigm on which to model their own dreams of modernity. In Japan they discovered a thoroughly modern vernacular literature, a literature created in East Asia, but tempered in the fires of modern Western aesthetics. The Chinese writers who perceived Japan as a model were savvy enough to recognize some of the significant differences between the two aesthetic traditions, and were willing to accept the Japanese model as nothing more than a practical template on which to superimpose their own radical ideas for a highly politicized and thoroughly modern literature.

During the interwar period, a group of writers, Chinese and Japanese, dared to dream. In attempting to realize that dream they created a milieu of cultural exchange so vital and vibrant, so multidimensional and mutually beneficial, that its influences were felt long after that period of direct exchange ended. The result of the termination of those relations in the late thirties was the emergence between the two literary communities and between the nations themselves of layers of denial, suspicion, resentment, and enmity, which resonate even to the present day.[7]

Nevertheless, the perceptions of the writers from both communities who participated in those exchanges were forever altered by their encounters with the other. The interwar period was, at its best, a period of hope and optimism. It is evident in the declarations of affinity produced at the outset of the period when a writer like Mushanokōji could say the following in regard to the young Chinese who read his translated work:

> I hope that my fears are their fears, that my joys are their joys, that my hopes are their hopes, and that in the future we may strive side-by-side toward common goals.[8]

Writers in the war period were attempting to respond to an increasingly volatile situation. Tanizaki Jun'ichirō, in "Yesterday and Today" offered the following:

> For writers like us, the political collision between our two countries, the economic imbalance, the popular boycotts of goods — those things that are destined to happen, must run their course, and writers are in no position to effect those things.[9]

When looking back on that era from the depths of war, Tanizaki still clung to the belief that the end of the conflict would bring a return to an age of engagement between Chinese and Japanese writers. Ironically, that hope was tied to the brush. Tanizaki's belief that things would improve was inspired by a young Chinese poet named Tang Lin, whom Tanizaki met during his visit to Ouyang Yuqian's home in 1926.

> There are often times when I whisper to myself the couplet from the poem that I had memorized: "Looking at the faces of others/one catches glimmers of the divine." At those times my thoughts drift back to recollections of the people I met on that distant evening.[10]

The dream of long-term engagement and mutual support ultimately remained unrealized. However, for a brief period, writers sought in the companionship of their art a safe haven and were able to transcend ancient prejudices and traditional modes of communication to engage in a dialogue beyond the conventions of brushtalk that enriched both sides and informed mutual conceptions of modernity and the role of the writer in a changed cultural landscape.

Notes

Introduction

1. Joshua Fogel, "Japanese Literary Travelers in Prewar China," *Harvard Journal of Asiatic Studies* 49: 2 (1989), 578.
2. It must be admitted that increasingly in East Asia, as elsewhere, spoken English is serving the intercessory function formerly served by written classical Chinese. Nevertheless, I witnessed my wife, who is Japanese and cannot speak Chinese, communicate via written characters at the market and elsewhere when we were living in Wenzhou, China.
3. Robert Borgen, "The Japanese Mission to China, 801–806," *Monumenta Nipponica* 37: 1 (Spring 1982), 1.
4. This type of communication within China was widespread until the advent of compulsory education made standard Chinese, *putonghua*, nearly universal.
5. Jonathan W. Best, "Diplomatic and Cultural Contacts between Paekche and China," *Harvard Journal of Asiatic Studies* 42: 2 (December 1982), 444.
6. Ibid., 449.
7. In the Six Dynasties period, this granting of titles was essentially a symbolic act, and there were ultimately few responsibilities incumbent upon either side. Ibid., 449.
8. Ibid., 448.
9. Ibid., 451.
10. Ibid., 451.
11. Ibid., 468.
12. Robert Borgen, *Sugawara no Michizane and the Early Heian Court* (Honolulu: University of Hawai'i Press, 1994), 6.
13. Ibid., 6.
14. Ibid., 227.
15. Ibid., 19.
16. Ibid., 2.
17. Borgen, "The Japanese Mission to China," 2.
18. Ibid., 4.
19. Ibid., 11.
20. The memorial to Kūkai in Xian is located at the Qinglongsi Temple southeast of the old city walls. The memorial jointly commemorates the contributions of Kūkai and

his master, the Chinese monk Huiguo. Interestingly, though it is a relatively modest temple by the grand standards of Xian, and rarely visited by most tourists, it is considered a must-see for Japanese visitors to the city.
21. Borgen, *Sugawara no Michizane*, 34.
22. Ibid., 97.
23. Ibid., 260.
24. The degree of Parhae's desire to be recognized by Japan can be gauged by the fact that they sent no fewer than thirty-three separate missions to Japan. See Borgen, *Sugawara no Michizane*, 227.
25. Ibid., 335.
26. Ibid., 6.
27. Interestingly and ironically, given his fate, Sugawara no Michizane's name became the rallying cry in the Tokugawa period for elements in the intellectual world concerned with asserting the importance of Chinese thought in determining Japanese social and cultural values. Consequently, the motto *wagon kansai* (Japanese spirit, Chinese learning) was incorrectly attributed to Michizane. Ibid., 6.
28. Ibid., 253.
29. It is not the goal of this study to examine this complex body of writing by *kangakusha*. Joshua Fogel has mined that field intensively, and those interested in this phenomenon should start by reading Dr. Fogel's *The Cultural Dimension of Sino-Japanese Relations: Essays on the Nineteenth and Twentieth Centuries* (Armonk, NY: M.E. Sharpe, 1995).
30. Ibid., 93. The *kangakusha* employed brushtalk in the traditional manner of exchanging official greetings as prescribed by Sinitic protocol. However, they also used the brush to communicate in more mundane ways as well, such as transactions in the marketplace. Joshua Fogel provides some examples of such exchanges in *The Cultural Dimension*, such as the exchange involving Hibino Teruhiro on page 81.
31. Ibid., 103.
32. Ibid., 105.
33. Ibid., 196.
34. Zheng Chun, *Liuxue beijing yu Zhongguo xiandai wenxue* (The Background of Overseas Study and Modern Chinese Literature) (Jinan: Shandong jiaoyu chubanshe, 2002), 32.
35. Ibid., 32.
36. Ibid., 33.
37. Ibid., 5.
38. For more about the question of the influence of Japanese on modern Chinese literary style, see Edward Gunn, *Rewriting Chinese: Style and Innovation in Twentieth-Century Chinese Prose* (Stanford: Stanford University Press, 1991).
39. For example, there were a great number of works in Japanese translation and original Japanese works available in Uchiyama Kanzō's bookstore in Shanghai at which Lu Xun and Tian Han, among others, regularly purchased books. See Wang Huoying, "Neishan Wanzao" [Uchiyama Kanzō] in *Lu Xun zawen cidian* (Lu Xun Miscellanea Dictionary) (Shandong: Shandong Xinhua shudian, 1986), 486. Moreover, these writers and other intellectuals also became conversant with Western political theory, including Marxist ideology, through Japanese translations. Sylvia Chan, "Realism or Socialist Realism? The 'Proletarian' Episode in Modern Chinese Literature, 1927–1932," *The Australian Journal of Chinese Affairs*, no. 9 (January 1983), 63.

40. Fang Changan, "Xingcheng, diaozheng yu zhibian: Zhou Zuoren 'Ren de wenxue' guanyu Riben wenxue de guanxi" (Form, Control, and Transformation: Perspectives on the Relationship of Zhou Zuoren's "Humane Literature" to Japanese Literature), *Literary Review*, 3 (2004), 95.
41. Wang Cheng, "Xiamu shushi wenxue zai Zhongguo de fanyi yu yinxing" (Lu Xun's Literature in Chinese Translation and Its Influence), *Fanyi Luntan*, 25.
42. One might conjecture that "Craig Sensei" appealed to Lu Xun on a personal level as well, as presenting a respected teacher figure, a mentor not unlike Fujino sensei, the teacher who had exerted a powerful influence on Lu Xun during his medical studies in Sendai. Interestingly, but not surprisingly, it was at Uchiyama's shop that Lu Xun purchased Sōseki's collected works. See Fuji Shōzō, "Lu Xun xinmuzhongde Xiamu Shushi (Natsume Sōseki in the Mind's Eye of Lu Xun), trans. by Ma Diji. *Lu Xun Studies Monthly*, vol. 2 (1991), 37.
43. Qin Gang, "Xiandai Zhongguo wentan dui Jiechuan Longzhijie de yijie yu zhishou," *Zhongguo xiandai wenxue yanjiu congkan*, 2 (2004), 248.
44. Liu Chenying. "Jiechuan Longzhijie zai Zhongguo" (Akutagawa Ryūnosuke in China), *Taidu xuekan* 3: 19 (2003), 2.
45. Inaba Shōzō, *Iku Tappu: sono seishun to shi* (Yu Dafu: His Youth and Poetry) (Tokyo: Tōhō senshu, 1982), 199.
46. The Creationists' tastes in modern Japanese literature, in fact, do not diverge very much from those of Lu Xun and Zhou Zuoren. See Xu Zidong, *Yu Dafu xinlun* (New Essays About Lu Xun) (Zhejiang wenyi chubanshe, 1984), 219.
47. Liu Boqing, "Lu Xun yi Riben xinsichaofa zuojia" (Lu Xun and Authors of the New Currents School), *Jilin Daxue shehui kexue xuebao*, 1 (1984), 51.
48. For more about the mission of the Senzaimaru to China and its significance in modern Sino-Japanese relations, see the chapter entitled "The Voyage of the *Senzaimaru* to Shanghai: Early Sino-Japanese Contacts in the Modern Era" in Joshua Fogel's book, *The Cultural Dimensions of Sino-Japanese Relations*, 79–94.
49. Leo Ou-Fan Lee, *Shanghai Modern: The Flowering of a New Urban Culture in China, 1930–1945* (Cambridge, MA: Harvard University Press, 1999), 4.
50. Joshua Fogel, "Japanese Literary Travelers," 579. See also Ogata Sadako, "Japanese Attitude Toward China," *Asian Survey* 5: 8 (August 1965), 391.
51. Fogel, "Japanese Literary Travelers," 585.
52. Ibid., 580.
53. Ibid., 580.
54. Susan Hamilton Nolte, "Individualism in Taishō Japan," *The Journal of Asian Studies*, 43: 4 (August 1984), 669.
55. Ibid., 677.
56. Also known by its Japanese name, Dongya tongwen shuyuan. Douglas R. Reynolds, "Chinese Area Studies in Prewar Japan: Japan's Tōa Dōbun Shoin in Shanghai, 1900–1945," *The Journal of Asian Studies* 45: 5 (November 1986), 945.
57. Ibid., 946.
58. Ibid., 950.
59. Ibid., 950.
60. Ian Nish, "An Overview of Relations between China and Japan, 1895–1945," *China Quarterly* 124 (December 1990), 601.
61. Ogata, "Japanese Attitude," 391.

62. Nish, "An Overview," 601.
63. Ogata, 390. For more about the background and significance of the term "Shina" see Joshua Fogel's essay, "The Sino-Japanese Controversy over *Shina* as a Toponym for China," in *The Cultural Dimensions of Sino-Japanese Relations*, 66–76.
64. Nish, "An Overview," 607.
65. Sydney Gifford, *Japan Among the Powers, 1890–1990* (New Haven, CT: Yale University Press, 1994), 50–51.
66. Immanuel C. Y. Hsu, *The Rise of Modern China* (New York: Oxford University Press, 1995), 494.
67. Nish, "An Overview," 609.
68. Ibid., 609–610.
69. Ibid., 610.
70. Ibid., 612.
71. Ibid., 613.
72. Ibid., 614.
73. Ibid., 616.
74. Ibid., 618.
75. Ibid., 619.
76. Sylvia Chen, "Realism or Socialist Realism?" 59.
77. Ibid., 62.
78. Ibid., 57.
79. Ibid., 65.
80. Nish, "An Overview," 622.

Chapter 1

1. It is difficult to assess the degree to which the influence of the Sinologist grandfather was to affect the direction that Uchiyama Kanzō's life was to take. Ozawa Masamoto, *Uchiyama Kanzōden* (Tokyo: Banchō shoten, 1972), 17.
2. Yoshida Hiroji, *Lu Xun no tomo: Uchiyama Kanzō no shōzō* (Lu Xun's Friend: A Portrait of Uchiyama Kanzō) (Tokyo: Shinkyō shuppansha, 1994), 54.
3. Ibid., 56.
4. Ibid., 59.
5. Ibid., 63.
6. Ibid., 64.
7. Ibid., 65.
8. Ozawa, *Uchiyama Kanzōden*, 30.
9. Makino Toraji, who would later hold several important administrative posts at prestigious Dōshisha University in Kyoto, was the favored disciple of the founder of Dōshisha, Nishima Jō. See Yoshida, *Lu Xun no tomo*, 65.
10. In later reminiscences, Uchiyama describes how upon deciding to fully embrace his newfound religion, he threw away the elegant ivory cigarette case which was the unofficial symbol of the merchant class in the Kansai region. Ibid., 65.
11. Ibid., 70.
12. Ibid., 73.
13. Ozawa, *Uchiyama Kanzōden*, 63.
14. Yoshida, *Lu Xun no tomo*, 76.
15. Ozawa, *Uchiyama Kanzōden*, 42.

16. Ibid., 46. Hankou stood at the point where the Han River merges with the Yangtze. Hankou was later combined with the smaller cities of Hanyang and Wuchang to comprise the present city of Wuhan. At the time of Uchiyama's visit, there were five foreign concessions in Hankou.
17. Ibid., 46.
18. Yoshida, Lu Xun no tomo, 80.
19. Ibid., 83.
20. Ibid., 87.
21. Ibid., 87.
22. Customers included Chinese, Japanese and Koreans. The Uchiyamas continued this policy in their new shop and the practice soon spread to other Japanese businesses in Shanghai. According to later reminiscences by Uchiyama Kanzō the only customers who occasionally took advantage of the good will of the Uchiyamas were Japanese businessmen. See Ozawa, Uchiyama Kanzōden, 75.
23. Yoshida, Lu Xun no tomo, 88.
24. Ozawa, Uchiyama Kanzōden, 76.
25. Ibid., 95.
26. Ibid., 96
27. Shih Shu-mei, The Lure of the Modern: Writing Modernism in Semicolonial China, 1917–1937 (Berkeley: University of California Press, 2001), 141.
28. Ibid., 141.
29. Ozawa, Uchiyama Kanzōden, 124.
30. Harriet Sergeant, Shanghai: Collision Point of Cultures 1918–1939 (New York: Crown Publishers, 1990), 237.
31. Ibid., 241.
32. Ozawa, Uchiyama Kanzōden, 84.
33. Yu Dafu, for example, studied in Japan from 1913 to 1922, Guo Moruo from 1913 to 1921, Zhang Ziping from 1912 to 1921, and Cheng Fangwu from 1910 to 1921. For more about the experiences of the Creation Society's members in Japan, see Chapter 1 of my book, The Subversive Self in Modern Chinese Literature (New York: Palgrave), 2004.
34. Uchiyama Kanzō, Kakōroku (A Record at Age Sixty) (Tokyo: Iwanami Shoten, 1981), 175.
35. Ibid., 193.
36. Ibid., 194.
37. Ibid., 167.
38. Ibid., 172.
39. Ibid., 172.
40. Wang Zili (ed.), Yu Dafu wenji (Yu Dafu's Writings), vol. 9 (Hong Kong: Joint Publishing, 1984), 401.
41. Ibid., 467.
42. Lu Xun, Lu Xun shuxin ji (Lu Xun's Collected Correspondences), vol. 2 (Beijing: renmin wenxue chubanshe, 1976), 1084.
43. Ibid., 1092.
44. Joshua Fogel, "Japanese Literary Travelers in Prewar China," Harvard Journal of Asiatic Studies 49: 2 (1989), 575–602.
45. Itō Toramaru (ed.), Iku Tappu shiryō hoben (A Companion of Yu Dafu Materials), vol. 2 (Tokyo: Tokyo Daigaku bunken sentaa, 1975), 201.

46. Ibid., 202.
47. One result of Lu Xun's move to Shanghai and this new era of productivity was the publication of a collection of translations of Japanese literature in 1929 called *Bixia yuecong* (Translations Beneath the Wall). See Yamada Keizō, *Rojin no sekai* (Lu Xun's World) (Tokyo: Oshū shoten, 1977), 215.
48. Uchiyama would later say that the anniversary of that meeting was the anniversary that he most cherished. Uchiyama Kanzō, *Kakōroku*, 156.
49. Sergeant, *Shanghai*, 235.
50. Ibid., 242.
51. Ibid., 240.
52. Ibid., 240.
53. Ibid., 239.
54. Yoshida, *Lu Xun no tomo*, 88.
55. Ibid., 117.
56. Ibid., 117.
57. Ibid., 118.
58. Sergeant, *Shanghai*, 238.
59. Ozawa, *Uchiyama Kanzōden*, 115.
60. The workshops themselves lasted two hours each day with the enthusiastic participation of young students, the majority of whom were from the Shanghai School of Art. Ibid., 115.
61. Ibid., 116.
62. W. J. F. Jenner, "Lu Xun's Last Days and After," *China Quarterly* 91 (September 1982), 428.
63. Ozawa, *Uchiyama Kanzōden*, 125.
64. Ibid., 125.
65. Lu Xun contributed a foreword for this collection in which he praised Uchiyama's contributions to understanding between the two nations. Ibid., 124.
66. Uchiyama Kanzō, *Shanhai mango* (Random Talk in Shanghai) (Tokyo: Kaizōsha, 1941), 2.
67. Ibid., 318.
68. Uchiyama, *Kakōroku*, 157.
69. Barak Kushner, *The Thought War: Japanese Imperial Propaganda* (Honolulu: University of Hawai'i Press, 2006), 15.
70. Yoshida, *Ro Jin no tomo*, 219.
71. Joshua Fogel, " 'Shanghai-Japan': The Japanese Residents' Association of Shanghai," *The Journal of Asian Studies* 59: 4 (November 2000), 942.
72. Ibid., 928.
73. Ibid., 249.

Chapter 2

1. Earl Miner, *Japanese Poetic Diaries* (Berkeley, CA: University of California Press, 1969), 8.
2. Ibid., 12.
3. The irony of the *kikōbun* form is the expectation that it at once be an intensely personal response to a place but also evocative of the site's cultural and historical associations. See Earl Miner et al., *The Princeton Companion to Classical Japanese Literature* (Princeton: Princeton University Press, 1985), 283.

4. Joshua Fogel, *The Cultural Dimensions of Sino-Japanese Relations* (Armonk, NY: M. E. Sharpe, 1995), 85.
5. Joshua Fogel, *The Literature of Travel in the Rediscovery of Japan, 1862–1945* (Stanford, CA: Stanford University Press, 1996), 33.
6. Sakaki Atsuko, "Japanese Perceptions of China: The Sinophilic Fiction of Tanizaki Jun'ichirō," *Harvard Journal of Asiatic Studies* 59: 1 (1999): 193.
7. Fogel, *The Literature of Travel*, 82.
8. Tanizaki's infatuation with the West was beginning to cool, and his ardor for Eastern traditions beginning to grow, just at the time of his first visit to China in 1918. See Ken Ito, *Visions of Desire: Tanazaki's Fictional Worlds* (Stanford, CA: Stanford University Press, 1991), 105–132.
9. Tanizaki Jun'ichirō, "Shina shumi to iu koto" (This Taste for Things Chinese), *Tanizaki Jun'ichirō zenshō* (Collected Works of Tanizaki Jun'ichirō), vol. 6 (Tokyo: Chūō kōronsha, 1969), 121. Unless otherwise noted, this and all of the translations in this study are mine.
10. For more about this body of fiction by Tanizaki, see Sakaki's article, "Japanese Perceptions of China."
11. The concept of "pilgrimage" in Tanizaki's writings, first to an imagined West and later in regard to his return to the East, are an important facet of his travel essays and fiction. For more about this phenomenon see Tsuruta Kin'ya, "Tanizaki Jun'ichirō's Pilgrimage and Return," *Comparative Literature Studies* 37: 2 (2000): 239–255.
12. Tanizaki, "Soshū kikō" (A Record of a Journey to Suzhou), *Tanizaki Jun'ichirō zenshū* (Collected Works of Tanizaki Jun'ichirō), vol. 6 (Tokyo: Chūō kōronsha, 1969), 223.
13. Sakaki, *Japanese Perceptions of China*, 201.
14. In the writings following Tanizaki's first trip to China he tends to exoticize China and the Chinese as he had the West in earlier writings. This objectification of the people and places he encounters is a quality on which a number of scholars comment. In fact, Atsuko Sakaki refers to the narrators in Tanizaki's fictional works from China as "Orientalists." Ibid., 201.
15. Ibid., 222.
16. Tanizaki, "Rozan nikki" (Lushan Diary), *Tanizaki Jun'ichirō zenshū* (Collected Works of Tanizaki Jun'ichirō), vol. 7 (Tokyo: Chūō kōronsha, 1969), 468.
17. Ibid., 470.
18. One feature of both the *nikki* and the *kikō*, which they share with other traditional prose forms such as the *monogatari* (tale literature) is the inclusion of poetry at moments involving an emotional encounter with the site's cultural significance. See Miner et al., *The Princeton Companion*, 292.
19. Miyauchi Junko, *Ikyō ōkan* (Travels to Foreign Lands) (Tokyo: Kokusho kankōkai, 1991), 84.
20. Tanizaki, "Shanhai kōyūki" (A Record of a Friendly Exchange in Shanghai), *Tanizaki Jun'ichirō zenshū* (Collected Works of Tanizaki Jun'ichirō), vol. 10 (Tokyo: Chūō kōronsha, 1969), 563.
21. Tanizaki's second visit to China coincided with his increasing fascination with the Kansai region, and his visit served to strengthen associations he had begun to make between the Kansai region as the cradle of traditional Japanese culture and China as the source of traditional Eastern culture. See Ken Ito, *Visions of Desire*, 111.
22. Interestingly, although Tanizaki met virtually all of China's important young writers during this visit, he was unable to meet Lu Xun, the writer he desired most to meet. See Fogel, *Japanese Literary Travelers*, 590.

23. Tanizaki, "Shanhai kōyūki," 589.
24. Ibid., 590.
25. Ibid., 591.
26. Jaroslav Prusek (ed.), *Dictionary of Oriental Literatures*, vol. 1 [East Asia] (London: George Allen and Unwin, 1974), 87.
27. Uchiyama, *Kakōroku*, 175.
28. Fogel, *Japanese Literary Travelers*, 589.
29. Nozaki Kan, "Tanizaki Jun'ichirō and Narrating 'Transcendental China'," *Journal of Modern Literature in Chinese* 7: 2 (December, 2005), 45.
30. These two works of fiction are simply the best known of Tanizaki's stories from the late teens and early twenties set in China. See Atsuko Sakaki, *Japanese Perceptions*, 199–200.
31. Nozaki, "Tanizaki Jun'ichirō," 49
32. Sakaki, *Japanese Perceptions of China*, 199.
33. "Shanhai kenbunroku" (A Record of Observations in Shanghai), *Tanizaki Jun'ichirō zenshū* (Collected Works of Tanizaki Jun'ichirō), vol. 22 (Tokyo: Chūō kōronsha, 1969), 553.
34. Tsuruta Kin'ya, "Tanizaki Jun'ichirō's Pilgrimage and Return," 244.
35. Ibid., 254.
36. Letter reprinted in *Tanizaki Jun'ichirō zenshū*, vol. 24: 245.
37. Sakaki, *Japanese Perceptions of China*, 196.
38. Ito, *Visions of Desire*, 136.
39. Ibid., 136.
40. From Noguchi Takehiko, "Tanizaki Jun'ichirō ron" (Concerning Tanizaki Jun'ichirō) (Tokyo: Chūō kōronsha, 1973), as cited in Ken Ito's *Visions of Desire*, 111.
41. Ibid., 110.
42. This essay was collected, at the end of 1942, in an anthology with earlier essays written after the completion of Tanizaki's first translation of *The Tale of Genji* under the title *Hatsu Mukashi, Kinō Kyō* (Not So Long Ago: Yesterday and Today). See Donald Keene, *Dawn to the West: Japanese Literature in the Modern Era* (Fiction) (New York: Holt, Rhinehart and Winston, 1984), 773.
43. Tanizaki Jun'ichirō, "Kinō kyō," in Itō Toramaru (ed.), *Tian Han zai Riben* (Tian Han in Japan) (Beijing: Renmin wenxue chubanshe, 1997), 180.
44. By emphasizing the importance of this exchange of poems at that gathering and the personal significance of the poem that he had received from Ouyang, Tanizaki is cleverly situating this encounter in the tradition of brushtalk communication and thereby providing the encounter with a time-tested framework.
45. Tanizaki, "Kinō kyō," 183.
46. Ibid., 184.
47. Ibid., 185.
48. Ibid., 185.
49. Ibid., 195.
50. Ibid., 195.
51. Ibid., 197.
52. Ibid., 193.
53. Tanizaki was not always willing to countenance compromise with the authorities. His unwillingness to compromise with *Sasameyuki* (The Makioka Sisters) in order to see it published, is well documented.

54. To a degree achieved by few other Japanese literary travelers of the era, Tanizaki was able in this essay to transcend the "fierce nationalism" of the day and engage Chinese writers in a direct way. Ibid., 599.

Chapter 3

1. "Xiongdi" documents the split between the Zhou brothers and portrays the selfless love of the older brother (Lu Xun) for the younger brother (Zuoren) juxtaposed with the feelings of hostility that emerge in the older brother at night toward his younger brother in the semi-conscious state of half sleep. For a translation of this story see Lu Xun, *Diary of a Madman and Other Stories,* translation by William A Lyell (Honolulu: University of Hawai'i, 1990), 363–376.
2. Another factor that distinguished the White Birch School from other late Meiji anti-naturalist coteries was its enduring influence. Even though the core of writers and artists associated with the White Birch School departed after only a few years, the school continued to exist in some form throughout the Taishō period (1912–1926), and its influence continued well into the Shōwa period (1926–1989). See Stephen W. Kohl et al., *The White Birch Society (Shirakabaha) of Japanese Literature: Some Sketches and Commentary* (Eugene, OR: Asian Studies Occasional Paper No. 2, 1975), 2.
3. The differences in educational background and values of the Shirakaba writers and the older generation of Japanese writers that includes Soseki and Ōgai can be seen in their respective reaction to the ritual suicide of Admiral Nogi and his wife in the wake of the death of the Meiji Emperor. While the older generation of Japanese writers expressed a general sympathy of this act bordering on reverence, Mushanokōji and other Shirakaba derided the suicide as a senseless waste. See Nakamura Mitsuo, *Nihon no kindai shōsetsu* (Modern Japanese Fiction) (Tokyo: Iwanami Shinsho, 1964), 176.
4. Kohl et al., *The White Birch Society,* 19.
5. *Shirakaba* likewise differed from the journals produced by other contemporary anti-naturalist coteries. The sheer scope of the magazine and the diversity of forms contained therein were atypical, and the inclusion of regular art works and photography was unique. *Shirakaba* was reprinted in its entirety in facsimile edition by Shirakabasha in Tokyo between 1969 and 1972.
6. Wang Jinghou, *Wusi: xinwenxue yu waiguo wenxue* (May Fourth: The New Literature and Foreign Literature) (Sichuan: Sichuan daxue chubanshe, 1989), 94.
7. Ibid., 94. The novelist Yu Dafu had become acquainted with Mushanokōji during one of Yu's visits to Japan in the latter part of the 1920s. They exchanged ideas and books as evidenced in the letter from Yu to Satō Haruo dated 1928. See Itō Toramaru (ed.), *Iku Tappu: shiryō hoben* (A Companion of Yu Dafu Materials), vol. 2 (Tokyo Daigaku bunken sentaa, 1975), 205.
8. Although it was Mushanokōji's uncle Kade no Kojisukeko, who introduced his nephew to Tolstoy's work, it was through the writings of the Meiji era author Tokutomi Rōka that Mushanokōji became truly familiar with Tolstoy's thought. See Takeda Torao, *Shirakaba* (Tokyo: Meiji Shoten, 1983), 1.
9. Kohl et al., *The White Birch School,* 93.
10. Eric Rothstein, "Diversity and Change in Literary Histories," in Jay Clayton and Eric Rothstein (ed.), *Influence and Intertextuality in Literary History* (Madison, WI: University of Wisconsin Press, 1991), 117.

11. Nakamura Mitsuo, *Nihon no kindai shōsetsu*, 182.
12. Shiga had planned to visit the mine in order to protest along with others who shared his concerns but was forbidden to do so by his father, who was indebted to the owner of the mine. See Donald Keene, *Dawn to the West*, 459.
13. Zhu Peichu, "Riben minyi yundong de changdaozhe: Liu Zongyue" (The Leader of the Japanese Folk Art Movement: Yanagi Sōetsu), *Art and Design*, 4 (1990): 419.
14. Interestingly, the house the two brothers rented in Nishikata had once belonged to the Japanese literary giant, Natsume Sōseki. See William Lyell, *Lu Xun's Vision of Reality* (Berkeley: University of California Press, 1976), 78.
15. Susan Daruvala, *Zhou Zuoren and an Alternative Chinese Response to Modernity* (Cambridge, MA: Harvard University Asia Center, 2000), 3.
16. Ibid., 61.
17. Nishihara Daisuke, "Zhou Zuoren's translations of two Japanese stories," *Hikaku bungaku: Journal of Comparative Literature*, vol. XXXVII (1994): 240.
18. Although the anthology is identified as an anthology of fiction (*xiaoshuo*), it in fact includes works that are clearly not fiction such as Arishima Takeo's essay, "Chiisaki mono e" (To the Little Ones). See Yamada Keizō, *Rojin no sekai* (Lu Xun's world) (Tokyo: Toshokan shoten, 1977), 205.
19. Ibid., 205.
20. Ibid., 209.
21. Nishihara Daisuke, "Zhou Zuoren's translations," 241.
22. Ibid., 239.
23. As translated by Nishihara Daisuke. Ibid., 238.
24. From Lu Xun's 1931 essay, "Fanyi de tongxin" (The Message of Translation). Translated by Nishihara Daisuke. Ibid., 235.
25. Ibid., 237. The two Akutagawa stories were "Rashōmon" and "Hana" (The Nose).
26. Ibid., 236. Other commentators, such as the Taiwanese scholar Lin Lianxiang, find the Zhou brothers' translations from the Japanese often inaccurate and "extremely clumsy" in general. Ibid., 236.
27. Nakamura Mitsuo, *Nihon no kindai shōsetsu*, 181.
28. Although Mushanokōji's writing might appear to us now as "pompous, naïve, or just plain silly" there is no doubt that he was an immensely popular and influential literary figure in his own day. See Kohl et al., *The White Birch School*, 42. Nevertheless, although Mushanokōji enjoyed a prominent career as a writer, thinker, painter and social reformer, it is as the spokesman for the ideas of the White Birch School that he is primarily remembered. Ibid., 42.
29. Tellingly, by the time of this translation, Mushanokōji had already pronounced, in typical dramatic fashion, that he had "graduated" from the stifling influence of Tolstoy and would thereafter advocate the thought and writing of the dramatist, Maurice Maeterlinck. See Keene, *Dawn to the West*, 451.
30. Zhou's essay about Mushanokōji's play was entitled "Du Muzhexiaoji qun zuo 'yige qingnian de meng'" (Reading Mushanokōji's "A Certain Young Man's Dream"). See Yamada Keizō, *Rojin no sekai*, 193.
31. Ibid., 193.
32. Ibid., 194.
33. Ibid., 194.
34. Odagiri Susumu (ed.), "Mushanokōji Saneatsu," in *Nihon kindai bungaku daijiten*, (Tokyo: Kōdansha, 1992), 1442.

35. "Aru seinen no yume" (A Certain Young Man's Dream), in *Mushanokōji Saneatsu zenshū* (Mushanokōji Saneatsu's Collected Works) (Tokyo: Shōgakukan, 1988), 499–607.
36. Ibid., 499.
37. Yamada Keizō, *Rojin no sekai*, 223. All four of the Mushanokōji pieces translated by Lu Xun were concerned with questions of self-expression and sincerity. Ibid., 221.
38. Fujii Shōzō, *Lu Xun bijiao yanjiu* (Lu Xun Comparative Research), trans. Chen Fuqiu (Shanghai: Shanghai jiaoyu chubanshe, 1997), 167.
39. Takeda Torao, *Shirakaba gunzō* (A Portrait of Shirakaba) (Tokyo: Meiji Shoten, 1983), 234.
40. Fujii, *Lu Xun bijiao yanjiu*, 167.
41. Ibid., 168.
42. Yamada Keizō, *Rojin no sekai*, 196.
43. Ibid., 197.
44. Although Zhou Zuoren shared these same concerns about the source of this idealistic, pacifist manifesto, he was ultimately more willing to accept this paradox than was his older brother. Ibid., 195.
45. Ibid., 195.
46. Ibid., 198.
47. Ibid., 200.
48. Fujii, *Lu Xun bijiao yanjiu*, 163.
49. Ibid., 174.
50. Yokomatsu Takashi, *Rojin: Minzoku no kyōshi* (Lu Xun: The People's Teacher) (Tokyo: Kawade shobō shinsha, 1986), 133.
51. Kohl et al., *The White Birch School*, 71.
52. Donald Keene, *Dawn to the West*, 473.
53. Ibid., 473.
54. In an article written after Arishima's death entitled "Haikyōsha toshite no Arishima" (Arishima the Apostate), Uchimura Kanzō admits having seen indications of Arishima's movement away from Christianity as early as 1907 when he visited his former student in Sapporo. See Kohl et al., *The White Birch School*, 83.
55. Keene, *Dawn to the West*, 492.
56. Kohl et al., *The White Birch School*, 71.
57. Arishima's essay appeared in the January 1918 issue of *Shinchō* (New Tide). Lu Xun apparently read it in October of the following year. See Lu Xun, *Lu Xun lun waiguo wenxue* (Lu Xun Discusses Foreign Literature), edited by Fujian shifan daxue Zhongwenxi (Beijing: Waiguo wenxue chubanshe, 1982), 232.
58. Ibid., 233.
59. Ibid., 234.
60. Yamada, *Rojin no sekai*, 211.
61. Ibid., 211.
62. Keene, *Dawn to the West*, 484.
63. Ibid., 475.
64. Yamada, *Lu Xun no sekai*, 207.
65. As quoted in Yamada, *Lu Xun no sekai*, 215.
66. Ibid., 220.
67. Lu Xun, "Mourning the Dead," in *Diary of a Madman and Other Stories*, trans. William A. Lyell (Honolulu: University of Hawai'i Press, 1990), 340.

68. Ibid., 340.
69. Yokomatsu, *Rojin: Minzoku no kyōshi*, 144.
70. Ibid., 146.
71. As quoted in Yamada, *Lu Xun no sekai*, 4.
72. Ibid., 226.
73. Ibid., 218.
74. Leith Morton, *Divided Self: A Biography of Arishima Takeo* (Sydney: Allen and Unwin, 1988), 199.
75. Ibid., 203–204.
76. Yamada, *Lu Xun no sekai*, 218–219.
77. Li Huoren, "Yu Dafu yu sixiaoshuo" (Yu Dafu and the *shishōsetsu*), *Zhongguo xiandai yanjiu* (March 1990): 208.
78. Yokomatsu, *Rojin: Minzoku no kyōshi*, 139.
79. Ibid., 141.
80. Ibid., 141.
81. Ibid., 140.
82. Yamada, *Lu Xun no sekai*, 227.
83. Ibid., 228.
84. Ibid., 228.
85. Yokomatsu, *Rojin: Minzoku no kyōshi*, 141.
86. This, however, did not signal the end of the influence of modern Japanese literature on the May Fourth literary community. An anthology of modern Japanese literature issued by Beixin shuju appeared as late as 1929. See Yamada, *Lu Xun no sekai*, 212.

Chapter 4

1. Stephen Kohl et al., *The White Birch School (Shirakabaha) of Japanese Literature: Some Sketches and Commentary.* Occasional Paper No. 2 (Eugene, OR: University of Oregon, 1975), 2.
2. Ibid., 11.
3. Ibid., 11.
4. This essay had an influence on Yu Dafu, one of the leaders of the Creation Society, who expressed similar ideas in an essay from 1927 entitled "Nongmin wenyi de tichang" (Advocating Literature by Peasants). See Li Huoren, "Yu Dafu yu Sixiaoshuo" (Yu Dafu and the *Shishōsetsu*), *Zhongguo xiandai wenxue* (March 1990), 208.
5. Kohl et al, *The White Birch School*, 86. Interestingly, among the ranks of the White Birch School the figure most disengaged from social concerns may have been Satomi Ton, the youngest of the three Arishima brothers. Satomi not only remained opposed to the eldest Arishima brother's stance of the social responsibility of the writer, he was also critical of Mushanokōji's involvement in the New Village Movement. Ibid., 93.
6. Odagiri Susumu (ed.), *Nihon kindai bungaku daijiten* (Dictionary of Modern Japanese Literature) (Tokyo: Kōdansha, 1992), 1442. The importance of Tolstoy's spirit in the creation of the village can be seen for example in the custom of celebrating Tolstoy's birthday as a holiday.
7. Included in Mushanokōji Saneatsu, *Jibun aruita michi* (The Road I Have Walked) in *Sakka no jiden* (Autobiographies of Writers) (Tokyo: Nihon tosho sentā, 1994), vol. 7.
8. Odagiri (ed.), *Nihon kindai bungaku daijiten*, 1442.

9. Leith Morton, *Divided Self: A Biography of Arishima Takeo* (Sydney: Allen and Unwin, 1988), 135.
10. Susan Daruvala, *Zhou Zuoren and an Alternative Response to Chinese Modernity* (Cambridge, MA: Harvard University Press, 2000), 50.
11. Morton, *Divided Self*, 136
12. Ibid., 137. The scholar Otsuyama Kunio maintains that since Arishima misunderstood Mushanokōji's intentions, the latter's reaction was justified. Arishima conceived of efforts of reform in terms of Japan as a whole, while Mushanokōji was purely concerned with the Hyūga project. See Otsuyama Kunio, "Atarashiki Mura no hankyō — Arishima Takeo no hihan o megutte" (Reaction to the New Village — Concerning Arishima Takeo's Criticism) *Bungaku* 42: 12 (1974), 1181–1182.
13. Derived from "Atarashiki Mura ni tsuite no taiwa" (A Dialogue about the New Village), 423.
14. Ibid., 50.
15. Lu Yan, *Re-understanding Japan: Chinese Perspectives, 1895–1945* (Honolulu: Association for Asian Studies and University of Hawai'i Press, 2002), 125.
16. Ibid., 3
17. Ibid., 3.
18. Zhou wrote several essays about his visit to the New Village including "Shuo Xincun shenghuo" (Discourse on Life in the New Village). See Qian Lijun, *Zhou Zuoren chuan* (A Biography of Zhou Zuoren) (Beijing: Beijing shiyue wenyi, 1993), 73.
19. Lu Yan, *Re-understanding Japan*, 126.
20. Ernst Wolff, *Chou Tso-jen* (New York: Twayne Pulishers, 1971), 4.
21. It should be pointed out that modern fiction was not Zhou's sole or even primary interest in Japanese literature. His voluminous essays and translations from Japanese literature cover everything from the Edo period novelist Takizawa Bakin (1767–1848) to the modern poet Ishikawa Takuboku (1886–1912). Zhou was particularly attracted to the haiku form, and it is interesting to note that not only did he write an essay about the haiku poet Kobayashi Issa (1763–1827), he also translated a brief play about Issa written by Mushanokōji Saneatsu. See Wolff, 68–69.
22. As quoted in Lu Yan, *Re-understanding Japan*, 126.
23. Qian, *Zhou Zuoren chuan*, 226.
24. Ibid., 226.
25. Fujii Shōzō, *Lu Xun bijiao yanjiu* (Lu Xun Comparative Research), translated by Chen Futai (Shanghai: Shanghai waiyu jiaoyu chubanshe, 1997), 166.
26. Ibid., 227.
27. Ibid., 231.
28. A few examples of the many essays that Zhou produced in this period about the New Village that might be cited include "Yishu yu shenghuo: Riben de xincun" (Art and Life: Japan's New Village) from 1919 and "Xincun de jingshen" (The Spirit of the New Village) which appeared in the November 23, 1919 issue of the newspaper *Minguo ribao*. See Qian, *Zhou Zuoren chuan*, 232.
29. Wang Jinhou, *Wusi: Xinwenxue yu waiguo wenxue* (May Fourth: New Literature and Foreign Literature) (Sichuan: Sichuan daxue chubanshe, 1989), 93.
30. Ibid., 93.
31. Ibid., 93. Originally appeared in *New Youth* (Xin qingnian), 7: 3 (1919).
32. Ibid., 231.

33. Ibid., 233.
34. Fujii, *Lu Xun bijiao yanjiu*, 165.
35. Ibid., 165.
36. Ibid., 165.
37. Ibid., 233.
38. Ibid., 233.
39. Translated by Ernst Wolff in the appendix of his work *Chou Tso-jen*, 100.

Chapter 5

1. Susanna Fessler, *Wandering Heart: The Work and Method of Hayashi Fumiko* (Albany, NY: State University of New York, 1998), 75.
2. There was, in fact, a crackdown on "lumpen writers" in the early 1930s due to their unflattering portrayal of contemporary Japanese society. See Joan E. Ericson, *To Be a Woman: Hayashi Fumiko and Modern Japanese Women's Literature* (Honolulu: University of Hawai'i Press, 1997), 63.
3. Kurahara's article originally appeared in the January 1928 issue of *Kaizō*. See Itō Toshihiko, "Kobayashi Takiji to Kurahara Korehito: Sakka to hyōronka no mondai" (December 15, 1990), in http://homepage2.nifty.com/tizu/proletarier, 8.
4. Ibid., 16.
5. Isogai Hideo, *Shinchō Nihon bungaku arubamu: Hayashi Fumiko* (Shinchō Japanese Literature Album: Hayashi Fumiko) (Tokyo: Shinchōsha, 1986), 40.
6. Fessler, *Wandering Heart*, 17.
7. Isogai, *Shinchō Nihon bungaku arubamu*, 40.
8. Fessler, *Wandering Heart*, 17.
9. Ibid., 17.
10. Ibid., 17.
11. Isogai, *Shinchō Nihon bungaku arubamu*, 45.
12. Ibid., 47.
13. Ibid., 47.
14. Ibid., 47. Yamamoto Sanehiko, the president of Kaizōsha Publishing House, which produced the large circulation journal *Kaizō*, was himself an intriguing figure in terms of Sino-Literary exchange. Not only did he publish the works of many of the Japanese writers of the interwar period treated in this study, he was also acquainted with a number of May Fourth writers as well including Lu Xun and Yu Dafu, whose work he included in *Kaizō*.
15. Fessler, *Wandering Heart*, 18.
16. Isogai, *Shinchō Nihon bungaku arubamu*, 47.
17. "Nikki" in *Hayashi Fumiko zenshū* (Collected Works of Hayashi Fumiko), vol. 29 (Tokyo: Shinchōsha, 1952), 102.
18. Sylvia Chan, "Realism or Socialist Realism: The 'Proletarian' Episode in Modern Chinese Literature, 1927–1932," *The Australian Journal of Chinese Affairs*, 9 (January 1983): 57.
19. Stephen Ching-Kiu Chan, "The Language of Despair: Ideological Representation of 'New Woman' by May Fourth Writers," in Tani E. Barlow (ed.), *Gender Politics in Modern China: Writing and Feminism* (Durham, NC: Duke University, 1993), 13.
20. Dian Xi and Zhong Xuequn (ed.), *Shiren nüren de Shanghai tan* (Ten Women Writers' Sojourns in Shanghai) (Beijing: New World Press, 2004), 191.

21. Yi-tsi Mei Feuerwerker, *Ding Ling's Fiction: Ideology and Narrative in Modern Chinese Literature* (Cambridge, MA: Harvard University Press, 1982), 19.
22. Ibid., 19.
23. Tani E. Barlow and George J. Bjorge (ed.), *I Myself Am a Woman: Selected Writings of Ding Ling* (Boston: Beacon Press, 1989), 49.
24. Ibid., 55.
25. Dian Xi and Zhong Xuequn (ed.), *Shiren nüren de Shanghai tan*, 193.
26. Ibid., 194.
27. Feuerwerker, *Ding Ling's Fiction*, 82.
28. Ibid., 8.
29. Ibid., 8.
30. Ericson, *To Be a Woman*, 63.
31. Isogai, *Shinchō Nihon bungaku arubamu*, 36.
32. The term was coined by Karl Marx in his essay from 1850, "The Class Struggle in France." Marx used this pejorative term to criticize sycophantic, non-productive members of society. See Ericson, 63.
33. Fessler, *Wandering Heart*, 56.
34. Isogai, *Shinchō Nihon bungaku arubamu*, 45.
35. Translation by Joan E. Ericson in *To Be a Woman*, 135.
36. In China, the utilization of the diary form as a form of fictional narrative to give expression to modern concerns had been established by the success of the first work of Chinese vernacular fiction, Lu Xun's "Kuangren riji" (Diary of a madman, 1916). For more about the impact of Lu Xun's seminal work see Benjamin I. Schwartz (ed.), *Reflections on the May Fourth Movement: A Symposium* (Cambridge, MA: Harvard University Press, 1973), 6.
37. As Yi-tsi Mei Feuerwerker notes, concerning the effectiveness of the diary form to articulate concerns of modern women writers, far from being a "transparent medium," a window through which to gaze upon the action of the story, the diary is self-reflexive, not just a means for self-investigation by the main characters but itself a subject for investigation. Feuerwerker, *Ding Ling's Fiction*, 50.
38. Certain qualities of Hayashi's diary hearken back to the Heian tradition of women's literary diaries. For instance, the protagonists remain largely anonymous in classical Japanese diaries as they do in Hayashi's fictional diary. See Ericson, *To Be a Woman*, 61.
39. Ibid., 60. Likewise, Ding Ling's *Miss Sophie's Diary* has been likened to Shen Fu's *Six Chapters of a Floating Life* in its depiction of the protagonist struggling to find direction in a love triangle in which he has become involved. Barlow and Bjorge (ed.), 49.
40. Ericson, *To Be a Woman*, 60.
41. Feuerwerker, *Ding Ling's Fiction*, 46.
42. Ericson, *To Be a Woman*, 79. Ironically, Hayashi's work won praise from Nakamura Mitsuo, who praised the work for its objectivity and calculated style, qualities that he identified as decidedly masculine. Ibid., 89.
43. Stephen Ching-Kiu Chan, "The Language of Despair," 30.
44. Lydia Liu, "Invention and Intervention: The Female Tradition in Modern Chinese Literature," in Tani E. Barlow (ed.), *Gender Politics in Modern China: Writing and Feminism* (Durham, NC: Duke University Press, 1993), 46.
45. Translated in Ericson, *To Be a Woman*, 149.
46. Feuerwerker, *Ding Ling's Fiction*, 19.

47. It is at this point in the narrative that Sophie, suffering from severe tuberculosis, moves into a damp apartment, merely to be closer to her beloved. Translated by Tani E. Barlow, in Barlow and Bjorge (ed.), *I Myself Am a Woman*, 55.
48. Feuerwerker, *Ding Ling's Fiction*, 20.
49. Sharon Hamilton Nolte, "Individualism in Taishō Japan," *Journal of Asian Studies*, 43: 4 (August 1984), 675.
50. Ericson, *To Be a Woman*, 104.
51. Ibid., 53.
52. Translated in Ericson, *To Be a Woman*, 181.
53. Feuerwerker, *Ding Ling's Fiction*, 43.
54. Barlow (ed.), *Gender Politics in Modern China*, 12.
55. Ibid., 12.
56. Ibid., 14.
57. Translation by Barlow and Bjorge (ed.), *I Myself am a Woman*, 59.
58. Wendy Larson, "The End of 'Funü Wenxue': Women's Literature from 1925 to 1935," in Tani E. Barlow (ed.), *Gender Politics in Modern China: Writing and Feminism* (Durham, NC: Duke University Press, 1993), 59.
59. Ibid., 59.
60. Ibid., 67.
61. Ibid., 67.
62. As quoted in Larson, "The End of 'Funü Wenxue'," 67.
63. Ibid., 69.
64. Sylvia Chan, "Realism or Social Realism?" 57.
65. Ibid., 57.
66. Ibid., 59.
67. Ibid., 64.
68. The strength of character that Ding exhibited in dealing with her loss and her subsequent enthusiastic involvement in political activities served to galvanize her popularity so that she became a "star" in the Shanghai scene in the early 1930s. See Dian Xi and Zhang Xuequn, *Shiren nüren de Shanghai tan*, 188.
69. Feuerwerker, *Ding Ling's Fiction*, 52.
70. Ibid., 19.
71. Ibid., 2.
72. Ibid., 2.
73. Fessler, *Wandering Heart*, 37.
74. Ibid., 80.
75. Ibid., 37.
76. Kobayashi Jirō, "Ding Ling zai Riben" (Ding Ling in Japan), in *Ding Ling yanjiu zai waiguo* (Ding Ling Research Abroad) (Hunnan renmin chubanshe, 1985), 365.
77. Ibid., 364.
78. Ibid., 364.
79. Ibid., 365. The same issue of *Nippon Hyōron* included a translated essay by Mao Dun entitled, "Onna sakka Ding Ling" (The Woman Writer Ding Ling), which reintroduced her to Japanese readers.
80. Ibid., 365. Many of these early translations can be credited to the Chūgoku bungaku kenkyūkai (Chinese Literature Research Society), which introduced and translated works of contemporary Chinese literature during and after the war.

81. Wang Cheng, "Riben nüxing wenxue jinru xinshidai" *Dongjing xinwen* (January 13, 1989): 52.
82. Jin Conglin, "Reqing de xianyi: jindai Riben wenxue zai Zhongguo," *Lu Xun yanjiu yuekan*, 2 (2001): 46–52.
83. The piece that resulted was entitled "Manmōyūki" (Record of a Voyage to Manchuria and Mongolia). See Joshua A. Fogel, "Japanese Literary Travelers in Prewar China," *Harvard Journal of Asiatic Studies*, 49: 2 (December 1989), 595.
84. Setouchi Harumi, *Tamura Toshiko* (Tokyo: Bungei shunju, 1983), 300.
85. Ibid., 300.
86. Ibid., 324.
87. Ibid., 303.
88. Ibid., 324.
89. Ericson, *To Be a Woman*, 63.
90. Ibid., 63.

Chapter 6

1. Mushanokōji's essay was an introduction to Zhou and included an explanation of his role in disseminating information about contemporary Japanese literary trends to Chinese readers. Mushanokōji Saneatsu, "Shū Sakunin" (Zhou Zuoren), *Nippon Hyōron* (March, 1938).
2. For more about the influence of Japanese literature on Yu Dafu and the relationship between Yu and Satō Haruo. see my book *The Subversive Self in Modern Chinese Literature: The Creation Society's Reinvention of the Japanese Shishōsetsu* (New York: Palgrave Macmillan, 2004).
3. For a comparison of *Rural Melancholy* and "Sinking" see Kurt W Radtke's essay, "Chaos or Coherence," in Adriana Boscaro, Franco Gatti, and Massimo Raveri (ed.), *Rethinking Japan*, vol. 1 (New York: St. Martin's Press, 1985), 86–101.
4. Ibid., 91.
5. Yu Dafu, "Sinking," in *Zhongguo xiandai wenxue daxi* (Compendium of Modern Chinese Literature), vol. 3 (Shanghai: Shanghai wenyi chubanshe, 1935), 2013.
6. Edward Fowler, *The Rhetoric of Confession: Shishōsetsu in Early Twentieth Century Japanese Fiction* (Berkeley, CA: University of California Press, 1988), xxvi.
7. Guo Laixun, *Yu Dafu yu Riben de ziwo xiaoshuo* (Yu Dafu and the Japanese "I-Novel"), in Yang Zhouhan (ed.), *Zhongguo bijiaowenxue niankan* (Chinese Comparative Literature Yearly) (Beijing: Beijing daxue chubanshe, 1987), 253.
8. Xu Zidong, *Yu Dafu xinlun* (New Essays about Yu Dafu) (Hangzhou: Zhejiang wenyi chubanshe, 1984), 216.
9. Ibid., 217.
10. Itō Toramaru, "Chuangzaoshe yu Riben wenxue" (The Creation Society and Japanese Literature), trans. Pan Shijingin. *Zhongguo xiandai wenxue* (March 1986), 213.
11. Itō Toramaru, "Zuoteng Chunfu yu Yu Dafu" (Satō Haruo and Yu Dafu), *Zhongguo xiandai wenxue* (February 1993), 208.
12. In 1920, Satō spent four months in Taiwan in which he exchanged poetry with the educator Chen Jingheng who acted as a guide in much the same way as Yu Dafu would eight years later during Satō's visit to Shanghai. Huang Meizi, *Satō Haruo to Taiwan, Chūgoku: "Hoshi" o Megutte* (Satō Haruo and Taiwan and China: Concerning "The Star") (Tsukuba, Japan: Tsukuba University Master's Thesis, 1983).

13. According to Satō Chieko's account, Yu came to greet the Satōs the day they arrived and guided them around on several occasions after that. This information appears in several letters from Satō Chieko to the Yu Dafu scholar Itō Toramaru describing the Satōs' 1927 visit. See Itō Toramaru, *Iku Tappu shiryō hoben* (Edited Materials of Yu Dafu), vol. 2 (Tokyo: Tokyo Daigaku bunken sentaa, 1975), 199–204.
14. Ibid., 201.
15. At this time Yu, an admirer of Akutagawa, sent a letter of condolence to Akutagawa's family out of deference to Satō Haruo. Ibid., 200.
16. From a letter dating from the third year of the Shōwa period (1928), the year following Satō's visit to China. See Ibid, 204.
17. Itō Toramaru, *Sōzōsha Shiryō* (Creation Society Materials) (Tokyo: Ajia shuppan, 1979), 1.
18. Although many Chinese writers who had experienced Japan as students exhibited a similar ambivalence toward Japan (Guo Moruo and Zhou Zuoren, for instance), no Chinese writer wrote as vehemently against Japanese imperialism, while simultaneously exhibiting genuine affection for Japanese culture as did Yu. Xu Zidong *Yu Dafu de xinlun* (New Essays about Yu Dafu) (Hangzhou: Zhejiang wenyi chubanshe, 1984), 219.
19. Ibid., 221.
20. Satō, "Ajia no ko" (Children of Asia), *Nippon hyōron* (March 1938), 193.
21. Ibid., 393.
22. Hasegawa Izumi, *Kindai bungei zasshi jiten* (Dictionary of Modern Literary Periodicals) (Tokyo: Shibundō, 1965), 2.
23. Yu Dafu, "Riben de wenshi yu changfu" (Japanese Literary Men and Whores), in *Yu Dafu wenji* (Collected Works of Yu Dafu), vol. 8 (Hong Kong: Joint Publishers, 1984), 294.
24. Ibid., 296.

Chapter 7

1. Immanuel C. Y. Hsu. *The Rise of Modern China* (New York: Oxford University Press, 1995), 582–583.
2. In fact, 1927–1937 is sometimes referred to as the "Leftist League Decade" due to the prominence of the league in the cultural and political affairs of China in that period. See Shu-mei Shih, *The Lure of the Modern: Writing Modernism in Semicolonial China, 1917–1937* (Berkeley: University of California Press, 2001), 238.
3. Sylvia Chan, "Realism or Socialist Realism?: The 'Proletarian' Episode in Modern Chinese Literature, 1927–1932," *The Australian Journal of Chinese Affairs*, No. 9 (January 1983), 57.
4. Ibid., 59.
5. Ibid., 59.
6. Ibid., 62.
7. And yet, Shanghai was also the home to a number of politically neutral writers as well. Prominent writers such as Ba Jin, Shen Congwen, Lao She and Wen Yiduo, kept their distance from the league and its activities.
8. Ibid., 155.
9. Shu-mei Shih, *The Lure of the Modern*, 234.
10. Bonnie S. McDougall and Kam Louie, *The Literature of China in the Twentieth Century* (New York: Columbia University Press, 1997), 25.

11. Ibid., 25.
12. Ibid., 27.
13. Ibid., 26.
14. Ibid., 27.
15. Yi-tsi Feuerwerker, *Ding Ling's Fiction: Ideology and Narrative in Modern Chinese Literature* (Cambridge, MA: Harvard University Press, 1982), 8.
16. Ibid., 8
17. Yi-tsi Feuerwerker, "The Changing Relationship between Literature and Life," in Merle Goldman (ed.), *Modern Chinese Literature in the May Fourth Era* (Cambridge, MA: Harvard University Press, 1987), 284. Twenty years after Hu's death Ding Ling revisited that event in the reminiscence "Yige zhengshi ren ji Hu Yepin" (The Life of an Upright Man, Hu Yepin).
18. Ibid., 287.
19. Feuerwerker, *Ding Ling's Fiction*, 2.
20. Harriet C. Mills, "Lu Xun: Literature and Revolution — From Mara to Marx," in Merle Goldman (ed.), *Modern Chinese Literature in the May Fourth Era* (Cambridge, MA: Harvard University Press, 1977), 214.
21. Ibid., 215. Lu Xun's abiding interest in Communism and the responsibilities of the writer can be seen, for example, in the case of a birthday celebration for Lu Xun in September of 1930, organized by Rou Shi in which Lu Xun used the occasion to lecture those in attendance about the lack of real proletarian writers in China. See Kirk A. Denton, "Lu Xun Biography," Modern Chinese Literature and Culture Resource website, http://mclc.osu.edu/rc/bios/lxbio.htm/.
22. From the essay, "The Revolutionary Literature of the Chinese Proletariat and the Blood of the Pioneers." See David E. Pollard, *The True Story of Lu Xun* (Hong Kong: Chinese University Press, 2002), 152.
23. Mills, "Lu Xun: Literature and Revolution," 216.
24. Ibid., 216.
25. Xu Zidong, *Yu Dafu xinlun* (Hangzhou: Zhejiang wenyi chubanshe, 1984), 221.
26. Originally contained in "Zuoyi zuojia lianmeng disici quanti dahui buzhi" (Supplement to the Minutes of the Fourth Convention of the League of Leftist Writers), *Hongqi ribao* (Red Flag Daily), November 22, 1930. In Lydia Liu, *Translingual Practice: Literature, National Culture, and Translated modernity — China, 1900–1937* (Stanford: Stanford University Press, 1995), 220.
27. W. J. F. Jenner, "Lu Xun's Last Days and After," *China Quarterly*, no. 91 (September 1982), 424.
28. Ibid., 428.
29. Ibid., 429.
30. Ibid., 428. Lu Xun was so consumed with woodblock print activities in his later years, in fact, that on the day that he died, during a visit with the Japanese leftist scholar Kaji Wataru at Kaji's home, the accomplishments of young Chinese woodblock artists was a main topic of discussion. Lu Xun expressed genuine pride in their accomplishments with the qualification that he wished they were better able to make the faces of their subjects appear more Chinese. Ibid., 426.
31. Ibid., 427.
32. Ibid., 430.
33. Ibid., 430.
34. Originally an essay of Feng's called "Huiyi" (Reminiscences). Ibid., 431.

35. Ibid., 431.
36. "Neishan Wanzao" [Uchiyama Kanzō], in *Lu Xun zawen cidian* (Lu Xun Miscellany Dictionary) (Shandong: Xinhua shudian, 1983), 238.
37. Uchiyama Kanzō, *Kakōroku* (A Record at Age Sixty) (Tokyo: Iwanami Shoten, 1981), 134.
38. As quoted in Fujii Shōzō, *Lu Xun hikaku kenkyū* (Lu Xun Comparative Research), trans. Chen Futai (Shanghai: Shanghai waiyu chubanshe, 1997), 171.
39. Ibid., 171.
40. W. J. F. Jenner, "Lu Xun's Last Days," 426.
41. Ibid., 433.
42. Ibid., 433.
43. Ibid., 433.
44. Ibid., 434.
45. Lu Yan, *Re-understanding Japan: Chinese Perspectives, 1895–1945*, (Honolulu: University of Hawai'i Press, 2002), 184.
46. Yoshida Hiroji, *Rojin no tomo: Uchiyama Kanzō no shōzō* (Lu Xun's Friend: A Portrait of Uchiyama Kanzō) (Tokyo: Shinkyō shuppansha, 1994), 189.
47. Ibid., 190.
48. Ibid., 190.
49. Ozawa Masamoto, *Uchiyama Kanzō den* (A Biography of Uchiyama Kanzō) (Tokyo: Banchō shobo, 1972), 156.
50. Ibid., 156.
51. Ibid., 159.
52. Ibid., 221.
53. Ibid., 179. The fact that he was chosen number one among all the candidates suggests the degree to which he was respected among the Japanese community in Shanghai. See Yoshida, *Rojin no tomo*, 248.
54. Ozawa, *Uchiyama Kanzō den*, 179.
55. Yoshida, *Rojin no tomo*, 249.
56. Ibid., 247. Originally in reminiscences by Kojima Toru.
57. Translated and quoted in Ken Ito, *Visions of Desire* (Stanford: Stanford University Press, 1991), 111.
58. The extent of Tanizaki's participation in the war effort was a radio talk on the fall of Singapore in 1942 and several half-hearted patriotic poems. See Donald Keene, *Dawn to the West: Japanese Literature in the Modern Era: Fiction*, vol. 3 (New York: Holt, Rinehart and Winston, 1984), 774.
59. Ibid., 773.
60. Ito, *Visions of Desire*, 186.
61. Ibid., 186.
62. Keene, *Dawn to the West*, 775.
63. Ibid., 773.
64. Ibid., 774.
65. Ibid., 773.
66. Ito, *Visions of Desire*, 190.
67. Keene, *Dawn to the West*, 774.
68. Joan Ericson, *Be a Woman: Hayashi Fumiko and Modern Japanese Women's Literature* (Honolulu: University of Hawai'i Press, 1997), 80.
69. Ibid., 80.

70. Keene, *Dawn to the West*, 1143.
71. Ericson, *Be a Woman*, 63.
72. Keene, *Dawn to the West*, 1143.
73. Ibid., 1143.
74. Ericson, *Be a Woman*, 81.
75. Keene, *Dawn to the West*, 1143.
76. Ibid., 1143.
77. Translated and included in Donald Keene, *Dawn to the West*, 456.
78. Stephen W. Kohl et al., *The White Birch School (Shirakabaha) of the Japanese Literature: Some Sketches and Commentary*. Occasional Paper No. 2 (Eugene: University of Oregon, March, 1975), 52.
79. Ibid., 53.
80. Suekawa Hiroshi (ed.), *Hōritsu* (Laws), in *Shiryō: Sengo nijūnen shi* (Materials: A History of the Twenty Years after the War), vol. III (Tokyo: Nihon hyōronsha, 1966–67), 35.
81. Quoted in Honda Shūgo, *Shirakaba no sakka to sakuhin* (The Authors and Works of the White Birch School), 80. Translated in Kohl et al., *The White Birch School*, 53.
82. Lu Yan, *Re-understanding Japan*, 181.
83. Ibid., 181.
84. Ibid., 186.
85. Ibid., 187.
86. Ibid., 187.
87. Yi-tsi Mei Feuerwerker, *Ding Ling's Fiction: Ideology and Narrative in Modern Chinese Literature* (Cambridge, MA: Harvard University Press, 1982), 8.
88. Hua Xianbiao, "Ding Ling," *Zhongguo xiandai wenxue shucang*, vol. I (Beijing: Xinhua shudian, 1987), 4.
89. Kobayashi Tsugio, "Ding Ling zai Riben" (Ding Ling in Japan), in Sun Ruichen and Wang Zhongqing (ed.), *Ding Ling yanjiu zai guowai* (Ding Ling Research Abroad) (Changsha: Hunan Renmin chubanshe, 1985), 365.
90. Ibid., 365.
91. Hua Xianbiao, "Ding Ling," 4.
92. Ibid., 5.
93. Lu Yan, *Re-understanding Japan*, 221.
94. Susan Daruvala, *Zhou Zuoren and an Alternative Response to Modernity* (Cambridge: Harvard University Press, 2000), 4.
95. Lu Yan, *Re-understanding Japan*, 230.
96. Ibid., 230.
97. Ibid., 230.
98. Ibid., 230.
99. Ibid., 231.
100. Ibid., 231.
101. Daruvala, *Zhou Zuoren and an Alternative Response*, 4.
102. Lu Yan, *Re-understanding Japan*, 231.
103. Ibid., 232.
104. These essays, which appeared in the newspaper *Yongbao* in Tianjin, were included in the column "Yaocaotang suibi" (Essays from the Medicine Hall). Ibid., 232.
105. Ibid., 239.

106. A complete description of the symposium held in Taiwan along with a transcript of selected proceedings is included in Itō Toramaru, *Iku Tappu shiryō hoben*, vol. 2: 218–228.
107. Ibid., 218.
108. Yu, in attempting to demonstrate affinities between the two literary communities, provided the example of Ōda Takeo (1900–79) who had won the Akutagawa Prize for *Jōgai* (Outside the Wall), a novel set in China. Yu admitted that he admired attempts such as these at the creation of truly cross-cultural literature, but feared problems of interpretation, given the linguistic and cultural differences. Ibid., 218.
109. Ibid., 227.
110. It is not clear from the records of these two journeys precisely which Chinese writers Satō visited during these journeys, but in reminiscences he mentions how he hoped to meet specific writers such as Hu Shi and Lu Xun. See Huang Meizi, *Satō Haruo to Taiwan, Chūgoku*, 4.
111. Yu Feng (ed.), *Yu Dafu haiwai wenji* (Anthology of Yu Dafu's Overseas Writings) (Beijing: Sanlian shudian, 1990), 517.
112. Ibid., 518.
113. Ibid., 519.
114. Woon Yoonwah, *Post-Colonial Chinese Literatures in Singapore and Malaysia* (Singapore: Department of Chinese Studies, National University of Singapore and Global Publishing Company, 2002), 85.
115. Ibid., 85.
116. Based on information contained in a letter from Ibuse to Itō Toramaru, which appears in Itō's *Iku Tappu shiryō hoben*, vol. 2: 213.
117. Woon Yoonwah, *Post-Colonial Chinese Literatures*, 89.
118. Ibid., 91.
119. Ibid., 92.
120. Ibid., 93.
121. Ibid., 96.
122. Christopher Bayly and Tim Harper, *Forgotten Armies: The Fall of British Asia, 1941–1945* (Cambridge, MA: The Belknap Press of Harvard University Press, 2005), 459.
123. The Japanese scholar Suzuki Masao, who interviewed Japanese military officials stationed in Bukit Tinggi at the time of Yu Dafu's death, has established that the Japanese military police executed Yu in order to silence a potentially articulate witness to their crimes. See Woon Yoon Wah, *Post-Colonial Chinese Literatures*, 83.

Epilogue

1. From a poem written by Lu Xun in March 1931 for Katayama Matsumo, Uchiyama Kanzō's sister-in-law, describing rapidly deteriorating conditions in China. See W. J. F. Jenner, *Lu Xun Selected Poems* (Beijing: Foreign Languages Press, 1982), 45 and 133.
2. As quoted in Christopher Bayley and Tim Harper, *Forgotten Armies: The Fall of British Asia, 1941–1945* (Cambridge, MA: The Belknap Press of Harvard University Press, 2005), 22.
3. Ōe Kenzaburo, "Japan, the Ambiguous, and Myself," in Tore Frängsmyr (ed.), *Le Prix Nobel* (Stockholm: Nobel Foundation Press, 1995).
4. Xing Lingjun, "Cunshang Chunju zai Zhongguo: dangdai Zhongguo wenxue sichao

xiade Cunshang rechushen," (Murakami Haruki in China: The Rage for Murakami in Contemporary Chinese Literary Thought) *Xibei Daxue xuebao* 35: 2 (March 2005), 169.
5. Ibid., 168.
6. Perhaps a better example of recent creative collaboration between artistic communities in China and Japan can be seen in the field of cinema in which there has been regular exchange between Chinese and Japanese filmmakers on a number of projects in the last two decades. One recent example of such collaboration is Zhang Yimou's 2005 film *Riding Alone for Thousands of Miles* starring the distinguished Japanese actor Takakura Ken in a bilingual production set in both countries and comprised of a Japanese and Chinese cast and crew. Both men have publicly described the opportunity to work together as the culmination of long-held dream.
7. Lu Yan, *Re-understanding Japan: Chinese Perspectives, 1895–1945* (Honolulu: University of Hawai'i Press, 2002), 253.
8. Fujii Shōzō, *Lu Xun bijiao wenxue* (Lu Xun's Comparative Literature) (Shanghai: Shanghai waiyu jiaoyu chubanshe, 1997), 169. Originally contained in Mushanokōji's open letter to *New Youth* entitled, "A Letter to Chinese Readers I Have Not Yet Met."
9. Tanizaki Jun'ichirō, "Kinō kyō" (Yesterday and Today), in Itō Toramaru (ed.), *Tian Han zai Riben* (Tian Han in Japan). (Beijing: Renmin wenxue chubanshe, 1997), 180.
10. Ibid., 182.

Appendix: Glossary of Selected Terms from Chinese and Japanese

Chinese terms

baihua 白話
Ba Jin (1904–1997) 巴金
Beidou 北斗
Benliu 奔流
bitan 筆談 "brushtalk" (see also Japanese *hitsudan*)
bufen 不分

Cai Yuanpei (1868–1940) 蔡元培
Chang'an 長安
Chen Duxiu (1879–1942) 陳獨秀
Chenbao 晨報
Chenbao fukan 晨報副刊
Cheng Fangwu (1897–1984) 成仿吾
"Chenlun" 沈淪
Chuangzao 創造
Chuangzaoshe 創造社
"Cong wenxue geming dao geming wenxue" 從文學革命到革命文學

dazi 大子
Ding Ling (1904–1986) 丁玲
"Ding Ling nüshi" 丁玲女士
Dongya Tongwen Shuyuan 東亞同文書院 (see also Japanese Tôa Dôbun shoin)
Du Fu (712–770) 杜甫

"Fang Riben xincun ji" 方日本新村記
"Fanyi de tongxin" 翻譯的通信
"Fengling" 風鈴
Funü wenxue 婦女文學

Gao Xingjian (1940–) 高行健
"Geming yu wenxue" 革命與文學
gerenzhuyi 個人主義
guocui 國粹
guojia yizhi 國家意識
Guomindang 國民黨
Guomin gongbao 國民公報
guomin wenxue 國民文學
"Guomin wenxue lun" 國民文學論
Guo Moruo (1892–1978) 郭沫若
Guoqu 過去

"Haishang tongxin" 海上通信
Heichao 黑潮
Henan 河南
Hong gaoliang 紅高粱
Hongloumeng 紅樓夢
Huaqiao ribao 華橋日報
huashen 化身
"Huise de niao" 灰色的鳥
"Hushang de beiju" 湖上的悲劇
Hunan jiaoyu yuekan 湖南教育月刊
Hu Feng (1902–1985) 胡風
Hu Shi (1891–1962) 胡適
Hu Yepin (1904–1931) 胡也頻
Hu Yuzhi (1896–1986) 胡愈之

Jia 家
"Jiechuan Longzhijie shi de Zhongguoguan" 芥川龍之介氏的中國觀
Jiefang ribao 解放日報
Jueju 絕句

Kang Youwei (1858–1927) 康有為
"Kuangren riji" 狂人日記
kuli 苦力
Kuzhuzhai 苦住宅

langmanzhuyi 浪漫主義
Lao She (1899–1966) 老舍
Liang Qichao (1873–1929) 梁啟超
Li Dazhao (1888–1927) 李大釗
Ling shan 靈山
lixiangde 理想的
Lu Xun (1881–1936) 魯迅
Lushan 廬山
lüshi 律詩

"Mangmang ye" 茫茫夜
Mao Dun (Shen Yanbing 沈雁冰) (1896–1981) 矛盾／茅盾
Mao Zedong (1893–1976) 毛澤東
Mengya 萌芽
"Minzuzhuyi wenyi yundong xuanyan" 民族主義文藝運動宣言
"Moluo shili shuo" 摩羅詩力說
"Mouye" 某夜
Mo Yan (1955–) 莫言
"Muqin" 母親

Nahan 吶喊
"Nan huan" 南還
Ni Huangzhi 倪煥之
Nüshen 女神

Ouyang Yuqian (1886–1962) 歐陽予倩

Pan Hannian (1906–1977) 潘漢年
"Piaoliu sanbuqu" 漂流三部曲
"Pingmin de wenxue" 平民的文學

Qianfeng yuebao 前風月報
Qian Qianwu 錢謙吾
qianze xiaoshuo 譴責小說
"Qingyan" 青煙

"Re feng" 熱風
"Ren de wenxue" 人的文學
"Riben de puluolietaliya yishu zenyang jingguo ta de yundong" 日本的普羅列塔利亞藝術怎樣經過他的運動

"Riben de qinlue zhanzheng yu zuojia" 日本的侵略戰爭與作家
"Riben de wenshi yu changfu" 日本的文士與娼婦
"Riben de xincun" 日本的新村
"Riben jin sanshinian xiaoshuo zhi fazhan" 日本近三十年小說之發展
"Riji wenxue" 日記文學

Shafei nüshi de riji 莎菲女士的日記
"Shanghai wenyi zhi yipie" 上海文藝之一瞥
"Shangshi" 傷逝
shehuizhuyi xianshizhuyi 社會主義現實主義
Shen Congwen (1902–1988) 沈從文
shi 詩
Shijie congshu 世界叢書
Shina 支那
Shina ju yanjiuhui 支那劇研究會
Shishi xinbao 時事新報
"Shui" 水
Sichuan lu 四川路
"Songzi" 松子

Taiwan shiminbao 台灣市民報
Taiyang zhao zai Sanggan he shang 太陽照在桑干河上
Tian Han (1898–1979) 田漢
Tianjin de Jueyusha 天津的覺悟社
Tianjin xueshu jiang yanhui 天津學術講演會
Tianping shan 天平山
Tiantai 天台 (see also Japanese Tendai)
"Toufa de gushi" 頭髮的故事

Wang Duqing (1898–1940) 王獨清
Wang Jingwei (1883–1944) 汪精衛
Wang Yangming (1472–1529) 王陽明
Wansuiguan 萬歲館
Wenxue daobao 文學導報
Wen Yiduo (1899–1946) 聞一多
Wenyi yanjiu 文藝研究
wenren 文人
wentan 文壇 (see also Japanese bundan)
wenti xiaoshuo 問題小說
wenxue 文學
Wenxue pinglun 文學評論
Wenxue xunkan 文學旬刊

Wenxue yanjiuhui 文學研究會
Wenxue zhoubao 文學週報
"Wenyijia de juewu" 文藝家的覺悟
Wenyi tongxuntuan 文藝通訊團
"Women de wenxue xin yundong" 我們的文學新運動
"Women xianzai zeyang zuo fuqin" 我們現在怎樣作父親
"Wo zai Xiacun de shihou" 我在霞村的時候
"Wo zai Xincun de shihou" 我在新村的時候
Wusong lu 吳淞路

Xiandai Riben xiaoshuoji 現代日本小説集
"Xiangchou" 鄉愁
Xiao Hong (1911–1942) 蕭紅
xiaopin 小品 (see also Japanese shōhin)
xiaoshuo 小説 (see also Japanese shōsetsu)
Xiaoshuo yuebao 小説月報
xiaozi 小子
Xinchao 新潮
Xincun Beijing zhibu 新村北京支部
"Xincun de jingshen" 新村的精神
"Xingyishan" 杏義山
Xingzhou ribao 星州日報
Xingzhou ribao banyuekan 星洲日報半月刊
Xin qingnian 新青年
Xin shiqi 新時期
Xintangshu 新唐書
Xinwenhua yundong 新文化運動
"Xin wenxue zhi jingzhong" 新文學之驚鐘
Xin xiaoshuo 新小説
Xinxieshizhuyi 新寫實主義
Xinyuekan 新月刊
Xin Zhongguo 新中國
"Xiongdi" 兄弟
Xu Zhimo (1896–1931) 徐志摩
"Xueye Riben guoqing de jishu: zizhuan zhi yi zhang" 學業日本國情的技術：自傳之一章
"Xuesheng zhi gongzuo" 學生之工作
Xueyi 學藝

Ye Shengtao (1894–1988) 葉聖陶
Yige ren de shengjing 一個人的聖經
"Yinhuise de si" 銀灰色的死
Yiwen 譯文
"Yiwen sijian" 藝文私見
Yuan Shikai (1859–1916) 袁世凱
Yu Dafu (1896–1945) 郁達夫

Yu Pingbo (1900–1990) 諭平伯
"Yu shina weizhi de youren" 與支那未知的友人
Yusishe 語絲社
"Yuwai xiaoshuo ji" 域外小説記
Yuzhoufeng 宇宙風

zashi 雜詩
Zhang Xueliang (1898–2001) 張學良
Zhang Ziping (1893–1959) 張資平
Zhang Zuolin (1873–1928) 張作霖
Zhao Lian 趙廉 (a late pen name for Yu Dafu)
Zheng Boqi (1895–1979) 鄭伯奇
Zhengfeng 正風
zhengzhi xiaoshuo 政治小説 (see also Japanese seiji shōsetsu)
Zhongguo wenhua 中國文化
Zhongguo xiandai wenxue yanjiu 中國現代文學研究
Zhou Enlai (1898–1976) 周恩來
Zhou Zuoren (1885–1967) 周作人
"Zisha riji" 自殺日記
"Ziji de yuandi" 自己的園地
zixu 自序
Ziye 子夜
Zuo Junzhi 左俊芝
Zuoyi zuojia lianmeng 左翼作家聯盟

Japanese terms

"Adauchi kinshirei" 仇討禁止令
"Aimaina Nihon no watashi" あいまいな日本の私
"Ajia no ko" アジアの子
Akahata 赤旗
Akutagawa Ryūnosuke (1892–1927) 芥川龍之介
An'ya Kōro 暗夜行路
Arishima Ikuma (1882–1974) 有島生馬
Arishima Takeo (1878–1923) 有島武郎
Aru Onna ある女
"Aru onna no gurimpusu" ある女のグリムプス
"Aru seinen no yume" ある青年の夢
Atarashiki mura 新しき村
Atarashiki mura undō 新しき村運動
"Atarashiki mura ni tsuite no taiwa" 新しき村についての対話
"Atarashiki mura no dōki" 新しき村の動機

Bakumatsu 幕末
"Bara no hana" 薔薇の花
bundan 文壇 (see also Chinese *wentan*)
Bungaku Hōkokukai 文学報国会
bungaku seinen 文学青年

chankoro チャンコロ
Chian iji hō 治安維持法
Chi'iki kenkyū 地域研究
"Chiisaki mono e" 小さき者へ
Chūgoku mandan 中国漫談
"Chūgoku no shitai o kataru" 中国の姿態を語る
Chūō kōron 中央公論

"Daihyō shin Chūgoku no josei sakka gun" 代表新中国の女性作家群
Daitōa kyōeiken 大東亜共栄圏
"Daitōa sensō shikan" 大東亜戦争私観
Den'en no yū'utsu 田園の憂鬱
dochakuha 土着派
Dōshisha 同志社

Fugen 普賢
Fujin kōron 婦人公論
Fujin kurabu 婦人倶楽部

Gankai 眼界
"Geijutsu o umu tai wa ai nomi" 芸術を生む胎は愛のみ
Genji monogatari 源氏物語
Gozan 五山
Gyokuteki fu 玉笛府

Hagita Ungai 萩田雲崖
haibun 俳文
"Hana" 鼻
Hana no machi 花の町
Hayashi Fumiko (1903–1951) 林芙美子
Hayashi Fusao (1903–1975) 林房雄
Heiankyō 平安京
heiwa no megami 平和の女神
Higuchi Ichiyō (1872–1896) 樋口一葉
Hinkyū Mondō 貧窮問答
Hiratsuka Raichō (1886–1971) 平塚らいちょう
"Hito no seikatsu" 人の生活
hitsudan 筆談 "brushtalk" (see also Chinese *bitan*)

Hitsuji o meguru bōken 羊をめぐる冒険
Honma Hisao (1886–1932) 本間久雄
Hōrōki 放浪記
Hyūga 日向

Ibuse Masuji (1898–1993) 井伏鱒二
"Ikanaru hoshi no moto ni" 如何なる星の下に
"Ikite iru Shina no sugata" 生きている支那の姿
"Ikite iru heitai" 生きている兵隊
Inoue Yasushi (1907–1991) 井上靖
Ishikawa Jun (1899–1987) 石川淳
Ishikawa Tatsuzō (1905–1985) 石川達三
Itō Katsugi 伊藤勝義

"Jibun no aruita michi" 自分の歩いた道
"Jindōshugi no bungaku" 人道主義の文学
Jōgai 城外
Josei 女性
Josei 女声
junbungaku 純文学

Kagerō nikki 蜻蛉日記
"Kain no matsuei" カインの末裔
kaishaha 会社派
Kaizō 改造
Kaizōsha 改造社
Kaji Wataru (1903–1982) 鹿地亘
Kammu (737–806) 桓武
kanbun 漢文
kangakusha 漢学者
kanji bunka 漢字文化
Kankanmushi かんかん虫
kanshi 漢詩
Kamo no Chōmei (1153–1216) 鴨長明
Kasai Zenzō (1887–1928) 葛西善蔵
Kataoka Teppei (1894–1944) 片岡鐵兵
Katsura Tarō (1848–1913) 桂太郎
Kawakami Hajime (1879–1946) 河上肇
Keizai ōrai 経済往来
Kentōshi 遣唐使
Kikōbun 紀行文
Kikuchi Kan (1889–1948) 菊池寛
"Kinosaki nite" 城崎にて
Ki no Tsurayuki (884–946) 紀貫之
Kiroku 記録
Kitchen キッチン

Kizoku no shakaishugi 貴族の社会主義
Kōbai kumiai 購買組合
Kobayashi Hideo (1902–1983) 小林秀雄
Kobayashi Takiji (1903–1933) 小林多喜二
Kōda Rohan (1867–1947) 幸田露伴
"Kodomo e no inori" 子供への祈り
Kōfukumono 幸福者
"Kohan no gashō" 湖畔の画商
kojin 個人
Kokoro 心
Kokyū Wasureubeki 故旧忘れ得べき
Konoe Fumimaro (1891–1945) 近衛文麿
Kōyūki 交遊記
Kūkai (774–835) 空海 (also Kōbō Daishi)
Kume Masao (1891–1952) 久米正雄
"Kureegu sensei" クレーグ先生
Kuriyagawa Hakuson (1880–1923) 厨川白村
Kyōsonkyōeishugi 共存共栄主義
Kyoto Kyōkai 京都教会

lumpen bungaku ルンペン文学

Mainichi shinbun 毎日新聞
Makino Toraji 牧野虎次
Manshūkoku 満州国
Mandan 漫談
Mango 漫語
manwa 漫話
Marusu no uta マルスの歌
Matsuo Bashō (1644–1694) 松尾芭蕉
meisho 名所
Mita bungaku 三田文学
"Miura Uemon no saigo" 三浦右衛門の最後
monogatari 物語
Mori Ōgai (1862–1922) 森鴎外
Murakami Haruki (1949–) 村上春樹
"Mushanokōji Kei e" 武者小路兄へ
Mushanokōji Saneatsu (1885–1976) 武者小路実篤

Nagayo Yoshirō (1888–1961) 長与善郎
Naitō Konan (1866–1934) 内藤湖南
Nakamura Mitsuo (1911–1988) 中村光夫
Nakamura Murao (1886–1949) 中村武羅夫
Nakamura Zekō (1867–1927) 中村是公
Nakano Shigeharu (1902–1979) 中野重治
Natsume Sōseki (1867–1916) 夏目漱石
"Neko to Shōzō to futari no onna" 猫と庄造と二人の女

Nihon Benkyōkai 日本勉強会
Niijima Jō (1843–1890) 新島襄
nikki 日記
"Ningyo no nageki" 人魚の嘆き
Nihon shoki (or *Nihongi*) 日本書紀
"Nihon shōsetsu no Shina yaku" 日本小説の支那訳
Ninin bikuni iro zange 二人比丘尼色懺悔
Nippon hyōron 日本評論
Nitobe Inazō (1862–1933) 新渡戸稲造
Noruwei no mori ノルウェイの森
Nyonin geijutsu 女人芸術

Oda Takeo (1900–1979) 小田岳夫
Ōe Kenzaburō (1935–) 大江健三郎
Oku no hosomichi 奥の細道
"Omatsu no shi" お末の死
Omedetaki hito お目出たき人
"Onna no nikki" 女の日記
Otoko wa tsurai 男はつらい
Ōtsu Junkichi 大津順吉
Ozaki Kazuo (1899–1983) 尾崎一雄

Pen butai ペン部隊

"Rozan nikki" 廬山日記
ryōsai kenbo 良妻賢母

Saichō (767–822) 最澄
Saku no kusabue 佐久の草笛
Santendō 参天堂
sanpitsu 三筆
Sasameyuki 細雪
sashie 挿絵
Satō Haruo (1892–1964) 佐藤春夫
Satomi Ton (1888–1983) 里見弴
"Seibei to hyōtan" 清兵衛と瓢箪
seiji shōsetsu 政治小説
"Seikatsu no geijutsuka" 生活の芸術化
"Seiko no tsuki" 西湖の月
Seisho no kenkyū 聖書の研究
Seitō 青鞜
Seiyūkai 政友会
"Sengen hitotsu" 宣言一つ
Senke Motomaro (1888–1948) 千家元麿
Shanhai 上海
"Shanhai kōyūki" 上海交遊記
"Shanhai mango" 上海漫語

"Shanhai manwa" 上海漫話
"Shanhai seikatsu nijūnen" 上海生活二十年
Shan Nippō 上日報
Shidehara Kijūrō (1872–1951) 幣原喜重郎
Shiga Naoya (1883–1971) 志賀直哉
Shimamura Hōgetsu (1871–1918) 島村抱月
Shimazaki Tōson (1872–1943) 島崎藤村
Shina 支那
Shina geki kenkyūkai 支那劇研究会
"Shina shumi to iu koto" 支那趣味という事
"Shina yūki" 支那遊記
Shingon 真言
Shin Nippon 新日本
Shinsei 新生
Shinshichō 新思潮
Shisōsen 思想戦
Shirakaba 白樺
Shirakabaha 白樺派
shishōsetsu 私小説 (see also watakushi shōsetsu)
Shitsuki gun 後月郡
shizenshugi 自然主義
shōhin 小品
Shōnan Taimuzu 湘南タイムズ
Shōsetsu no kakenu shōsetsuka 小説の書けぬ小説家
shōsetsu no kamisama 小説の神様
"Shōsetsu shinzui" 小説神髄
Shufu no tomo 主婦の友
Shumi 趣味
"Sono imōto" その妹
"Soshū kikō" 蘇州紀行
"Soshū kikō maegaki" 蘇州紀行前書き
Sotoyama Gorō 外山五郎
Subaru スバル
Sugawara no Kiyokimi (770–842) 菅原清公
Sugawara no Michizane (845–903) 菅原道真

Taigyaku Jiken 大逆事件
Tairiku bungaku sōsho 大陸文学叢書
Taishō Democracy 大正デモクラシー
"Taiwan fūkei" 台湾風
"Taiwan no subuniiru" 台湾のスブニール
Takami Jun (1907–1965) 高見順
Takamura Kōtarō (1883–1956) 高村光太郎
Takeda Taijun (1912–1976) 武田泰淳
Tanaka Giichi (1864–1929) 田中義一
Tanizaki Jun'ichirō (1886–1965) 谷崎潤一郎

Tayama Katai (1871–1930) 田山花袋
Tendai 天台 (see also Chinese Tiantai)
tenkō 転向
Terauchi Masatake (1852–1919) 寺内正毅
Tōa dōbun shoin 東亜同文書院 (see also Chinese Dongya Tongwen shuyuan)
Tochi 土地
Tōhō kaigi 東方会議
Tokuda Shūsei (1871–1943) 徳田秋声
"Tōkyō o omou" 東京を思う
"Torusutoishugi" トルストイ主義
Tosa nikki 土佐日記
Tsubouchi Shōyō (1859–1935) 坪内逍遥
Uchimura Kanzō (1861–1930) 内村鑑三
Uchiyama Kanzō (1885–1959) 内山完造
Uchiyama Miki (1892–1945) 内山美喜
Uno Tetsuto (1875–1974) 宇野哲人
Ukigumo 浮雲

wakon kansai 和魂漢才
Waseda bungaku 早稲田文学
"Washi mo shiranai" わしも知らない
watakushi shōsetsu 私小説 (see also shishōsetsu)

Yamamoto Sanehiko (1885–1952) 山本実彦
Yanagi Sōetsu (1889–1961) 柳宗悦
Yanagita Kunio (1875–1962) 柳田國男
Yokomitsu Ri'ichi (1898–1947) 横光利一
Yomiuri shimbun 読売新聞
Yosano Akiko (1878–1942) 与謝野晶子
Yoshimoto Banana (1964–) 吉本ばなな
Yūjō 友情
"Yume jūya" 夢十夜

Zaiya gakuha 在野画派
zuihitsu 随筆

Bibliography

Barlow, Tani E., ed. *Gender Politics in Modern China: Writing and Feminism.* Durham, NC: Duke University Press, 1993.
Barlow, Tani E. and George J. Bjorge, eds. *I Myself Am a Woman: Selected Writings of Ding Ling.* Boston: Beacon Press, 1989.
Bayly, Christopher Alan and Timothy Harper. *Forgotten Armies: The Fall of British Asia, 1941–1945.* Cambridge, MA: Belknap Press of Harvard University Press, 2005.
Best, Jonathan W. "Diplomatic and Cultural Contacts between Paekche and China." *Harvard Journal of Asiatic Studies* 42: 2 (December 1982): 443–501.
Borgen, Robert. "The Japanese Mission to China, 801–806." *Monumenta Nipponica* 37:1 (Spring 1982): 1–28.
———. *Sugawara no Michizane and the Early Heian Court.* Honolulu: University of Hawaii Press, 1994.
Bosaro, Adriana, Gatti Franco and Massimo Raveri, eds. *Rethinking Japan.* New York: St. Martin's Press, 1991.
Chan, Sylvia. "Realism or Socialist Realism?: The 'Proletarian' Episode in Modern Chinese Literature, 1927–1932." *The Australian Journal of Chinese Affairs,* No. 9 (January 1983): 55–74.
Cheng, Ching-mao. "The Impact of Japanese Literary Trends on Modern Chinese Writers." In *Modern Chinese Literature in the May Fourth Era,* ed. Merle Goldman. Cambridge, MA: Harvard University Press, 1977, 63–88.
Ching-Kiu, Stephen Chan. "The Language of Despair: Ideological Representations of 'New Woman' by May Fourth Writers." In *Gender Politics in Modern China: Writing and Feminism,* ed. Tani E. Barlow. Durham, NC: Duke University Press, 1993.
Daruvala, Susan. *Zhou Zuoren and an Alternative Chinese Response to Modernity.* Cambridge: Harvard University Press, 2000.
Denton, Kirk A. "Lu Xun Biography," *Modern Chinese Literature and Culture Resource Homepage* (http://mclc.osu.edu/rc/bios/lxbio.htm), 2002.
Dian Xi 田茜 and Zhang Xuequn 張學君, eds. *Shiren nuren de Shanghai tan* 十人女人的上海灘 (Ten Women Writers' Sojourns In Shanghai). Beijing: New World Press, 2004.
Dolezalova, Anna. *Yü Ta-fu: Specific Traits of His Literary Creation.* London: C. Hurst and Company, 1971.

Egan, Michael. "Yu Dafu and the Transition to Modern Chinese Literature." In *Modern Chinese Literature in the May Fourth Era*, ed. Merle Goldman. Cambridge, MA: Harvard University Press, 1977, 209–238.

Ericson, Joan E. *Be a Woman: Hayashi Fumiko and Modern Japanese Women's Literature*. Honolulu: University of Hawaii Press, 1997.

Fang Changan 方長安. "Xingcheng, diaozheng yu zhibian: Zhou Zuoren 'Ren de wenxue' guan yu Riben wenxue de guanxi" 形成、凋整與質變：周作人"人的文學"觀與日本文學的關係 (Form, Control, and Transformation: Perspectives on the Relationship of Zhou Zuoren's "Humane Literature" to Japanese Literature) *Literary Review* 3 (2004).

Fessler, Susanna. *Wandering Heart: The Work and Method of Hayashi Fumiko*. Albany, NY: State University of New York, 1998.

Feuerwerker, Yi-tsi Mei. *Ding Ling's Fiction: Ideology and Narrative in Modern Chinese Literature*. Cambridge, MA: Harvard University Press, 1982.

———. "The Changing Relationship between Literature and Life." In *Modern Chinese Literature in the May Fourth Era*, ed. Merle Goldman. Cambridge, MA: Harvard University Press, 1977.

Fogel, Joshua A. *The Cultural Dimensions of Sino-Japanese Relations: Essays on the Nineteenth and Twentieth Centuries*. Armonk, NY: M.E. Sharpe, 1994.

———. "Japanese Literary Travelers in Prewar Japan." *Harvard Journal of Asiatic Studies* 49: 2 (1989): 575–602.

———. *The Literature of Travel in the Japanese Rediscovery of China: 1862–1945*. Stanford, CA: Stanford University Press, 1996.

———. " 'Shanghai-Japan': The Japanese Residents' Association of Shanghai." *The Journal of Asian Studies* 59: 4 (November 2000): 927–950.

Fowler, Edward. *The Rhetoric of Confession: Shishōsetsu in Early Twentieth Century Japanese Fiction*. Berkeley, CA: University of California Press, 1988.

Fujii Shōzō 藤井省三. *Chūgoku bungaku kono hyakunen* 中国文学この百年 (The Last Hundred Years of Chinese Literature). Tokyo: Shinchōsha, 1991.

———. *Lu Xun bijiao yanjiu* 魯迅比較研究 (Lu Xun Comparative Research). Translated by Chen Fukang. Shanghai: Shanghai waiyu jiaoyu chubanshe, 1997.

———. "Lu Xun xinmuzhong de Xiamu Shushi" 魯迅心目中的夏目漱石 (Natsume Sōseki in the Mind's Eye of Lu Xun). Translated by Ma Diji. *Lu Xun Studies Monthly*, Vol. 2 (1991).

Guo Laixun 郭來舜. "Yu Dafu yu Riben de ziwoxiaoshuo" 郁達夫與日本的自我小說 (Yu Dafu and the Japanese "I-Novel"), ed. Yang Zhouhan, *Zhongguo bijiaowenxue nianjian* 中國比較文學年鑑 (*Chinese Comparative Literature Yearly*). Beijing: Beijing Daxue chubanshe, 1987, 252–253. Originally appeared in *Wenxue Pinglun* (April 1983).

Hamilton Nolte, Sharon. "Individualism in Taishō Japan." *The Journal of Asian Studies* 43: 4 (August 1984): 667–684.

Hayashi Fumiko 林芙美子. "Nikki" 日記 (A Diary) in *Hayashi Fumiko zenshū* 林芙美子全集 (Collected Works of Hayashi Fumiko), Vol. 19. New York: Shinchōsha, 1952.

Hoston, Germaine A. "The State, Modernity, and the Fate of Liberalism in Prewar Japan." *The Journal of Asian Studies* 51:2 (May 1992): 287–316.

Huang Meizi 黃美滋. *Satō Haruo to Taiwan, Chūgoku: "Hoshi" o megutte* 佐藤春夫と台湾、中国：「星」を巡って (Satō Haruo and Taiwan and China: Concerning "The Star"). Tsukuba, Japan: Tsukuba University Master's Thesis, 1983.

Hsu, Immanuel C. Y. *The Rise of Modern China*. New York: Oxford University Press, 1995.
Imai Nobuo 今井信雄. *Shinchō Nihon bungaku arubamu* 新潮日本文学アルバム (Shinchō Japanese Literary Albums), Vol. 10 [Mushanokōji Saneatsu]. Tokyo: Shinchōsha, 1984.
Inaba Shoji 稲葉昭二. *Iku Tappu: sono seishun to shi* 郁達夫：その青春と詩 (Yu Dafu: Youth and Poetry). Tokyo: Toho senshu, 1982.
Isogai Hideo 磯貝英夫. *Shinchō Nihon bungaku arubamu* 新潮日本文学アルバム (Shinchō Japanese Literary Albums), Vol. 34 [Hayashi Fumiko]. Tokyo: Shinchōsha, 1986.
Ito, Ken K. *Visions of Desire: Tanizaki's Fictional Worlds*. Stanford, CA: Stanford University Press, 1991.
Itō Toramaru 伊藤虎丸. "Chuangzaoshe yu Riben wenxue" 創造社與日本文學 (The Creation Society and Japanese Literature). Translated by Pan Shijingin. *Zhongguo xiandai wenxue* (March 1986): 210–216.
———. *Iku Tappu shiryō hoben* 郁達夫資料補編 (Companion of Yu Dafu Materials), Vol. 2. Tokyo: Tokyo Daigaku bunken sentā, 1975.
———. *Sōzōsha shiryō* 創造社資料 (Creation Society Materials). Tokyo: Ajia shuppan, 1979.
———. et al., ed. *Tian Han zai Riben* 田漢在日本 (Tian Han in Japan). Beijing: Renmin wenxue chubanshe, 1997.
———. "Zuoteng Chunfu yu Yu Dafu" 佐藤春夫與郁達夫 (Satō Haruo and Yu Dafu). *Zhongguo xiandai wenxue* (February 1993): 206–214.
Izu Toshihiko 伊豆利彦. "Kobayashi Takiji to Kurahara Korehito: sakka to hyōronka no mondai" 小林多喜二と蔵原惟人：作家と評論家の問題 (Kobayashi Takiji and Kurahara Korehito: An Author and Critic Issue) (December 15, 1990) (http://homepage2.nifty.com/tizu/proletarier/takiji@kurhara.htm), 1–21.
Jenner, W. J. F. "Lu Xun's Last Days and After." *China Quarterly* 91 (September 1982): 424–445.
———. translator. *Lu Xun Selected Poems*. Beijing: Foreign Languages Press, 1982.
Jin Conglin 靳叢林. "Reqing de xuanze: jindai Riben wenxue zai Zhongguo" 熱情的選擇：近代日本文學在中國 (Fervent Choices: Modern Japanese Literature in China) *Lu Xun yanjiu yuekan*, Vol. 2 (2001): 46–52.
Karatani Kōjin. *Origins of Modern Japanese Literature*. Translated by Brett de Bary. Durham, NC: Duke University Press, 1993.
Kawaguchi, Hisao 川口久夫. *Heianchō kanbungaku no kaika: shijin Kūkai to Michizane* 平安朝漢文学の開花：詩人空海と道真 (The Flowering of Chinese Literary Studies in the Heian Court: The Poets Kūkai and Michizane). Tokyo: Yoshikawa kobunkan, 1991.
Keene, Donald. *Dawn to the West: Japanese Literature in the Modern Era: Fiction*. New York: Holt, Rinehart and Winston, 1984.
———. *Landscapes and Portraits: Appreciations of Japanese Culture*. Tokyo: Kodansha, 1971.
———. *Modern Japanese Diaries: The Japanese at Home and Abroad as Revealed Through Their Diaries*. New York: Columbia University Press, 1998.
———. *Travelers of a Hundred Ages: The Japanese as Revealed Through 1,000 Years of Diaries*. New York: Holt and Company, 1999.
Kobayashi Fukuko. "Women Writers and Feminist Consciousness in Early Twentieth-Century Japan." *Feminist Issues* 11: 2 (Fall 1991): 1–15.
Kobayashi Futao 小林二男. "Ding Ling zai Riben" 丁玲在日本 (Ding Ling in Japan). In *Ding Ling yanjiu zai guowai* 丁玲研究在國外 (Ding Ling Studies Overseas), ed. Sun Ruizhen and Wang Zhongchen. Changsha: Hunan Renmin chubansha, 1985.

Kohl, Stephen W. et al. *The White Birch School (Shirakabaha) of Japanese Literature: Some Sketches and Commentary.* Occasional Paper No. 2, University of Oregon, March 1975.

Kushner, Barak. *The Thought War: Japanese Imperial Propaganda.* Honolulu: University of Hawai'i Press, 2006.

Larson, Wendy. "The End of 'Funü Wenxue': Women's Literature from 1925 to 1935." In *Gender Politics in Modern China: Writing and Feminism,* ed. Tani E. Barlow. Durham, NC: Duke University Press, 1993.

Lee, Leo Ou-Fan. *Shanghai Modern: The Flowering of a New Urban Culture in China, 1930–1945.* Cambridge, MA: Harvard University Press, 1999.

Li Huoren 黎活仁. "Yu Dafu yu sixiaoshuo" 郁達夫與私小説 (Yu Dafu and the Shishōsetsu). *Zhongguo xiandai wenxue* (March 1990): 200–218.

Liu Boqing 劉柏青. "Lu Xun yu Riben xinsichao zuojia" 魯迅與日本新思潮派作家 (Lu Xun and Shinshichō Authors). *Jilin Daxue shehui kexuebao* 1 (1983): 49–55.

Liu Chunying 劉春英. "Jiechuan Longzhijie zai Zhongguo" 芥川龍之介在中國 (Akutagawa Ryūnosuke in China). *Tangdu xuekan* 3: 19 (2003): 1–6.

Liu, Lydia. "Invention and Intervention: the Female Tradition in Modern Chinese Literature." In *Gender Politics in Modern China: Writing and Feminism* ed. Tani E. Barlow. Durham, NC: Duke University Press, 1993.

———. *Translingual Practice: Literature, National Culture, and Translated Modernity — China, 1900–1937.* Stanford, CA: Stanford University Press, 1995.

Liu Xianbiao 劉獻彪. "Ding Ling" 丁玲. In *Zhongguo xiandai wenxue shucong* 中國現代文學手冊 (Compendium of Modern Chinese Literature), Vol. 1. Beijing: Xinhua shoushang, 1987.

Lu Xun 魯迅. *Lu Xun lun waiguo wenxue* 魯迅論外國文學 (Lu Xun's Discussions about Foreign Literature), ed. Fujian Shihan Daxue Zhongwenxi. Beijing: Waiguo wenxue chubanshe, 1982.

———. "Zhi Zhou Zuoren" 致周作人 (To Zhou Zuoren). In *Lu Xun Quanji* 魯迅全集 (Collected Works of Lu Xun). Beijing: Renmin Wenxue Chubanshe Chuban, 1981.

Lu Xun Bowuguan 魯迅博物館 ed. *Lu Xun: 1881–1936* 魯迅：1881–1936 (Lu Xun: 1881–1936). Beijing: Xinhua shudian faxing, 1976.

Lu Yan. *Re-understanding Japan: Chinese Perspectives, 1895–1945.* Honolulu: Association of Asian Studies and University of Hawai'i Press, 2004.

McDougall, Bonnie S. and Kam Louie. *The Literature of China in the Twentieth Century.* New York: Columbia University Press, 1997.

Mills, Harriet C. "Lu Xun: Literature and Revolution — From Mara to Marx." In *Modern Chinese Literature in the May Fourth Era,* ed. Merle Goldman. Cambridge, MA: Harvard University Press, 1977.

Miner, Earl. *Japanese Poetic Diaries.* Berkeley, CA: University of California Press, 1969.

———. *The Princeton Companion to Classical Japanese Literature* ed., Hiroko Odagiri and Robert Morrell. Princeton: Princeton University Press, 1985.

Minichiello, Sharon A., ed. *Japan's Competing Modernities: Issues in Culture and Democracy, 1900–1930.* Honolulu: University of Hawai'i Press, 1998.

Miyauchi Junko 宮内淳子. *Ikyō ōkan* (Travels to Foreign Lands) 異郷往還. Tokyo: Kokusho Kankōkai, 1991.

Mizuta Noriko. "In Search of a Lost Paradise: The Wandering Woman in Hayashi Fumiko's *Drifting Clouds.*" In *The Woman's Hand: Gender and Theory in Japanese Women's Writing,* ed. Paul Gordon Schalow and Janet A. Walker. Stanford, CA: Stanford University Press, 1996.

Morton, Leith. *Divided Self: A Biography of Arishima Takeo*. Sydney: Allen and Unwin, 1988.
Mushanokōji Saneatsu 武者小路実篤. "Aru seinen no yume" ある青年の夢 (A Certain Young Man's Dream). In *Mushanokōji Saneatsu Zenshū* (Collected Works of Mushanokōji Saneatsu), Vol. 2. (Tokyo: Shogakkan, 1988).
———. *Jibun no aruita michi* 自分の歩いた道 (The Road I Have Walked). In *Sakka no jiden* 作家の自伝 (Autobiographies of Writers), Vol. 7. Tokyo: Nihon tosho sentā, 1994.
Nakajima Midori 中島碧. "Tei Rei ron" 丁玲論 (Concerning Ding Ling). In *Ding Ling yanjiu zhiliao* 丁玲研究資料 (Ding Ling Research Materials), ed. Biao Liangshun. Tianjin: Tianjin renmin chubanshe, 1995.
Nish, Ian. "An Overview of Relations between China and Japan, 1895–1945." *China Quarterly* 124 (December 1990): 601–623.
Nishihara Daisuke, "Zhou Zuoren's Translation of Two Japanese Stories." *Hikaku Bungaku: Journal of Comparative Literature,* Vol. XXXVII. (1994): 239–242.
Noguchi Takehiko 野口武彦. "Tanizaki Jun'ichirō ron" 谷崎潤一郎論 (Concerning Tanizaki Jun'ichirō). Tokyo: Chūō kōronsha, 1973.
Nozaki Kan 野崎歓. "Guqi Xunyilang yu 'Gaogui de dalu' yuyan" 谷崎潤一郎與 "高貴的大陸" 語言 (Tanizaki Junichirō and Narrating "Transcendental China"). *Journal of Modern Literature in Chinese* 7:2 (December 2005): 45.
Ōe Kenzaburo. "Japan the Ambiguous, and Myself." In *Le Prix Nobel*, ed. Tore Frängsmyr. Stockholm: Nobel Foundation Press, 1995.
Ogata Sadako, "Japanese Attitude toward China." *Asian Survey* 5: 8 (August 1965): 389–398.
Otsuyama Kunio 大津山邦夫. "Atarashiki Mura no hankyō — Arishima Takeo no hihan o megutte" 新しき村の反響—有島武郎の批判を巡って (Reaction to the New Village — Concerning Arishima Takeo's Criticism). *Bungaku* 42: 12 (1974): 1181–1182.
Ozawa Masamoto 小澤正元. *Uchiyama Kanzō Den* 内山完造伝 (A Biography of Uchiyama Kanzō). Tokyo: Banchō shoten, 1972.
Pollard, David E. *The True Story of Lu Xun*. Hong Kong: Chinese University Press, 2002.
Prusek, Jaroslav, ed. *Dictionary of Oriental Literatures, Volume I: East Asia.* London: George Allen and Unwin, 1974.
Qian Liqun 錢理群. *Zhou Zuoren zhuan* 周作人傳 (Biography of Zhou Zuoren). Beijing: Beijing Shiyue Wenyi, 1993.
Qin Gang 秦剛. "Xiandai Zhongguo wentan dui Jiechuan Longzhijie de yijie yu jieshou" 現代中國文壇對芥川龍之介的譯介與接受 (The Reception and Critical Interpretation of Akutagawa Ryūnosuke in the Modern Chinese Literary Community). *Zhongguo xiandai wenxue yanjiu congkan*, Vol. 2 (2004): 246–259.
Rabson, Steve. "Yosano Akiko on War: To Give One's Life or Not: A Question of Which War." *The Journal of the Association of Teachers of Japanese* 25: 1 (April 1991): 45–74.
Radtke, Kurt W. "Chaos or Coherence." In *Rethinking Japan*, ed. Adriana Boscaro, Franco Gatti, and Massimo Raveri, Vol. 1.New York: St. Martin's Press, 1985, 86–101.
Reynolds, Douglas R. "Chinese Area Studies in Prewar China: Japan's Tōa Dōbun Shoin in Shanghai, 1900–1945." *The Journal of Asian Studies* 45:5 (November 1986): 945–970.
Sakaki, Atsuko. "Japanese Perceptions of China: The Sinophillic Fiction of Tanizaki Jun'ichirō." *Harvard Journal of Asiatic Studies* 59: 1 (1999): 187–218.

Satō Haruo 佐藤春夫. "Ajia no ko" 亜細亜の子 (Children of Asia). *Nippon hyōron* 日本評論 (March 1938).

Sergeant, Harriet. *Shanghai: Collision Point of Cultures, 1918–1939*. New York: Crown Publishers, 1990.

Setouchi Harumi 瀬戸内晴美. *Tamura Toshiko* 田村俊子. Tokyo: Bungei Shunjū, 1983.

Shih, Shu-mei. *The Lure of the Modern: Writing Modernism in Semicolonial China, 1917–1937*. Berkeley, CA: University of California Press, 2001.

Silverberg, Miriam. *Changing Song: The Marxist Manifestos of Nakano Shigeharu*. Princeton, NJ: Princeton University Press, 1990.

Suekawa Hiroshi 末川宏 ed. *Hōritsu* 法律. In *Shiryō: Sengo nijūnenshi* 資料：戦後二十年史 (Materials: The Twenty Years Following the War), Vol. III. Tokyo: Nihon hyōronsha, 1967.

Takeda Torao 武田寅雄. *Shirakaba gunzō*「白樺」群像 (A Portrait of Shirakaba). Tokyo: Meiji shoten, 1983.

Takenouchi Shizuo 竹之内静雄, ed. *Satō Haruo shū* 佐藤春夫集 (Satō Haruo Collection). In *Gendai bungaku taikei* 現代文学大系 (Compendium of Modern Literature), Vol. 29. Tokyo: Chikuma shobō, 1967: 456–457.

Tanizaki Jun'ichirō 谷崎潤一郎. "Kinō kyō" きのうきょう (Yesterday and Today). In *Tian Han zai Riben* 田漢在日本 (Tian Han in Japan), ed. Itō Toramaru. Beijing: Renmin Wenxue Chubanshe chuban, 1997, 180–195. Originally appeared in *Bungei shunjū* (June to November, 1942).

———. "Rozan nikki" 廬山日記 (Lushan Diary), *Tanizaki Jun'ichirō zenshū* 谷崎潤一郎全集 (Collected Works of Tanizaki Jun'ichirō), Vol. 7. Tokyo: Chūō kōronsha, 1969, 463–469.

———. "Shanhai kenbunroku" 上海見聞録 (A Record of Observations in China). *Tanizaki Jun'ichirō zenshū* 谷崎潤一郎全集 (Collected Works of Tanizaki Jun'ichirō), Vol. 22. Tokyo: Chūō kōronsha, 1969, 553.

———. "Shanhai kōyūki" 上海交遊記 (A Record of a Friendly Exchange in Shanghai). *Tanizaki Jun'ichirō zenshū* 谷崎潤一郎全集 (Collected Works of Tanizaki Jun'ichirō), Vol. 10. Tokyo: Chūō kōronsha, 1969, 562–598.

———. "Shina shumi to iu koto" 支那趣味ということ (This Taste for Things Chinese). *Tanizaki Jun'ichirō zenshū* 谷崎潤一郎全集 (Collected Works of Tanizaki Jun'ichirō), Vol. 6. Tokyo: Chūō kōronsha, 1969, 121–123.

———. "Soshū kikō" 蘇州紀行 (A Record of a Journey to Suzhou). *Tanizaki Jun'ichirō zenshū*. 谷崎潤一郎全集 (Collected Works of Tanizaki Jun'ichirū), Vol. 6. Tokyo: Chūō kōronsha, 1969, 223–243.

Tsuruta, Kinya. "Tanizaki Jun'ichirō's Pilgrimage and Return." *Comparative Literature Studies* 37: 2 (2000): 239–255.

Uchiyama Kanzō 内山完造. *Kakōroku*. 花甲録 (A Record at Age Sixty). Tokyo: Iwanami shoten, 1981.

———, *Shanhai Mango*. 上海漫語 (Idle Chatter in Shanghai). Tokyo: Kaizōsha, 1941.

Wang Cheng 王成. "Riben nüxing wenxue jinru xinshidai" 日本女性文學進入新時代 (Period of the Emergence of Japanese Women's Literature). *Dongjing xinwen* (January 13, 1989), 79–80.

———. "Xiamu Shushi wenxue zai Zhongguo de fanyi yu yingxiang" 夏目漱石文學在中國的翻譯與影響 (Natsume Sōseki's Literature in Chinese Translation and Its Influence). *Fanyi Luntan* (2002): 25–26.

Wang Chunlin 王春林, ed. *Lu Xun wenxian tuchuan* 魯迅文獻圖傳 (An Illustrated Record of Lu Xun's Literary Contributions). Guangzhou: Daxiang chubanshe, 1998.
Wang Huoying 王炳英. "Neishan Wanzao" [Uchiyama Kanzō] 內山完造. In *Lu Xun zawen cidian* 魯迅雜文辭典 (Lu Xun Miscellanea Dictionary). Shandong: Shandong xinhua shudian, 1986, 485–486.
Wang Jinhou 王錦厚. *Wusi: xinwenxue yu waiguo wenxue* 五四：新聞學與外國文學 (May Fourth: The New Literature and Foreign Literature). Sichuan: Sichuan Daxue chubanshe, 1989.
Wang Wenying 王文英, ed. *Shanghai xiandai wenxueshi* 上海現代文學史 (A Literary History of Modern Shanghai). Shanghai: Shanghai renmin chubansha, 1999.
Wolff, Ernst. *Chou Tso-jen*. New York: Twayne Publishers, 1971.
Woon Yoon Wah. *Post-Colonial Chinese Literatures in Singapore and Malaysia*. Singapore: Department of Chinese Studies, The National University of Singapore and Global Publishing Company, 2002.
Xing Lingjun 邢靈君. "Cunshang Chunshu zai Zhongguo: dangdai Zhongguo wenxue sichao xiade Cunshang rechutan" 村上春樹在中國：當代中國文學思潮下的村上熱初探 (Murakami Haruki in China: The Rage for Murakami in Contemporary Chinese Literary Thought). *Xibei Daxue xuebao* 35: 2 (March 2005):168–170.
Xu Zidong 許子東. *Yu Dafu xinlun* 郁達夫新論 (New Essays about Yu Dafu). Hangzhou: Zhejiang wenyi chubanshe, 1984.
Yamada Keizō 山田敬三. *Ro Jin no sekai* 魯迅の世界 (Lu Xun's World). Tokyo: Taishūkan shoten, 1977.
Yokomatsu Takashi 橫松崇. *Ro Jin: minzoku no kyōshi* 魯迅：民族の教師 (Lu Xun: The People's Teacher). Tokyo: Kawade shobo shinsha, 1986.
Yoshida Hiroji 吉田曠二. *Lu Xun no tomo: Uchiyama Kanzō no shōzō* 魯迅の友：內山完造の肖像 (Lu Xun's Friend: A Portrait of Uchiyama Kanzō). Tokyo: Shinkyō shuppansha, 1994.
Yu Dafu 郁達夫. "Riben de wenshi yu changfu" 日本的文士與娼婦 (Japanese Literary Men and Whores). In *Yu Dafu wenji* 郁達夫文集 (Collected Works of Yu Dafu), Vol. 8. Hong Kong: Joint Publishers, 1984.
———. "Chenlun" 沈淪 (Sinking). In *Zhongguo xiandai wenxue daxi* 中國現代文學大系 (Compendium of Modern Chinese Literature), ed. Zheng Boqi, Vol. 3. Shanghai: Shanghai wenyi chubanshe, 1935.
Yu Feng 郁風, ed. *Yu Dafu haiwai wenji* 郁達夫海外文集 (Anthology of Yu Dafu's Oversea's Writings). Beijing: Sanlian shudian, 1990.
Yu Yun 郁雲. *Wo de fuqin Yu Dafu* 我的父親郁達夫 (My Father Yu Dafu). Taipei: Lanting shudian, 1986.
Zheng Chun 鄭春. *Liuxue Beijing yu Zhongguo xiandai wenxue* 留學背景與中國現代文學 (The Study Abroad Background and Modern Chinese Literature). Jinan, Shandong: Shandong jiayu chubanshe, 2002.
Zhu Peichu 朱培初. "Riben minyi yundong de changdaozhe: Liu Zongyue" 日本民藝運動的倡導者：柳宗 (The Leader of the Japanese Folk Art Movement: Yanagi Sōetsu). *Art and Design*, 4 (1990): 36–42.

Index

NB: In this index a continuous discussion over two or more pages is indicated by a span of page numbers, e.g. "57–59." *Passim* is used for a cluster of references in close but not continuous sequence.

"Adauchi kinshirei" (Proscription on Revenge), 12
"Aimaina Nihon no watashi" (Japan the Ambiguous and Myself), 158
"Ajia no ko" (Children of Asia), 117, 124–127, 145, 150
Akahata (Red Flag), 113, 143
Akutagawa Ryūnosuke, 12, 14, 33, 35, 65, 72, 180n15
An Lushan, 7
Analects, 91
Arishima Ikuma, 76
Arishima Takeo, 66, 88, 175n12; relationship with Lu Xun, 76–83
Aru onna (A Certain Woman), 77 *passim*
"Aru onna no gurinpusu" (A Glimpse of a Certain Woman), 77
Aru seinen no yume (A Certain Young Man's Dream), 66, 74 *passim*, 136, 172n30
Asahi shimbun (Asahi News), 150
Ashikaga Shogunate, 7
Atarashiki mura (New Village), 21–22, 85 *passim*; impact on Chinese Communist Party, 93–95
"Atarashiki mura" (The New Village), 87, 92
"Atarashiki mura no dōki" (Motivation for the New Village), 88
"Atarashiki mura no taiwa" (A Dialogue about the New Village), 87

Ba Jin, 19
baihua (vernacular literature), 71, 160
"Bara no hana" (The Rose), 71
Bashō (*see* Matsuo Bashō)
Beidou (Big Dipper), 105
Beijing University, 105, 148
Berlin Film Festival, 159
Bing Xin, 110
bitan (*see also* "brushtalk"), 2
Blake, William, 118
brushtalk, 2, 9, 170n44
bufen, 6
Bukit Tinggi, 151–152
bundan (literary community) (*see also* *wentan*), 8, 117, 123; of the Meiji Period, 33
Bungaku hōkokukai (Literature Patriotic Association), 149
Bungei shunjū (Literary Quarterly), 31, 59, 61

Chang'an, 4–6
chankoro, 16
Chen Duxiu, 22, 33, 67, 89, 93
Chenbao (Morning News), 12, 114
Cheng Fangwu, 111
"Chenlun" (Sinking), relation to Satō Haruo's *Rural Melancholy*, 118 *passim*
"Chiisaki mono e" (To the Little Ones), 77, 172n18

Chijin no ai, (A Fool's Love), 58
Chinese Communist Party, 19, 67, 92–95, 130, 132
Choson Dynasty, 8
Chuangzaoshe (Creation Society), 53, 54, 111, 130, 138, 146, 167n33
Chūgoku bungaku kenkyūkai (Chinese Literary Research Society), 178n80
Chūgoku no shitai o kataru (Talking about the State of China), 135
Chūō Kōron (Central Review), 31, 48, 49, 88, 141
Confucius, 9, 91
"Cong wenxue geming dao geming wenxue" (From Literary Revolution to Revolutionary Literature), 111

"Daihyō shin Chūgoku no josei sakkagun" (Group of Representative New Women Writers in China), 113
Daitōa kyōeiken (Greater East Asian Coprosperity Sphere), 18, 62, 144
"Daitōa sensō shikan" (Private Views on the Great East Asian War), 145
Dalu wenxue congshu (Compendium of Continental Literature), 113
da wo (greater self), 95
Dazaifu, 6
Den'en no yū'utsu (Rural Melancholy), 22, relation to Yu Dafu's "Sinking," 118
Ding Ling, 22, 37, 99–100, 103 *passim*, 112, 131–133, 178n68; activities during the war, 147
dōbun dōshu (common script, common race), 16
dochakuha (native clique), 42
"Doll's House," 79, 108
Dongya dongwen shuyuan (East Asia Common Culture Academy), 160, 165n56

enpon (one yen books), 31
Enzan sosui (Mountains of North China and the Rivers of South China), 8

"Fang Riben xincunji" (Record of a Visit to the New Village), 93
Feng Xuewen, 132

Fogel, Joshua, 3, 46, 114
Fugen (Bodhisattva), 121
Fujin kōron (Ladies' Review), 109
Fujin kurabu (Ladies' Club), 109
Fukuoka Asian Literature Prize, 159
funü wenxue (women's literature), 110
Futabatei Shimei, 33

Gakushūin, 76
Gankai (Vision), 71
Gao Xingjian, 159
"Geijutsu o umu tai wa ai nomi" (Only Love Can Give Birth to Art), 79
Genji monogatari (Tale of Genji), 47, 58, 62, 141–142
Gozan (five mountain) poetry, 7
Guandong Army, 18
Guo Moruo, 10, 31, 52, 53, 54, 61–62, 117; activities during the war, 146–147; as portrayed in *Children of Asia*, 124–127
Guomindang, 38, 130, 140
Guoqu (The Past), 124
Gyokuteki fu (Poems of the Jade Flute), 128

Hagita Ungai, 23
"Haikyōsha toshite no Arishima" (Arishima the Apostate), 54
"Haishang tongxin" (Correspondence from the Sea), 122
Han Dynasty, 3
"Hana" (The Nose), 12
Hana no machi (City of Flowers), 144
Hankou, 26, 167n16
Hara Kei, 1
Hatano Akiko, 7
Hayashi Fumiko, 22, 33, 151; activities during the war, 143–144, 149; biographical details, 97 *passim*; interactions with writers in Shanghai, 100–103
Hayashi Fusao, 127
Heian Period, 5
Heiankyō, 6
Heichao (Black Tide), 160
Hibino Teruhiro, 8
Higuchi Ichiyō, 109
Hinkyū mondō (Dialogue on Poverty), 121
Hiratsuka Raicho, 109

"Hito no seikatsu" (Human Life), 92
Hitsudan (*see also* "brushtalk"), 2
Hitsuji o meguru bōken (Wild Sheep Chase), 159
Hong gaoliang (Red Sorghum), 159
Hong Genpei, 152
Hōrōki (Diary of a Vagabond), 97, 99, 101; Chinese translation of, 143; comparison with Ding Ling's *Miss Sophie's Diary*, 103–111
Hu Qiuyuan, 131
Hu Shi, 123
Hu Yepin, 37, 112, 131, 147, 181n17
Hu Yuzhi, 152
Huang Deshi, 150
Huangpu Military Academy, 80
Huaqiao zhoubao (Overseas Chinese Weekly), 151
Hunan jiaoyu yuekan (Hunan Education Monthly), 93–94
Hyūga, 87

Ibsen, Henrik, 79, 108
Ibuse Masuji, 13, 144, 151
Ikanaru hoshi no moto ni (Under What Star), 121
Ikite iru heitai (Living Soldiers), 144
Ikite iru Shina no sugata (Portrait of a Living China), 39
"implied reader" of literary diary, 107
Inoue Yasushi, 146
International Settlement (Shanghai), 13, 38
interwar period, 1–2, 157, 160–161
Ishikawa Jun, 121
Ishikawa Takuboku, 175n21
Ishikawa Tatsuzō, 144
Isogai Hideo, 106
Itō Katsugi, 24
Ito, Ken, 58
Itō Toramaru, 122

Jia (Home), 19
Jiang Jieshi (Chiang Kai-shek), 125
Jibun no aruita michi (The Road I Have Walked), 145
Jiefang ribao (Liberation Daily), 147
Jiga kaiki (return to the self), 59
"Jindōshugi no bungaku" (Humanistic Literature), 87

Jōgai (Outside the Wall), 184n108
joryū sakka (women writers), 114
Josei (Woman), 52
junbungaku (pure literature), 18, 159

Kagero nikki (Diary of Gossamer Years), 107
"Kain no matsuei" (Descendents of Cain), 78
kaishaha (company clique), 42
Kaizō (Reform), 31, 35, 40, 80, 105, 113, 121, 146, 176n14
Kakōroku (A Record of Sixty Years), 36, 40
Kammu Emperor, 5
kanbun (Chinese language prose), 6
kangakusha (scholar of Chinese learning; Sinologist), 8–9, 23, 46, 164n30
kanji bunka (culture of Chinese characters), 13
Kankan mushi (Rust Clippers), 78
Kankō Kiyū (Trip Report), 8
kanshi (Chinese language poetry), 5, 7
Kasai Zenzō, 121
Kataoka Teppei, 149
Katsura Taro, 160
kentōshi, 5, 13
Ki no Tsurayuki, 45
kikōbun (travel diary), 21, 45 *passim*, 63, 168n3, 169n18
Kikuchi Kan, 12, 52, 61
"Kinō kyō" (Yesterday and Today), 59 *passim*, 64, 170n42
Kitchin (Kitchen), 159
kizoku no shakaishugi (aristocratic socialism), 75
Kōbai kumiai (Buyer's Association), 32
Kobayashi Issa, 92, 175n21
Kobayashi Takiji, 18, 99
Kōbō Daishi (*see* Kūkai)
"Kodomo e no inori" (A Prayer for Children), 71
Kōfukusha (The Happy One), 72
Koguryo, 3, 7
"Kohan no gashō" (The Art Dealer on the Lakeshore), 136
Kokyū wasureubeki (Should Auld Acquaintance Be Forgot), 121
Konoe Fumimaro, 18, 160
kōyūki (friendly exchange), 53

"Kuangren riji" (Diary of a Madman), 73, 177n36
Kūkai (also Kōbō Daishi), 5–6, 163n20
kuli (coolie), 24, 26
Kurahara Korehito, 99
"Kureegu Sensei" (Craig Sensei), 12, 165n42
Kurihara Thomas, 52
Kuzhu zhai (Living-in-bitterness studio), 148
kyōson kyōeishugi (co-existence and co-prosperity), 17
Kyoto, 23–25, 139
Kyoto Kyōkai (Kyoto Church), 24, 25, 26

Lao She, 150
League of Leftist Writers (see Zuoyi zuojia lianmeng)
Li Dazhao, 93, 96
Liang Qichao, 67
Lin Lianxiang, 172n26
Ling shan (Ghost Mountain), 159
"Literature in a Revolutionary Age," 80
lixiang de (idealistic), 94
Lu Yan, 147
Lu Xun, 2, 10, 11, 12, 21, 31, 33, 65, 69, 70, 71, 73 passim, 157, 168n47; death and its impact on Sino-Japanese relations 133–138; education in Japan, 30; relationship with Uchiyama Kanzō, 34 passim, 137; relationship with Arishima Takeo, 76–83; relationship with Hayashi Fumiko, 102, role in League of Leftist writers, 131–132
lūshi (regulated verse), 60

Ma Xuefeng, 105
Mainichi shinbun (Daily News), 14, 143, 150
Makino Toraji, 24–25, 27, 166n9
Manchuguo, 18
Manchuria, 15, 16, 18, 32, 48, 139
mandan (random discussions), 34, 39
mango (random chatter), 39–40
"Manmōyūki" (Record of a Voyage to Manchuria and Mongolia), 179n83
Mao Dun, 18, 150
Mao Zedong, 94

Marusu no uta (Song of Mars), 121
Matsuo Bashō, 45
May Fourth Period, 10–11, 37, 69
Meiji Period, 8, 11, 75, 80
Mengya (Sprout), 132
Miao Bin, 148
Midaregami (Tangled Hair), 114
Mingei undō (Folk Art Movement), 69
"Minzhuzhuyi wenyi yundong xuanyan" (Declaration by the Nationalist Literary Movement), 131
Mita bungaku (Mita Literature), 66, 113
"Miura Uemon no saigo," 12
Miyamoto Yuriko, 102
Mo Yan, 159
Mori Ōgai, 66
Mukden Incident, 18, 131
Muqin (Mother), 113
Murakami Haruki, 159
"Mushanokoji Kei e" (To Mushanokoji), 88
Mushanokoji Saneatsu, 11, 21, 33, 52, 66, 69, 75 passim, 84, 123, 161, 179n1; activities during the war, 144–145, 149; relationship with Lu Xun, 136; status in Japanese literary world, 85, 172n28

Nagayo Yoshirō, 149
Nahan (Call to Arms), 83
Naitō Konan, 8, 46
Nakamura Mitsuo, 108
Nakamura Zeko, 14
Nakano Shigeharu, 121
Natsume Sōseki, 11–12, 14, 33, 65, 66, 172n14
Neko to Shōzo to futari no onna (A Cat, Shōzō and the Two Women), 141
New Culture Movement, 17
"new woman," literary representation of, 102–103
Ni Huangzhi, 19
Nichinichi shinbun (Daily News), 113
Nihon benkyōkai, 32
Nihon shoki, 4
"Nihon shōsetsu no Shina yaku" (A Chinese Translation of Japanese Stories), 72
Nikki (literary diary), 21, 45 passim, 51, 63, 169n18, 177n38
"Ningyo no nageki" (Lament of a Mermaid), 47, 55

Nippon hyōron, 113, 117, 126
Nitobe Inazo, 76
Noble Prize for Literature, 158, 159
"Nongmin wenyi de tichang" (Advocating a Literature by Peasants), 81, 174n4
Noruwei no mori (Norwegian Wood), 159
Nūsheng (Woman's Voice), 114
Nyonin geijutsu (Women's Arts), 105, 109

Ōda Takeo, 34, 184n108
Ōe Kenzaburo, 158–159
Oka Senjin, 8, 46
Oku no hosomichi (Narrow Road to the Deep North), 45
Omedetaki hito (An Innocent), 75
Onna no nikki (A Woman's Diary), 97
Osaka mainichi shinbun (Osaka Daily News), 148
Ouyang Yuqian, 32, 33, 54, 60, 161, 170n44
Ozaki Hideki, 94

Padang, 151
Paekche, 3–4, 5
Pan Hannian, 146
Parhae, 7, 164n24
Pen butai (Pen Squadron), 113, 115, 143
"Pingmin de wenxue" (Popular Literature), 95
Post-Modernism, 159
Proletarian movement, 18, 19, 86, 121
"psychological warfare," 16
"Puroretaria rearizumu e no michi" (The Path to Proletarian Realism), 99
putonghua, 163n4

Qianfeng yuebao (Vanguard Monthly), 131
Qianshao (Outpost), 132
Qinglongsi, 163n20
Qu Qiubai, 132

"Re feng" (Hot Wind), 77
"Ren de wenxue" (Humane Literature), 11, 95
"Riben de qinlue zhanzheng yu zuojia" (Japanese War of Invasion and Writers), 150
"Riben de wenshi yu changfu" (Japanese Literary Men and Whores), 117, 126–127

"Riben de xincun" (Japan's New Village), 92
"Riben jin sanshinian xiaoshuo zhi fazhan" (Developments in Japanese Fiction in the Last Thirty Years), 11, 90, 114
Rou Shi, 37, 132, 181n21
"Rozan nikki" (A Diary of Lushan), 47, 49 *passim*
"runpen bungaku" (hobo literature), 97, 106, 176n2, 177n32
ryōsai kenbo (good wife, wise mother), 109

Saga Emperor, 5
Saichō, 5
"Saikin no puroretaria bungaku to shinsakka" (Recent Proletarian Literature and New Authors), 99
Sakaki Atsuko, 46
Saku no kusabue (Reed Flute of Saku), 128
Santendō, 25–28
Sapporo Agricultural School, 76
Sasameyuki (Makioka Sisters), 58, 142–143, 170n53
Satō Chieko, 180n13
Satō Haruo, 22, 33, 151, 179n12; 1927 visit to Shanghai, 35; activities during the war, 145–146, 150; relationship with Yu Dafu, 122, 149, 179n2
Satomi Ton, 76, 86, 174n5
"Seibei to hyōtan" (Seibei and the Gourd), 71
"Seiko no tsuki" (Moon on the West Lake), 47, 55
Seisho no kenkyū (Biblical Research), 25
Seitō (Blue Stocking), 109
"Sengen hitotsu" (A Manifesto), 80–82
Senzaimaru, 8, 13, 46, 165n48
Shafei nūshi de riji (Miss Sophie's Diary), 22; comparison with Hayashi Fumiko's *Hōrōki,* 103–111, 147
Shandong, 16–17
Shanghai, 1, 8, 13, 41, 122, 158, 180n7; appeal for Tanizaki Jun'ichirō, 56–57; Uchiyama's activities during the war, 140–141
"Shanhai kenbunroku" (Record of Observations in Shanghai), 56
"Shanhai kōyūki" (Record of Friendly Exchange in Shanghai), 52–54, 63

"Shanhai mango" (Random Chatter in Shanghai), 36, 39–40
"Shanhai manwa" (Random Talk in Shanghai), 36
"Shanhai seikatsu nijū nen" (Twenty Years Living in Shanghai), 35
Shangshi (Mourning the Dead), 79 *passim*
Shaw, George Bernard, 37, 135
Shidehara Kijūrō, 17
Shiga Naoya, 66, 69, 86, 127, 150, 172n12
Shimamura Hōgetsu, 109
Shimazaki Tōson, 11, 127
Shin Nippon (New Japan), 127
Shina, 16, 166n63
Shina bunmei ki (A Record of Civilization in China), 9
Shina geki kenkyūkai (Chinese Drama Research Society), 30, 35
"Shina kinyūkai" (The Chinese Financial World), 40
"Shina shumi to iu koto" (This Taste for Things Chinese), 47, 169n9
Shin'ei bungaku sōsho (Collection of New Literature), 110
Shinshichō (New Tide), 12
shintaishi (new style verse), 114
Shirakaba, 88, 89, 120, 171n5
Shirakaba-ha (White Birch School), 21, 65 *passim*, 76, 80–84, 85 *passim*, 171n2, 171n3
Shishōsetsu (I-Novel), 69, 119, 121
shisōsen (thought war), 41
Shitsuki (Okayama Prefecture), 23
Shōnan Taimuzu (Shōnan Times), 151
Shōsetsu no kakenu shōsetsuka (A Novelist Who Cannot Write Novels), 121
shōsetsu no kamisama (god of fiction), 69
Shōsetsu no shinzui (Essence of the Novel), 90
"Shui" (Water), 113
Silla, 3
Singapore, 144, 151–152, 158
Sino-Japanese War, 16
Six Dynasties, 3, 163n7
Social Darwinism, 82
socialist realism (*shehuizhuyi xianshizhuyi*), 15, 19, 99
"Solitary Reaper," 118

"Songzi" (Pine), 113
"Sono imōto" (The Younger Sister), 72
"Soshū kikō" (Record of a Visit to Suzhou), 47 *passim*, 169n12
South Manchurian Railway (SMR), 14, 114, 139
Spencer, Herbert, 82
study abroad, in Japan by Chinese writers, 10–11
Su Wen, 131
Subaru (Pleiades), 66
Sugawara no Kiyokimi, 6
Sugawara no Michizane, 5–7, 164n27
Sui Dynasty, 4–5
Sumatra, 151
Sun Yat-sen, 160
Suzhou, 48, 49

Tachibana no Hayanari, 5
Tade kuu mushi (Some Prefer Nettles), 55, 57–59
Taigyaku jiken (High Treason Incident), 83
Tairiku bungaku sōsho (Compendium of Continental Literature), 147
"Taishō Democracy" 1, 2, 66
Taishō Period, 11, 13
"Taiwan fūkei" (Taiwanese Landscape), 101
"Taiwan no subuniiru" (Souvenir from Taiwan), 101
Taiwan shiminbao (Taiwan People's News), 149
Taizang Emperor, 4
Takami Jun, 121
Takamura Kōtaro, 68
Takasugi Shinsaku, 8
Takeda Taijun, 146
Takezoe Shin'ichiro, 8
Tamura Toshiko, 114–115
Tanaka Giichi, 17
Tang Dynasty, 4–5, 7
Tang Lin, 161
Tanizaki Jun'ichirō, 2, 11, 13, 21, 29, 33, 34, 150, 161–162, 182n58; 1918 visit to China, 47–51; 1926 visit to Shanghai, 52 *passim*
Tao Jingsun, 115
Tayama Katai, 11
Tendai (Chinese Tiantai), 5

tenkō (conversion), 19, 113, 143
Terauchi Masatake, 16–17
"Thorns cover the plain," 157
Tian Han, 10, 30, 31, 32, 33, 52, 53, 54, 61
Tianping, 48
Tōa Dōbun Shoin, 14–15
"Tochi" (The Land), 87
Tōhō kaigi (Eastern Conference), 17
Tokugawa Period, 8, 13
Tokyo Imperial University, 133
"Tokyo o omou" (Thinking of Tokyo), 141
Tolstoy, Leo, 25, 65, 68, 93, 171n8, 172n29, 174n6
"Tomoda to Matsunaga no hanashi" (Tale of Tomoda and Matsunaga), 55, 57
"Torusutoishugi" (Tolstoyism), 87
Tosa Nikki (Tosa Diary), 45, 97
"Toufa de gushi" (Story about Hair), 95
translations, Japanese of Western works, 9, 164n39
"True story of Ah Q," 11
Tsubouchi Shōyō, 90
"Twenty-one Demands," 16, 28, 74

Uchimura Kanzō, 25, 76
Uchiyama Kakichi, 38–39
Uchiyama Kanzō, 2, 21, 115, 123, 182n53; early years, 23–26 *passim,* move to Shanghai, 26–27; as cultural liaison between the Chinese and Japanese literary communities, 33, 42, 52; politics of, 40–42; relationship with Lu Xun, 34 *passim,* 168n48
Uchiyama Miki (nee Inoue), 26 *passim*
Uchiyama Shudian (Uchiyama Bookstore), 23, 27, 42, 167n22; cultural activities on the second floor of, 31 *passim;* final days of operation; impact on Chinese writers, 29 *passim;* move to Sichuan Road, 28
Ukigumo (Drifting Clouds), 143
Uno Tetsuto, 9

Waka, 7
Wang Baolian, 38
Wang Jingwei, 148
Wansuiguan, 35
Waseda bungaku (Waseda Literature), 120

"Washi mo shiranai" (I Too Don't Know), 72
Watanabe Kazuo, 158
Weiss, Ruth, 39
Wenxue daobao (Literary Guide), 132
Wenyi yanjiu (Literary Research), 132
Wo zai Xiacun de shihou (When I Was at Xia Village), 147
"Women xianzai zeyang zuo fuqin" (How Should We Depict the Contemporary Father?), 77
woodblock print making, 38–39, 134, 181n30

Xi'an, 6, 163n20
Xiao Hong, 110
xiao wo (small self), 95
"Xiayi shan" (Mount Xiayi), 102
Xibei War Zone Service Corps, 147
Xie Liuyi, 32
Xihu (West Lake), 122
Xin qingnian (New Youth), 11, 91, 93
Xincun Beijing zhibu (Beijing New Village Support Division), 91–92
"Xincun de jingshen" (Spirit of the New Village), 94
Xincun yundong (New Village Movement), 92
Xing Lingjun, 159
Xingzhou ribao (Singapore Daily), 151
Xinxieshizhuyi (Neorealism), 159
"Xiongdi" (Brothers), 66, 171n1
Xu Guangping, 140
Xu Zhimo, 133
"Xuesheng zhi gongzuo" (Duty of Students), 94

Yamada Yoshio, 142
Yamamoto Sanehiko, 102, 135, 151, 176n14
Yanagi Sōetsu, 69, 86
Yanagita Kunio, 66
Ye Shengtao, 19
Yenan, 113, 147
Yi Dynasty (*see* Choson)
Yi Zhen, 104
Yige ren de shengjing (One Man's Bible), 159
"Yishu yu shenghuo: Riben de xincun" (Art and Life: Japan's New Village), 175n28

Yokohama, 56
Yomiuri Symposium, 128, 149, 184n106
Yosano Akiko, 109, 114
Yoshimoto Banana, 159
Yoshiya Nobuko, 143
Yu Dafu, 22, 33, 34, 117; activities during the war, 149–152; ambivalent feelings about Japan, 180n18; death, 20, 184n123; portrayed in *Children of Asia*, 124–127; relationship with Satō Haruo, 122–123; role in the League of Leftist Writers, 132–133
"Yu Shina weizhi de pengyou" (A Letter to Chinese Friends I Do Not Yet Know), 93
Yuan Shikai, 16
Yuezhou, 6
Yūjō (Friendship), 75
"Yume jūya" (Ten Nights of Dreams), 12
Yuzhou feng (Cosmic Wind), 148

zaya gakuha (independent artists and intellectuals), 14
Zen Buddhism, 7
Zhang Xueliang, 18
Zhang Yimou, 185n6
Zhang Ziping, 31
Zhao Lian (as alias of Yu Dafu), 151
Zhaoyi Distillery, 151
Zhejiang Province, 4
Zheng Boqi, 133
Zhengfeng Movement, 147
Zhongguo wenhua (Chinese Culture), 147
Zhongwenguan (Chinese Academy), 4
Zhou Enlai, 92, 94
Zhou Zuoren, 11, 12, 21–22, 33, 52, 96 173n44, 175n21; activities during the war years, 147–149; education in Japan, 30, 65, 67 *passim*; attraction to the New Village, 85, 87 *passim*, 175n18; relationship with Mushanokōji Saneatsu, 117
"Ziji de yuandi" (Our Own Garden), 95
Ziye (Midnight), 19
Zuihitsu, 39
Zuoyi zuojia lianmeng (League of Leftist Writers), 19, 22, 111, 123, 130–133, 180n2

www.ingramcontent.com/pod-product-compliance
Ingram Content Group UK Ltd.
Pitfield, Milton Keynes, MK11 3LW, UK
UKHW021826140426
5217IPUK00012B/145/J